A Social Theory
of Congress

A Social Theory
of Congress

Legislative Norms in
the Twenty-First Century

Brian Alexander

LEXINGTON BOOKS
Lanham • Boulder • New York • London

Published by Lexington Books
An imprint of The Rowman & Littlefield Publishing Group, Inc.
4501 Forbes Boulevard, Suite 200, Lanham, Maryland 20706
www.rowman.com

6 Tinworth Street, London SE11 5AL, United Kingdom

British Library Cataloguing in Publication Information Available

Library of Congress Cataloging-in-Publication Data

Library of Congress Control Number: 2021931435

ISBN 978-1-7936-0127-8 (cloth)
ISBN 978-1-7936-0129-2 (pbk)
ISBN 978-1-7936-0128-5 (electronic)

For Caroline, Kitty, and Phoebe,
with all my love.

Contents

List of Figures

List of Tables

Preface

A New Way of Thinking about Congress

The role of norms in American politics has been the subject of renewed attention over recent years. The presidency of Donald Trump comes to mind, with its frequently unconventional and purportedly norm-breaking behavior. But the U.S. Congress is also an institution in which norms are a key aspect of how the legislature functions or not. Historically, Congressional professionals and scholars alike pointed to norms identified by Donald Matthews's (1960) work on Senate "folkways" such as apprenticeship, legislative work (over showmanship), specialization, reciprocity, courtesy, and institutional patriotism. Yet, in the modern Congress, we can identify numerous instances where old norms are broken or just do not seem to apply. Think of instances such as South Carolina Republican Representative Joe Wilson shouting "You lie!" at President Barack Obama during a 2009 address to Congress, or the 2016 Democratic sit-in in the House over gun control. These seeming differences between the normative era that Matthews studied and our own warrant renewed attention.

Speaker of the House Sam Rayburn (D-Texas) famously provided advice to junior members of Congress, "You've got to go along to get along" (Lingeman 1975). This statement captures much of the essence of the "agreement-oriented context" (Rybicki 2003, 15) of the post–World War II U.S. Congress. Through much of the second half of the twentieth-century, the Congress was predominated by deliberation, compromise, and commitment to the resolution of legislation (Fenno 1966: 164). Despite underlying political divisions in American politics, on Capitol Hill the context of that increasingly bygone era was one where norms of cooperation flourished.

By the end of the century, norms of cooperation were rivaled by those of conflict. In the twenty-first century, some members, rather than abiding Speaker Sam's admonition, increasingly favored an attitude of "neither go along, nor get along." Norms of conflict have taken hold in the modern Congress. Today, we see these norms widely present, reflecting not only broader political conflict in American society, but the changing of members' fundamental ideas of what it means to be a lawmaker.

The emergence of norms of conflict threatens to further erode vestiges of cooperation and adds to the problems of a legislature already dominated by partisan polarization and gridlock. However, close inspection of congressional norms of the twenty-first century suggests that norms of cooperation are surprisingly resilient and widely shared among members in both chambers, Republicans and Democrats alike. It is perhaps in part because of the enduring presence of norms of conflict that the modern Congress is not even more conflict-addled than it already is. Without these norms of cooperation, dysfunction in Congress could be even worse.

This book focuses specifically on two normative contexts of the modern Congress, which exist simultaneously. In doing so, it borrows from the field of constructivism, which has been prevalent in political science subfields of comparative politics and international relations for at least the past two decades, to examine what members of Congress want, why they want it, and how they behave as a consequence. The answer includes empirical work to identify what norms exist in the Congress of the twenty-first century— updating work that started with Matthews and periodically revisited, but which has been largely untouched in recent years. These norms—the unwritten rules of Congress—serve many purposes. Some purposes of norms are instrumental, helping the institution to function and helping strategic members successfully achieve what they want. This behavioralist model is how political scientists have conventionally thought of norms. But to more fully understand the role played by congressional norms, this book proposes an alternate model for thinking about Congress and its members.

What has not been examined is a constructivist approach. In this, the manner in which shared ideas inform members' preferences, the beliefs they have about what is appropriate behavior as a lawmaker, and the very identity of what it is to be a member of Congress, inform a social theory of Congress. To understand the behavior of members of Congress in this model, it is not sufficient to focus exclusively on strategic, goal-oriented action toward reelection, power, or ideological outcomes. In a social theory of Congress, norms have both a causal and a constitutive effect on congressional behavior—they may act as constraints on rational lawmakers' decision-making, but they also form the basis of ideas that inform members' identities, preferences, and action. By giving consideration to congressional norms from a constructivist perspective, we can gain insight into the ideas that inform what it is that members of Congress want. A social theory of Congress allows us to craft an understanding of the institution that complements the dominant behavioralist models of congressional behavior and allows us to bring norms back into the study of Congress.

By examining the norms present in the modern Congress, updating the canon of norms that were found in the Congress of the past, and presenting a social theory of how these norms function, this book refreshes our knowledge of contemporary congressional norms while also arguing on behalf of a new theoretical perspective. A social theory of Congress helps us address a perennial question, "Do ideas or interests drive our politics?" On the political science podcast, *Politics in Question*, U.S. Senator Mike Lee (R-Utah) was asked that very question. He answered, "I don't think you can separate one from the other. It's a little like the distinction between cognitive and normative thoughts. You can't really tell where one ends and the other begins. It is certainly possible and it is always ideal for ideas to influence institutions, and even to affect and have a mediating influence on interests and the way that interests have an impact on institutions" (Azari, Drutman, and Wallner 2020, 2:17). A social theory of Congress posits the answer that it is a combination of both, but by studying the role ideas play in shaping preferences we can gain a better understanding of the relationship between ideas and interests.

Introducing concepts of constructivism to the scholarly discipline of congressional studies is no small task. The field is dominated by superlative work premised in rational choice and economic theories and backed by the rigors of the scientific method and quantitative analyses. A constructivist approach to Congress looks in many ways different from this behavioralist tradition in political science. However, virtually every other field in the social sciences and humanities has undertaken some form of ''postmodern turn,'' resulting in many new insights as well as new controversies. What follows is certainly not the last word in this new way of thinking about Congress, but I hope it gets the conversation started.

Acknowledgments

On the surface, this is a book about the modern Congress, and specifically about the role that norms play in the institution. For this, I hope it serves well the community of congressional scholars, professionals, and ordinary citizens interested in this important aspect of American politics. On another level, this book is the result of a lengthy intellectual journey, some of which began way back in my undergraduate years, but which came to fore in my career in public policy and, finally, academia. Along the way, there have been numerous people who supported me, encouraged me, indulged me, and, often, inspired me as I grew in the knowledge and experience that I hope is reflected in the modest manuscript that follows.

My most immediate debt is to the wonderful people at George Mason University, who welcomed me as an older working policy professional into their enriching community of political scientists. Their mentorship and encouragement both edified and inspired me throughout the entire experience of becoming a PhD. It was while working on my dissertation that the contours of this book took shape. At Mason, I am particularly grateful to Jennifer Victor, Tim Conlan, Rob McGrath, Suzanne Robbins, Pris Regan, Peter Mandaville, Anne Ludwick, Eric McGlinchey, Sonia Ben Ouagrham, Ahsan Butt, and the many other faculty and administrators whom I count as friends. A special shout-out goes to Peg Koback for her wonderful kindness and uncanny ability to keep me on track to meet all my degree requirements. The library staff at Mason was essential to work that began during my time there and which finally made it to print here, so I thank Debbie Kermer, Helen McManus, and Anne Brennan for their readiness to always help.

In 2015, I was honored to be awarded an American Political Science Association (APSA) Congressional Fellowship. The APSA Congressional Fellowship was one of the most rewarding experiences of my life. Through the fellowship, I met too many people to name, but at APSA I am particularly grateful to Betsy Super, Kara Abramson, and Barbara Walthall, whose support and friendship have made APSA one of my favorite places in Washington. I am also indebted to a grant from the William A. Steiger Fund for Legislative Studies, through which I was able to achieve an invaluable jump start on this project in the beautiful setting of the APSA building in downtown DC. As an APSA Congressional Fellow, I had the privilege of serving in the office of U.S. Senator Jack Reed (D-Rhode Island) and the incomparable intellectual and civic experience of working as a staff member on Capitol Hill. It is one of the great honors of my life to have worked for a man of such decency and integrity. I will always be grateful to the Senator and his kind, hardworking, and wonderful staff. Go Team Reed!

During the period I was writing this book, I have had the great pleasure of joining the faculty of the Department of Politics at Washington and Lee University, in Lexington, Virginia. Nothing could provide me greater professional satisfaction than to call W&L home. The fellowship of faculty, students, and alumni of this wonderful university makes it a truly special place. There are countless people encountered every day on campus and beyond who make teaching, writing, and research here a delight. In particular, I would like to thank Lucas Morel, who offered numerous bits of advice on writing a book but topped it all with the encouraging reminder to write the book I felt it was important to write. Bill Connelly is a good friend, mentor, and always ready-ally in defending Congress as *the* great institution of American democracy. Stu Gray always provides engaging conversation that keeps my mind attuned to a bigger picture, beyond Congress. Zoila Ponce de Leon provided much-needed assistance on statistical modeling and generously walked through some questions that were thorny to me but which she easily made clear. Additional gratitude goes to the limitlessly helpful librarians at Leyburn Library, such as Dick Grefe, Elizabeth Teaf, Emily Cooke, and each of the twenty-four-hour library people who make it always possible to, when in doubt, go to the library. Finally, W&L students are exceptional individuals and provided me much food for thought and encouragement through classroom discussions and on-campus conversations. In particular, I want to extend my appreciation to Luke Basham, who served as my summer research assistant in 2019. Luke's service on this project was immensely valuable and demonstrated his own extraordinary potential as a political scientist.

This book would not be possible if it were not for dozens of congressional professionals with whom I conducted anonymous interviews as part of the research, and the hundreds more who responded to my e-mails to complete the research survey. The willingness of so many current and former members of Congress and staff to share not just their insights but their time is testimony to the high caliber and decency of individuals working on behalf of the American people in Washington, DC. I am committed to your anonymity, but please know that I am grateful for your invaluable participation in this project. A number of political scientists and congressional scholars also provided encouragement, thoughtful insights, resources, and time in helping me at various stages of this research. I would like to extend particular gratitude to Sarah Binder, Martha Finnemore, Matt Green, Kevin Kosar, Francis Lee, Burdett Loomis, Nate Monroe, Mark Oleszek, Walter Oleszek, David Rohde, Colleen Shogan, and Sean Theriault. Betty Koed and Kate Scott of the Senate Historical Office and Matthew Wasniewski of the House Office of the Historian are wonderful for their enthusiasm and knowledge about the U.S. Congress and their readiness to help others understand the institutions they serve so well. In addition, dozens of conversations and encounters at political science conferences, policy events, and other meetings have proven invaluable to this project and remind me of what a strong community of scholars I am fortunate to be a part.

Going further back, I have been forever indebted to Miami University professors Nancy Nicholson, who encouraged me "to see the forest for the trees," and Jim Sosnoski who laid so much of the foundation for my later intellectual pursuits. At the University of Cincinnati, I am grateful for the support and mentorship of Richard Harknett and Abraham Miller. For my friend Alison Harvey, this is all part of one conversation that began at a Vienna courtyard, many years ago. A special thank you is also warranted to Howard Davis, Steve Kittrell, and my friends at Gentle East Taekwondo who help me keep a clear mind and to persevere in the face of the many challenges that go into a project of this sort.

In my family, I am grateful for Jack and Angela Finke whose enthusiasm for my efforts is a source of joy and inspiration and Tom Webb and Tom Maffeo, who each thoughtfully talked with me in many conversations about the topics herein. A special dedication is made to Marvis Maffeo, my mother-in-law, who passed away while this manuscript was being completed and who is sorely missed. I wish to thank my mom, for her love and support and for making this project easier by babysitting the kids, and my dad whose name is even in the title. Most of all, I write this for Kitty and Phoebe, to encourage you to do what you believe in, and do it to the best of your ability (while also making time every night for bedtime stories), and for Caroline, whose love makes everything I do not only possible, but worth it.

Chapter 1

Bringing Norms Back into the Study of Congress

The relevance of norms in American politics has been the topic of heightened attention in the period since the 2016 presidential election cycle and its aftermath. Much of this focus has been spawned by the many instances in which Donald Trump as a candidate and then president has been perceived as thwarting conventional wisdom about how a contender and a holder of the office of president ought to conduct herself (McCarthy 2018). Seemingly unconstrained by informal rules and guidelines on what is proper or appropriate behavior, Trump's conduct frequently calls attention to the unwritten rules—the norms—that presumably guide and constrain the attitudes and actions of national office holders in American politics, as well as the role that norms play in the functioning of American political institutions and the maintenance of democratic values in American society (Masket 2016; Jamieson and Taussig 2017; Schwartz 2017; Yglesias 2017).

Heightened interest regarding norms and concern over the effects of violations of long-held norms has extended to observers of the U.S. Congress (Drutman 2017; Lesniewski 2017). It is not uncommon nowadays to hear concerns over a "breakdown" of congressional norms (Huder 2017; Ornstein 2018). The urgency surrounding the role of norms in the functioning of American political institutions expressed among political analysts, pundits, and practitioners comes at a time when scholarship on norms in the U.S. Congress in political science research has been relatively silent. Central works on legislative norms date to the 1950s, with only periodic attention to the topic from varying perspectives during the years since. In 1995, Heinz Eulau wrote, "The systematic study of norms is one of the more neglected areas of research" in legislative studies (Eulau 1995, 585). More than two decades later, this statement remains true.

But how should scholars of Congress study norms? Quality work of the past, while frequently illuminating and instructive, does not fully address the context of the modern Congress. Norms identified in this previous literature may be outmoded, definitions inconsistent, methods for identifying norms analytically problematic, and a general theory of how norms affect congressional behavior underdeveloped. Previous research leaves open many relevant questions about the role of norms in the organization and behavior of the U.S. Congress and of its members in the opening decades of the twenty-first century.

The rise over the past several decades of partisan polarization, heightened political tensions within Congress and the country as a whole, and several high-profile breaches of courtesy in both the House and Senate suggest that a return to the study of norms in the scholarly discussion on congressional behavior is overdue. In his seminal study of Senate "folkways," Donald R. Matthews set out to answer questions such as "What, specifically, do the unwritten rules say? Why do they exist? In what ways do they influence the behavior of senators? How, concretely, are they enforced?" (Matthews 1959, 1064). Such questions remain important and, in many senses, open, ripe for fruitful research on the role that norms play in the contemporary Congress. This book embarks on this agenda, addressing requirements such as establishing an operational definition of norms, outlining a manner for the identification of contemporary norms, and exploring the empirical outcomes of congressional norms—that is, if norms exist, what difference do they make? Over time, norms have been studied through qualitative field research, quantitative surveys, and game theoretic behavioralism. The strengths and weaknesses of these approaches are considered, and a path is proposed for fruitful, ongoing study of congressional norms.

HOW DO WE DEFINE LEGISLATIVE NORMS?

If we are going to talk about congressional norms, it is necessary to arrive at an adequate definition of the concept of "norm" itself. Definitions of norms from congressional literature, other subfields of political science, and sociology help inform a conceptualization of norms that enables us to identify what norms are, which norms exist, and how norms function to affect the behavior and organization of Congress and its members. To look at the meaning as well as the limits of the definitions of norms in congressional scholarship, we can begin at the beginning with Donald Matthews's 1960 book-length treatment of the U.S. Senate: "The Senate of the United States, just as any other group of human beings, has its unwritten rules of the game, its norms of conduct, its approved manner of behavior. Some things are just not done, others are met with widespread approval . . . the standards to which senators are expected to conform" (Matthews 1960, 92). Calling these phenomena "folkways," he states, "these unwritten rules of behavior are normative . . . they define how a senator ought to behave" (Ibid., 116). In the 1959 journal article that preceded the book, Matthews offered a slightly different take, which contains terms generally implied and assumed in his and other subsequent work on legislative norms: "unwritten but generally accepted and informally enforced norms of conduct in the chamber" (Matthews 1959, 1064). In Matthews, we see key elements of an understanding of congressional norms that has informed subsequent discussion of the topic, even if inconsistently: norms are viewed as informal, unwritten rules about how lawmakers ought to behave or face the possibility of some form of sanction if they do not. They are different from formal rules, say of decorum or those governing the filibuster, which are part of written, enforceable guidelines of behavior. But the concept of congressional norms requires greater articulation if it is to help us identify and understand their role.

Norms are prescriptive. One meaning of norms implies that they are *descriptive*, in that they account for uniformity, statistical regularity, or repeated patterns of certain types of behavior (Blake and Davis 1964, 456; Gibbs 1965; Rohde 1988; Thomas 2000). However, in another view, norms are *prescriptive* in that they obligate social actors to certain behaviors they should follow and imply the possibility of some form of reprobation if they do not. It is the latter, prescriptive sense that is closer to what we have in mind when we discuss norms in Congress.[1] Echoes of Matthews are found throughout the literature on congressional norms which convey this prescriptive meaning. Richard Fenno speaks of congressional norms as comprising expectations and the prospects of sanctions for violating those expectations among members in legislative roles in the appropriations committees and process (Fenno 1966). Herbert Asher employs this definition: "A norm has been defined herein as a rule or standard of conduct appropriate to a person in a specified situation within a group. The norm describes the type of behavior expected by almost all of the other members of the group and often, though not necessarily, has associated with it sanctions for deviance" (Asher 1973, 500). Eulau refers to norms as "informal, unwritten, and, to an extent, even unspoken understanding[s] . . . of what is proper and improper conduct. These normative understandings orient and channel otherwise discretionary personal and/or interpersonal behavior in a socially mandated direction and call for expressions of approval or disapproval on the part of group members" (Eulau 1995, 585). Such terms pertaining to informality, obligation, appropriateness, how lawmakers *ought* to behave and an expectation of conformity are frequently expressed or implied in other conceptualizations of legislative norms (e.g., Hebert and McLemore (1973), Rohde (1988), Pettit

(1990), Choate (2003)). Borrowing a definition from comparative politics, norms serve as a kind of informal institution, comprised of "socially shared rules, usually unwritten, that are created, communicated, and enforced outside officially sanctioned channels" (Helmke and Levitsky 2004, 725). Put another way, in this logic, norms are *causal*: they lead to certain behavior that otherwise would not occur in their absence.[2]

Norms entail costs and benefits. The possibility of sanction for violating a norm is an intrinsic quality of the concept itself (e.g., Hebert and McLemore 1973). Some scholarly work on norms focuses on the obligation to adhere to norms as a strategic choice entailing costs and benefits. This approach is rooted in behavioralist and rational choice theories of Congress, seeing norms as a sense of what is agreed upon as proscribed or prescribed that act as constraints on strategic individual behavior (Coleman 1990). Norm adherence or rejection brings with it costs or benefits that a rational actor will weigh in determining whether to follow a norm, based on what is strategically beneficial (Knight 1992), a function of the capacity for sanction (Sinclair 1989), and because the expected payoff for doing so is greater than the benefits of not doing so (Weingast 1979). The expectation among members is that norm adherence will derive benefits to norm followers (Rohde, Ornstein, and Peabody 1985). "These rules are enforced by sanctions, positive and negative, that affect status, project success, and other valued outcomes" (Azari and Smith 2012, 40). This strategic logic is captured by Philip Pettit, who speaks of norms as being followed if "it is in people's individual interest, economic or social, to honor them" (Pettit 1990, 726).

Norms serve institutional purposes. The emergence of norms themselves may be based upon a need to solve collective action problems that help institutions function. This rational, strategic nature of norm adherence is also viewed as a means by which norms endure: "Norms are the outcome of learning in a strategic context; hence, they are a function of individual choices and, ultimately, of individual preferences and beliefs" (Bicchieri 1990, 839). Norms are "a cluster of expectations . . . a conditional choice based on expectations about other people's behavior and beliefs" (Ibid., 840). The sense of obligation to adhere to norms is driven by threat of sanction and game-theoretic calculations of costs and benefit of adherence or defection, but also because norms imply "a sort of action such that everyone is better off if everyone adopts it" (Pettit 1990, 738). The puzzle that Mancur Olson identified and subsequent research on prisoner's dilemma reaffirmed is that "individuals cannot overcome collective action problems and need to have externally enforced rules to achieve their own long-term self-interest" (Ostrom 2000, 137). Norms are unwritten rules that provide the logic by which cooperation emerges in social situations of competing, self-interested individuals or "rational egoists" (Ibid., 143). Ostrom's assessment comports with the Barbara Sinclair's proposition regarding Congress: "The existence of norms implies that the institution or its members collectively benefit from the behavior prescribed by those norms and therefore have an interest in promoting that behavior" (Sinclair 1989, 14).

Albeit driven by individual choice, norms may serve both individual legislators and the institution as a whole, "provid[ing] stability to an institution . . . [operating] to strengthen the power of an institution, facilitating the achievement of the goals of its members . . . or they may give power or perpetuate the power of certain members within the institution" (Rohde, Ornstein, and Peabody 1985, 149). Norms can provide an informal basis for institutional functionality which provides stability for members (March and Olsen 1989, 53), fulfilling Matthews's contention that folkways "provide motivation for the performance of legislative duties that, perhaps, would not otherwise be performed" (Matthews 1959, 1074). Norms fill gaps, coordinate operations, and regulate political behavior in formal institutions (Azari and Smith 2012). Norm adherence, in this view, becomes a function of a kind of collective trust, wherein some (indeterminate) level of defection among actors results in widespread abandonment of the norm as the benefits of adherence become less predictable and less probable, while sanctions for violation become less certain and more diffuse.

Norms are constitutive. Norms open the study of Congress to thus far unchartered intellectual territory. On the one hand, as discussed above, a conventional understanding of norms treats them as informal rules of behavior about which rational, strategic actors make calculated decisions when adhering to or rejecting a norm (e.g., Weingast 1979; Sinclair 1989). Ontologically, this is fairly rote ground for economic and behavioralist approaches to the study of political actors and institutions, premised on rational actors making strategic or economic choices toward maximizing utility in outcomes. In behavioralist models, if a norm exists, rational actors will make strategic decisions about the costs and benefits of following it. From another perspective, however, the study of norms opens to the field of congressional studies an interdisciplinary and constructivist understanding of congressional organization and the behavior of members of Congress (Alexander 2016). Here, the conventional rational actor perspectives are inadequate and a social theory of Congress becomes possible. Norms have not just a causal but also a constitutive effect on congressional behavior. That is, norms have an ideational basis in which shared ideas shape lawmaker identities, preferences, and actions. In this sense, norms are not simply an additional causal variable that explains congressional behavior. They are constitutive of the very idea of what it is to be a lawmaker and which preferences and behaviors are considered appropriate to being a member of Congress.

In a constitutive understanding of norms, norm adherence is not exclusively strategic; the sense of what is appropriate, of "fulfilling obligations in a role in a situation" (March and Olsen 1989, 160) is not an external constraint but, rather, fundamental to lawmakers very identity as lawmakers. Overby and Bell observe that "[as] norms become internalized over a long period they outlive the expiration of purely rational considerations and continue to exercise an influence on behavior even when individual utility concerns may dictate otherwise" (Overby and Bell 2004, 921–922). In proposing a social theory of Congress, I am explicitly adopting and applying concepts and language of constructivism in international relations to the field of congressional studies. A social theory of Congress articulates how norms matter both materially and constitutively in congressional behavior. Shared ideas (e.g., a norm of cooperation) and material factors (e.g., electoral or institutional constraints) interact to create preferences. Preferences, in this regard, are social structures. Ideas are "constitutive" because they are shared among social actors and form the basis upon which identities and interests are formed and by which related rational, strategic, and consequentialist decision-making and action occurs. Indeed, constructivist definitions of norms speak to the way in which norms are not simply preferences, but part of the identities that comprise the basis of preferences. Constructivist theorists define norms as "standards of appropriate behavior for actors with a given identity" (Finnemore and Sikkink 1998, 891) and "collectively held beliefs that shape actors' preferences and 'legitimate social purpose' and constrain and enable their behavior in a complex . . . system" (Evers 2017, 787).

From a constitutive perspective derived from constructivist theory, norms are not just instrumental, material constraints that limit the behavior of rational egoists. Rather, norms serve to form the identities and the interests of the actors themselves. In this sense, norms do not work in the service of instrumentality; they serve to create the ideas that inform interests in the first place. They are "the means which allow people to pursue goals, share meanings, communicate with each other, criticize assertions, and justify actions" (Kratochwil 1989, 11). Norms are "guidance devices which are designed to simplify choices and impart 'rationality' to situations by delineating the factors that a decision-maker has to take into account" (Ibid. 10). Beyond a functional or strategic role alone, in other words, norms help inform the nature of preferences from which other activity follows. Such an understanding of norms invites an alternative (although not mutually exclusive) interpretation of cooperation in the U.S. Congress. For example:

> A constructivist analysis of cooperation . . . would concentrate on how the
> expectations produced by behavior affect identities and interests. The process
> of creating institutions is one of internalizing new understandings of self and

other, of acquiring new role identities, not just of creating external constraints
on the behavior of exogenously constituted actors. Even if not intended as such,
in other words, the process by which egoists learn to cooperate is at the same
time a process of reconstructing their interests in terms of shared commitments
to social norms. (Wendt 1992, 417)

In this constructivist sense, norms become part of the identities of members
of Congress themselves and serve to shape preferences irrespective of the
instrumental outcomes they may produce.

Norms are ambiguous social facts. Post–Matthews political science, as
well as sociological literature (e.g., Blake and Davis 1964; Gibbs 1965),
focus on shared understandings and the possibility of sanctions for violations thereof as fundamental aspects of social norms. Yet there is an implicit
ambiguity about the specific qualities of a given norm as well as the prob-
ability of being sanctioned or rewarded for violating or adhering to it. That
is, norms themselves are inherently ambiguous, and such ambiguity is part
of their nature and their effect. Norms, as is often stated, are not explicit
rules or laws; they are not conventions or values around which statements of
belief are expressly stated or clearly communicated (Gilbert 2008). Schneier
indicates such when he writes, regarding the persistence of legislative norms,
"norm observance was not universal and the boundaries marking deviant
behavior were not clearly staked" (Schneier 1988, 118). What's more, the
appetites and tolerance for deviance as well as for imposing sanctions vary
among lawmakers in ways that are not universal, clear, or even predictable.
Where Sinclair observes that norms change and fall by the wayside "unless
most members understand each other and keep their word most of the time"
(Sinclair 1989, 98), there remains an expectation that most but not all of the
time a norm can be counted on to be followed. Some members of Congress
may have higher tolerance for punishment (Schneier 1988, 130) while others may base their careers in part on being normative outliers and mavericks
(Huitt 1961). Matthews states outright: "in the Senate there are occasional
careers to be made out of deliberate nonconformity" (Matthews 1959, 1064),
a statement as true of the Congress today as it was of the Senate of the 1950s.

Norms, as we understand the imperatives or obligations they imply as well
as the possibility of sanctions for their violation, are by their nature *ambiguous social facts*. What we *should* do and the penalty we *may* incur for not
doing so is expressly indeterminate in norms and normative behavior. Rules
are matched with penalties for their violation; norms entail ambiguous terms
of adherence and uncertain costs if they are disregarded. For instance, Gibbs
(1965) composes a taxonomy of nineteen possible attributes of norms, and
Crawford and Ostrom (1995) place norms in the context of no fewer than
sixteen concepts of normative motivation. Without questioning the analytic

rigor and validity of such taxonomic and epistemological work, when a social concept is so detailed and complex that it requires a dozen or more conceptual distinctions to identify it, the terms of adherence and rejection become even harder to render unambiguously in a dynamic social context populated by mere mortal minds (where not all of us are Nobel Prize-winning Elinor Ostrom). Even within such rich analysis of the nature and dynamics of norms, ambiguity is a fundamental part of norms as social facts: norms "are *ad hoc* and lack a generalized rationale in that they do not explicitly identify the dimensions to which their components might be referable" (Gibbs 1965, 588). Where Bicchieri assigns game theoretic rationality to norm conformity, the "cluster" of expectations around normative behavior in a social setting contains, by necessity, an element of uncertainty over the behavior of other rational actors (Bicchieri 1990). In another example, Hebert and McLemore define norms as "expectations which more or less effectively define the boundaries of appropriate conduct for the members of the legislature" (Hebert and McLemore 1973, 506). Boundaries of behavior that are "more or less" defined provide intrinsic leeway regarding when to follow them and when they will be enforced. Thus, ambiguity is part of the very essence of norms. Norms are what we *should* do in social behavior under the threat of the possible but uncertain penalty that may result if we do not, but there always remains ambiguity about what should be done and the consequences of not doing so. This ambiguity is a key distinguishing feature of norms as compared to law, regulations, formal rules, and other shared social understandings like conventions or values. The imperatives and the penalties of norms are inherently contextual and unclear.

In sum, based on the literature on norms across fields of congressional studies, sociology, and constructivism, an operational definition of legislative norms can be stated as such: *Legislative norms are informal prescriptive rules, often unwritten or unspoken, about how lawmakers should or ought to behave in the functioning of the institution, violations of which may result in some form of reprobation or sanction. Such norms may be constitutive, in that they form the basis of the identities or preferences that lawmakers hold with regard to their role as lawmakers. These informal prescriptive rules are inherently ambiguous social facts—the exact terms of the rule and the conditions upon which violations thereof may be met with sanction is intrinsically inexact.*

WHAT LEGISLATIVE NORMS EXIST?

With an adequate definition of norms in hand, we can ask, what norms currently exist in the U.S. Congress? This, however, raises several issues. First, any norms previously identified or newly uncovered would need to meet the terms of the definition in some sufficient fashion. This is not a daunting task in its own right—the present definition, while it adds such factors as ambiguity and the possibly constitutive nature of norms—otherwise contains generally accepted concepts regarding what legislative norms are. The greater challenge lies in epistemological and methodological questions about how we identify the existence of a norm and which, if any, previously identified congressional norms can be said to exist in the modern Congress. This latter concern raises related questions about the methodology by which any—past or present—study of norms may be adequate to sufficiently establish the existence of a given norm.

Matthews set the course for the study of legislative norms by identifying six "folkways" of the U.S. Senate of 1956 and 1958: apprenticeship, legislative work, specialization, courtesy, reciprocity, and institutional patriotism. These folkways have, as Eulau puts it, "an almost canonical quality and impact" (Eulau 1995, 588), appearing in the subsequent literature "with monotonous regularity, first as almost self-evident truths, later as guideposts to record change" (Ibid.). Indeed, this cannon should be challenged. Not only has the congressional context changed and our conceptualization of legislative norms become more highly articulated than in Matthews's day, methodologically this work operated under a different style and standard of rigor than is acceptable today. While contemporary research would probably benefit if there were more field interviews and *in situ* observation, by relying almost exclusively on such data, Matthews is vulnerable to common critiques regarding reproducibility and observer bias of such approaches to data gathering and hypothesis testing. Moreover, sixty-years out, when so much else has changed about Congress, a fresh look at active, existing norms merits undertaking.

In the intervening years, much research on norms either confirms the persistence of some set of Matthews's original six (e.g., Rohde 1988) or uses those norms as a starting point to explore how those norms have evolved or fallen out of favor in both the House and Senate (e.g., Schneier 1988; Uslaner 1993; Choate 2003). There is a strong research commitment to the norms first spelled out by Matthews in the congressional literature, with only a few additional norms repeatedly identified or empirically investigated. Asher's study of how members learn legislative norms borrowed an open-ended question from Wahlke et al. (1962) but focused on evidence of norms that members of the House quickly assimilate norms that Matthews and Fenno identified, "specialization, reciprocity, legislative work, courtesy, and aspects of apprenticeship" (Asher 1973, 500). Loomis and Fishel used survey research of members of the House to find evidence of the conditional resilience of norms of seniority and apprenticeship in following 1970s reforms (Loomis and

Fishel 1981). Rohde, Peabody, and Ornstein (1985) identify substantial continuity in the 1970s and early 1980s among the Senatorial norms of Matthews's folkways. Choate, based on interviews with members of the House in the 104th Congress, finds "the continuing importance of [such] norms [as seniority, specialization, and reciprocity] in the minds of members" (Choate 2003, 140). Even Sinclair's groundbreaking work, which departed from functionalism and how norms act as informal institutions toward game-theoretic and rational choice modeling of norm adherence (and the evolution of the Senate to a more outward-facing, individualistic institution), relied upon Matthews's folkways to illustrate her argument (Sinclair 1989).

Matthews's norms are not, of course, the only norms identified by congressional scholars. Huitt pointed to the normative aspects of party loyalty to nominees by presidents of the same party (Huitt 1957). In the 1960s, scholars looked to legislative norms that facilitated committee integration and functionality. Fenno, for example, identified three norms that functioned in the House of the 1950s and 1960s to "promote harmony and reduce conflict among subcommittees": specialization, reciprocity, and subcommittee unity (Fenno 1962, 316). Manley identified a normative context in House committee settings that included "restrained partisanship, responsible lawmaking, and reasonable behavior" (Manley 1965, 935–936). Polsby speaks to normative aspects of an agreement-oriented context of the pre-reform committee system of the 1950s and 1960s (Polsby 2004, 114–124). Uslaner addresses the decline of the norm of comity in Congress, a function of not only changes in the institution but also the deterioration of civility in American political discourse in general (Uslaner 1993). Overby and Bell (2005) identify evidence for norms of cooperation and consent in the use of the Senate filibuster in the period 1975–1993: "retiring senators do not entirely and en masse disregard the chamber's norms of comity and cooperation in order to pursue narrowly personal legislative goals" (Overby and Bell 2005, 920). Senate obstruction, the "replacement of a majoritarian informal rule with a supermajoritarian one," in which use of the cloture rule has become common place over the period of the 1970s to the present may be attributable, at least in part, because "senators have replaced one shared understanding of acceptable practice—one unwritten rule—with another" (Azari and Smith 2012, 46). It is not that structural and strategic factors play no role, but evidence of a normative basis in such behavior exists as well. There are, no doubt, other cases where scholars have identified congressional norms that this author has overlooked.

Other research illustrates the methodological difficulty of finding consensus around the existence of specific legislative norms. For instance, open-ended interview questions result in a bevy of identified norms. Wahlke et al. identify no fewer than forty-two "rules of the game" based on interviews with legislators in four states (Wahlke et al. 1962). Hebert and McLemore, in a survey of Iowa state legislators, find at least nineteen norms but little by way of consensus with respect to which particular norms are operative and when (Hebert and McLemore 1973). This can be attributed to the variance in responses and terminology endemic to interview questioning as well as the statistical difficulty of identifying significant consensus around a particular norm or set of norms. Such diversity in norm identification and variance in the acceptance rates of particular norms suggests the difficulty of substantiating the existence of any specific norm and the possibility of consequences for violating it.

The congressional context has changed dramatically in the intervening decades since political scientists first started writing about norms in Congress. Our understanding of norms is more sophisticated, and past methodological approaches of interviews and direct observation to identify norms are not without shortcomings. While much work has been conducted over the years to test the existence, evolution, or extinction of legislative norms, a productive avenue for future research is to look afresh at the institutional context of the modern, post-1994 reform, leadership-dominated, polarized Congress to identify norms that currently exist, and which meet the conditions of a definition that encompasses the prescriptive, institutional, constitutive qualities of norms. In the chapters that follow, such work begins. While not every possible existing congressional norm is identified, a combination of methodological approaches and a focus on the modern Congress finds a context dominated by norms of cooperation, conflict, and those of a changing culture. Prevalent norms of the early twenty-first century include norms previously identified which facilitate cooperation, such as apprenticeship, reciprocity, and cooperation, and norms of conflict that include nonconformity, and partisanship. In addition, norms of a changing culture have affected practices on Capitol Hill, which include sexual propriety and sobriety.

DO NORMS MATTER?

The question of what norms exist is tied to ontological presuppositions about the nature of norms in a social system; that is, what place do norms hold in how people understand the world and the way they make decisions on how to act in it? In the definition of norms provided here, norms may have several different effects on the organization and behavior of Congress and its members. In a research agenda exploring the nature of norms in the contemporary Congress, the effect of norms would vary based on the aspect of norms one is seeking to identify, as well as the institutional contexts of the House and Senate. Norms, as explained, may be causal or constitutive. They exist as social facts—shared understandings—that constrain individual strategic behavior, solve institutional collective action problems, or are the ideational bases of identities and preferences. Norms are also intrinsically ambiguous, so any evidence of their existence or their effects is subject to uncertainty and unexpected variance. Evidence of norms and their effects may, therefore, be identified in multiple ways, but the aspect of norms being examined must be stated carefully so as to avoid confusion and the epistemological strategies to identify norms and their effects must be clear and related to that purpose. Meanwhile, the methodological challenges of identifying norms and norm-based outcomes are significant but not insurmountable.

To date, there has been substantial research on instrumental aspects of norms, premised on their prescriptive nature in which they act as constraints on strategic behavior, often in the service of institutional functionality. Research beginning with Matthews (1959; 1960), and scholars who subsequently sought evidence of his "folkways" in the performance of the institution, committees, or leadership (e.g., Asher 1973; Rohde, Peabody, and Ornstein 1985; Choate 2003) indicate the way norms help the institution of Congress function, disincentivizing individual members from defecting from unwritten, prescriptive rules (Weingast 1979; Sinclair 1989). Much of this research focuses on how Matthews's norms have changed or endured through periods of institutional change, such as through the reforms of the 1970s (e.g., Rohde 1988; Schneier 1988).

On the other hand, unexamined avenues exist for the exploration of norms and their effects in the contemporary Congress. Surveys conducted by John Wahlke and his collaborators in the 1960s, Herbert Asher in the 1970s, and Judd Choate in the 1990s offer opportunities to replicate research on the existence of specific norms previously identified and assess their persistence, while potentially uncovering new norms not previously discovered or in existence. Moreover, given the transformation of the institution over the previous six decades, and given at least fifteen years since the last book-length treatment of Matthews's norms (Choate 2003), old norms have likely evolved or dissolved while new ones will have emerged. Creative approaches to identifying norms are also necessary, but in limited supply in current research. Exceptions are Marvin Overby and Lauren Bell, who examine norms of cooperation and consent by looking at variance in filibuster activity of retiring Senators for evidence of normative versus strategic motivation of filibustering in the Senate (Overby and Bell 2005). Julia Azari and Jennifer Smith find evidence of the emergence of a supermajoritarian norm in the Senate by looking at usage of the cloture rule (Azari and Smith 2012). Other scholars are using computer-based textual analysis of linguistic patterns to find relationships between normative attitudes and governance in the presidential rhetoric of Donald J. Trump, with as possible application in future congressional studies (Jamieson and Taussig 2017). Political ethnography, often out of favor or the subject of methodological controversy among political scientists (Sohn 2016), entails participant observation, semistructured interviews, and mixed methods. This approach has been a cornerstone of some of the formative research on norms in legislative studies (e.g., Matthews 1959; Fenno 1966; Asher 1973; Loomis and Fishel 1981) and can be continually fruitful in the identification of contemporary congressional norms and their effects. Research for the present study, for instance, relies heavily on participant observation and first-person accounts of primary congressional players to draw its findings and conclusions.

Evidence presented in the chapters to follow points to the simultaneous existence of norms of cooperation and conflict in the modern Congress. While older norms of cooperation such as courtesy are present, norms of conflict such as nonconformity have emerged in the period since the 1990s, providing a countervailing normative milieu to the one that dominated Congress for much of the middle part of the twentieth century. Interviews about legislative norms with current and former members Congress and congressional staff point to an erosion of norms of cooperation in favor of norms of conflict. Through much of the post–World War II era an agreement-oriented context existed in which norms of deliberation, compromise, and commitment to the resolution of legislation (Fenno 1966, 617) underscored much of the behavior in Congress. However, beginning in the 1990s, this agreement-oriented context eroded, and saw the rise of norms favoring conflict, in which obstructionism and individualistic behavior are among the shared expectations members hold regarding one another, coinciding with a period of heightened partisan polarization and stalemate in the U.S. Congress. The U.S. Senate captured in Matthews (1960) characterizes the is characterized by norms of cooperation, whereas more recent work on the culture of Congress embodies norms of conflict (Wolfensberger 2012). As one former member of Congress stated, "partisan patriotism has trumped institutional patriotism" (Interview 2016).[3] A former senior staffer said, "norms to me are the manner in which people work with each other, especially across the aisle. And those norms have eroded terribly" (Interview 2016).

Additional questions arise as to whether such behavior is normative as compared to more purely instrumental or strategic, serving self-interest in a postreform context of strong party leaders, ideological conflict, and partisan polarization. The challenge, as Overby and Bell put it, is "to draw analytical distinctions between behavior that is motivated by accession to norms and behavior that is driven purely by self-interest" (Overby and Bell 2005, 911). Evidence from surveys and interviews provides insight into what lawmakers understand as appropriate attitudes or behaviors. Such attitudes inform what is appropriate, informing them how to respond to particular ideological or strategic contexts. Not all ideological or strategic contexts lead to inevitable choices on preferences or which behaviors are appropriate. Norms inform such choices. Evidence points to the independent effect of a norm of partisan conflict where members no longer face sanctions for individual, obstructionist behavior, and partisan conflict is the informal rule to which members are expected to adhere. There is an instrumental component to this norm—members are incentivized to adhere to a norm of partisan conflict. There is also a constitutive aspect of such norms, in which the very identities of lawmakers are no longer that of a deliberative legislator of an older cooperation-oriented context, but of that of a partisan warrior, where identities, preferences, and expectations are structured around partisan conflict. The norm of partisanship affects which behaviors are appropriate given particular partisan ideological or strategic contexts.

THE CHAPTERS AHEAD

Speaking to reporters in the fall of 2017, Republican Senator Marco Rubio of Florida warned of the deterioration of norms in the U.S. Senate. "We have to understand that a republic really can't function unless there are some norms of behavior that are not legally prescribed or in the law. It's just the way human beings should conduct themselves in interacting with one another," he said (Lesniewski 2017). Intuitively, Senator Rubio understands what political scientists have meant regarding legislative norms in the U.S. Congress and how they serve to constrain individual behavior and help the Congress function as an institution. His statement implies an understanding that norms are informal rules about shared understandings of what is valued and what is appropriate.

The purpose of the present research is to go beyond intuitive understandings to provide clearer definitions of concepts relating to norms, identify examples of the normative phenomena under question, and assess the effects of norms on the institution of the U.S. Congress. If, as Sarah Binder suggests, "history and norms become embedded into institutions and then come to shape lawmakers' preferences and priorities" (Binder 2015, 7), the nature and effects of norms—both causal and constitutive—warrant our attention.

At a time when political norms in the United States and, in particular, the U.S. Congress have evolved or are potentially under attack, it is imperative to turn our attention to what these norms are, what effects they have, and what, if anything, would be lost if existing norms change or go away altogether. As scholars, the opportunity is ripe to undertake much original research on congressional norms to address old questions worth reexamination and new questions heretofore unexplored. As citizens, if warnings by Senator Rubio are accurate, it is imperative that we undertake such research for the sake of American democracy itself. The chapters ahead begin to lead us on this journey.

NOTES

1. A key distinction is made between two common usages of the term "norms" in common language. On the one hand, patterns of observed behavior are referred to as "the norm," which is distinct from what behavior is expected (Rohde 1988). Norms in the sense we mean here imply a kind of social imperative, an expectation, and a sense of what is appropriate. A pattern of observed behavior cannot be assumed to be indicative of a norm without other corroborating evidence or at least the assumption that an observed behavior is based on an expectation. Illustrating the difference, for example, David Rohde quips that in the era of 1970s and 1980s Democratic control of the House there could have been considered a norm against being Republican because Democrats achieved more legislative successes (Ibid., 140–141).

2. Heinz Eulau suggests that congressional norms exist along one end of a continuum of formality. "At one end are enacted, or positive, rules of varying duration that are always subject to instant reform through amendment or new rules of formal nature" (Eulau 1995, 585). On the other end are norms.

3. Interviews conducted by author during period 2016–2020. Interviewees granted the author permission to quote responses anonymously, without attribution.

Chapter 2

A Constructivist Approach
to Congressional Norms

Simply stated, the theory I am putting forward is that norms have both a causal and a constitutive effect on congressional behavior. On the one hand, we can see how norms act as constraints on a rational lawmaker's decision-making, akin to other material constraints such as electoral imperatives or the strategic requirements of obtaining power in Congress and achieving policy goals. On the other hand, norms have an ideational basis in which shared ideas shape lawmaker identities, preferences, and actions. In this sense, norms are not simply an additional causal variable that explains congressional behavior. They are constitutive of the very idea of what it is to be a lawmaker and the behaviors considered appropriate as a member of Congress.

In Congress itself, two major normative contexts have dominated the period since World War II: a normative context of cooperation and a context of conflict. Understanding the material and ideational aspects of norms of cooperation and conflict provides insight into the rational and strategic grounds of such behavior as well as the constitutive basis from which preferences originate and norms of appropriate behavior are formed. In addition, norms of a changing culture, particularly social mores pertaining to gender and socializing, are also evident in the modern Congress, affecting both formal rules and informal constraints.

In proposing a social theory of Congress, I am explicitly adopting and applying concepts and language of constructivism in international relations to the field of congressional studies (e.g., Kratochwil 1989; Onuf 1989; Wendt 1992, 1999; Finnemore 1996; Katzenstein 1996). It is curious that this discussion has not occurred before now. Virtually every field in the social sciences and the humanities over the past half-century has undertaken some form of "postmodern turn," in which it is examined how ideas, identities, and norms inform interests, preferences, and behavior among communities of political agents. Within political science itself, the fields of international relations, comparative politics, political theory, and American political development have each had productive, often spirited, debates regarding norms and the material and ideational determinants of political behavior and outcomes (e.g., Finnemore and Sikkink 2001; Orren and Skowronek 2004; James, Bertucci, and Hayes 2018). Meanwhile, although Americanists are no strangers to protests over the dominance of behavioralism (Petracca 1991; Green and Shapiro 1996; Monroe 2005; Luke 2013) congressional studies, amidst a tremendously productive period of data-driven and rational choice research, has all but tabled discussion of norms.

The constructivist paradigm offers great promise for the study of Congress. To accept norms as ideas that inform actors' identities and their senses of what is appropriate allows us to look beyond the rational, strategic, and consequentialist thinking of the dominant schools of thought in American political science on how we think about Congress. This is not to replace or disprove such approaches, but to complement them. In nonacademic terms, a social theory of Congress allows us to see how members of Congress—those who wield the formal power of the legislative branch—are not fully strategic, Machiavellian, or grounded in clear and deep ideological principles. Rather, like all humans, the beliefs and behaviors of members of Congress are also rooted in the ambiguities of culture, socialization, and an unarticulated, almost subconscious sense of appropriateness. In other words, beyond rationality, members of Congress are driven by norms.[1]

A social theory of Congress articulates how norms matter both materially and constitutively in congressional behavior. Shared ideas (e.g., a norm of courtesy) and material factors (e.g., electoral or institutional constraints) interact to create preferences. Preferences, in this regard, are social structures. Ideas are "constitutive" because they are shared among social actors and form the basis upon which identities and interests are formed. Ideas underlie the choices and actions of lawmakers based on a shared understanding of what is appropriate or valued; this may include, but not necessarily, related rational, strategic, and consequentialist decision-making and actions. A social theory of Congress does not dismiss the roles, for example, of parties, ideological conflict, or institutions in accounting for strategically or consequentially bound congressional behavior and policy outcomes. The rational choice framework upon which theories of Congress are based is both theoretically productive and a necessary component of explaining the behavior of the institution and its members. However, I propose that a more robust theory of Congress includes both materialist and ideational approaches to norms and the origins of preferences in Congress. Just as norms may constrain, they may guide behavior as well. Matthew Green suggests, "[e]xisting norms and practices matter, too: some tactics gradually accrete until they develop a sort of 'autonomous motivational dynamic,' done simply because they always have been done and there is an unquestioned faith that they work" (Green 2015, 19). When Binder suggests, "history and norms become embedded into institutions and then come to shape lawmakers' preferences and priorities" (Binder 2015, 7), then addressing the causal and constitutive nature and effects of norms provides a more complete understanding of the U.S. Congress.

In what follows, I discuss the contrast between behavioralist approaches and constructivism, articulate how we can understand a constructivist approach to Congress, and identify empirical research strategies for identifying norms and applying the theory, queuing up cases where norms play a constitutive role in Congress that are examined in the chapters ahead.

CONSEQUENTIALISM AND CONGRESSIONAL NORMS

The predominant approach in political science to studying norms in Congress treats norms as informal rules of behavior about which rational, strategic actors make calculated decisions in adhering to or rejecting a norm. Ontologically, this is rooted in economic and behavioralist approaches to the study of political actors and institutions (Downs 1957; Riker 1962; Olson 1965; Ordeshook 1986). In this "consequentialist" approach, norms act as constraints on strategic behavior of individual members of Congress. Norm adherence or rejection brings with it costs or benefits that a rational actor will weigh in determining whether to follow a norm. In this sense, norm adherence is instrumental based on what is strategically beneficial (Knight 1992), a function of the capacity for sanctions (Sinclair 1989), and because the expected payoff for doing so is greater than the benefits of not doing so (Weingast 1979). The expectation among members is that norm adherence will derive benefits to norm followers (Rohde, Ornstein, and Peabody 1985). "These rules are enforced by sanctions, positive and negative, that affect status, project success, and other valued outcomes" (Azari and Smith 2012, 40).

In the instrumental sense, norm adherence or rejection is based on a logic of consequences: following a norm is a function of a calculation of the likelihood of benefits or costs of being sanctioned for such action. In rational actor models, norm adherence is rooted in the ability of other actors to impose sanctions and the relative cost of those sanctions, as weighed against the costs of norm rejection. Thus, the rational choice framework places norms along a hierarchy of preferences (Coleman 1990, 274). This logic accounts for why autonomous strategic actors would adhere to an informal rule, or social convention, such as a norm. Jack Knight provides a thorough account of this approach:

The key feature of a social convention is that adherence to its rules is beneficial for the actors in a particular interaction. Each of the actors prefers to coordinate (either implicitly or by explicit agreement) on one of the beneficial conventions, as opposed to arriving at an outcome that involves a failure to coordinate. The rules of the convention provide the information about the future actions of others necessary to achieve that coordination. In formal terms, the convenient constitutes an equilibrium outcome for the actors in the game: Compliance with the convention is their best reply to the strategic choices of the other actors. Hence, if they can coordinate on a particular rule, the rule will be self-enforcing. That is, as long as the individual actor can do better for himself or herself by acting in accordance with the institution than he or she can do by abandoning the institution, that actor will continue to respect its constraints, regardless of the absence of an external-enforcement mechanism. (Knight 1992, 98)

Norm adherence, therefore, is strategically sensible when lawmakers pursue a hierarchy of preferences and action in a context of repeated interaction. In this materialist framework, norm adherence may lead to behavior inconsistent with other interests if their payoff is greater than the alternative of defecting from the norm. A norm may oppose "the actor's own interests, either directing him toward doing something he would not otherwise want to do or toward not doing something he would otherwise want to do" (Coleman 1999, 250).

Norms, therefore, become obligations, but they implicitly provide a net benefit to those who adhere to them or those whose behavior they constrain, as Barbara Sinclair explains:

[T]he concept of norms incorporates the notion of obligation; norms do not simply specify instrumental behavior of no particular interest to anyone else. In a modern institution, the existence of norms implies that the institution or its members collectively benefit from the behavior prescribed by those norms and therefore have an interest in promoting that behavior. That norms have this obligatory aspect also implies that abiding by norms involves some cost to the individual. (Sinclair 1989, 14)

Thus, in the materialist or consequentialist approach to norms, an actor may adhere to a norm for strategic, instrumental purposes, even though the immediate behavior or the norm in question may entail costs or contradict other interests. Norm adherence remains "rational" in that it is part of a broader hierarchy of preferences and cost-benefit analysis.

Norm adherence in the Senate, for instance, can be explained by the game theoretic logic of the prisoner's dilemma. Sinclair illustrates this by applying the logic Robert Axelrod's *The Evolution of Cooperation* (1984) to the adherence to senatorial norms. "Abiding by norms involves some cost; not conforming results in a higher payoff whatever other senators do" (Sinclair 1989, 15), which raises a puzzle as to why senators would incur the costs of adhering to a norm. The answer, Sinclair explains, lies in a strategic calculation of costs versus benefits: the temptation of payoff (T) is greater than the reward (R) for mutual cooperation (T>R) and the punishment (P) for mutual defection is greater than the sucker's payoff (S), (P>S). "On the other hand, the cost of conforming is not too high," in that the reward for mutual cooperation is greater than the punishment for mutual defection (R>P). In other words, "everyone is better off if everyone conforms" (Ibid.).

Such logic is analogous to the strategic calculus of states in the international system, as explained in international relations theory. For example, in neorealism (e.g., Waltz 1979) the interests of states are presumed to be determined by the material factors, in particular but not limited to state survival, that structure the international system. Individual states are autonomous actors who derive their interests based on such external factors of the international system as the balance of power, the imperatives of survival, among others. Actions, in this context, are consequentialist in that they are rational or strategic means toward ends, based on a calculation of how such actions will help an actor achieve particular goals that are consistent with preexisting (that is, ontologically *a priori*) interests (Wendt 1999, 34). Similar to neorealism, in behavioralist or economic approaches to Congress, such as Sinclair or Weingast put forward, interests drive immediate action toward consequences—anticipated ends such as reelection, power in Congress, particular policy or partisan outcomes, and electoral advantage (Mayhew 1974; Fenno 1978; Lee 2009; Koger and Lebo 2017). Such rational choice theories, whether from international relations or congressional studies, assume autonomous actors with fixed, hierarchical preferences around which cost-benefit calculations are made to best advance interests and optimize outcomes. In behavioralism, or the consequentialist approach, norms are just one aspect of this economic calculus.

It is along consequentialist terms that, for example, the norm of courtesy can be understood to function in the U.S. Congress. A 2005 essay by the *CQ* publisher and longtime congressional observer Robert Merry captures the consequentialist logic of the courtesy norm, both its spirit and function, in the Senate:

[T]he mores and folkways of an institution that for more than two centuries has stood as the country's bulwark against flighty or ill-considered governmental action. It has never been easy getting legislation through this most august of governmental bodies, and so the smart senator always knew that collegiality and cooperation had to transcend ideology or partisan impulse. You never knew when you might need the help of another senator, however divergent his view of the world might be from yours. And this gave shape to the cultural sensibility that has guided senatorial behavior through the decades: the elaborate courtesies, the political patience and perseverance, the institutional reverence, and the understanding that all of these things. (Merry 2005)

In other words, from an instrumentalist perspective, courtesy pervades Congress because it is advantageous to behave courteously. This aspect of the courtesy norm is understood by those on the Hill. A senior Democratic staff captured both the norm as well as the instrumental purposes to following it: "In the Senate there is a principle of comity, which is essentially the ability to get along and disagree without being disagreeable. I think there is some sort of unofficial scoreboard on keeping your word, nothing is ever really recorded, but members do keep track" (Interview 2019).

In this logic of consequences, norms help self-interested actors maximize individual gain while achieving shared common outcomes—cooperation is a desired individual behavior because the individual outcomes of cooperating are superior to those of not cooperating. From a consequentialist perspective, the norm of courtesy embodies this reasoning: "Conformity involved some cost to the individual, but by and large, if everyone conformed, everyone was better off" (Sinclair 1989, 21). Members choose to adhere to the norm—courtesy, in this case—because they view the consequences of norm adherence as superior to those of being norm rejection. In this respect, the norm is a means toward some other end. To draw a Kantian analogy, the courtesy norm under the logic of consequences is a hypothetical imperative chosen not because it embodies a good manner of being, but because it is instrumental in obtaining some other objective. But consequentialist logic is not enough to fully explain norms in Congress.

Consequentialist logic is contrasted to the role of ideas in forming interests and identities in Alexander Wendt's work, *A Social Theory of International Relations* (1999). Wendt's account of realist scholars in international relations theory is analogous to the rational choice approaches to norms in congressional studies (e.g., Weingast 1979; Sinclair1989), which "treat ideas as 'variables' that interact with material forces to produce outcomes. They ask 'how much variance in behavioral outcomes is explained by ideas as opposed to power and interest?' This is a causal question and it captures an important aspect of the difference that ideas make" (Wendt 1999, 78). Norms in the rational choice, or consequentialist framework, are just another causal independent variable, the effects of which can be looked for in widely utilized quantitative and qualitative methods and the logic of inference (see, for instance, King, Keohane, and Verba 1994). But in a social theory of international relations norms shape "actions and beliefs by constituting actors' identities and interests" (Hoffman 2017, 1). In the constructivist approach, "the manner in which the material world shapes and is shaped by human action and interaction depends on dynamic normative and epistemic interpretations of the material world" (Adler 1997, 322). This, of course, is not to say that material reality is not consequential but the manner in which actors, whether states in international relations or legislators in the institution of Congress, interact with material constraints is based on how identities and interests are shaped by norms.

The logic of consequences assumes particular interests or goals and agents who behave strategically to achieve them. Such consequentialist thinking, in which utility maximization is the objective, stands in contrast to a "logic of appropriateness," where "social structures of norms and rules govern the kinds of action that will be contemplated and taken" (Finnemore 1996, 29). Norms of courtesy or cooperation, for instance, shape lawmakers' preferences when faced with particular ideological or strategic contexts. Cultural norms affect what is understood as appropriate in, for instance, gender relations in offices on Capitol Hill. The logic of appropriateness is evident in the congressional setting in senses of duties and obligations and, in effect, the nature of interests and preferences themselves. Evidence of such thinking is present in some scholarship on congressional norms, although it has not been articulated as directly as I am doing here. For instance, adherence to norms in Congress has been seen not as strategic, but rather "fulfilling obligations in a role in a situation" (March and Olsen 1989, 160)—or what is agreed upon as proscribed or prescribed (Coleman 1990). The logic of appropriateness can be observed in the Senate, for instance, in the reluctance of retiring members to overindulge the use of the filibuster, when "norms become internalized over a long period they outlive the expiration of purely rational considerations and continue to exercise an influence on behavior even when individual utility concerns may dictate otherwise (Overby and Bell 2004, 921–922). Relating these ideas back to Finnemore, a sense of what is appropriate, as embodied in a norm, can "prompt behavior even in the absence of any functional reason for it" (Finnemore 1996, 30).

A CONSTRUCTIVIST APPROACH TO CONGRESS

How do members of Congress know what they want? Like Martha Finnemore's question about states in the international system (Finnemore 1996, 1), a social theory of congress articulates the role that ideas play in defining preferences and constituting understandings and knowledge of material and social realities of Congress. Finnemore and Sikkink summarize the key concepts of constructivism in international relations in a manner that provides a summary that can be used in applying constructivist ideas to the study of Congress:

[C]onstructivism is an approach to social analysis that asserts the following: (a) human interaction is shaped primarily by ideational factors, not simply material ones; (b) the most important ideational factors are widely shared or 'intersubjective' beliefs, which are not reducible to individuals; and (c) these shared beliefs construct the interests and identities of purposive actors. (Finnemore and Sikkink 2001, 392–393)

Constructivism, in other words, emphasizes ideational factors, not just material ones, shared among actors and that "construct the interests and identities of actors" (Bertucci, Hayes, and James 2018, 18).

The constructivist approach to Congress, as in its international relations theory counterpart, focuses on the way preferences are constructed by ideas (Wendt 1999, 22–29). In a constructivist approach to Congress—like in the constructivist approach to international relations—the material basis of reality matters (the logics of consequences are rooted in the materiality of outcomes: reelection, power in Congress, and policy outcomes are all material outcomes). But the way those material outcomes are understood and the way they affect action is a consequence of the ideas that actors hold about that material reality and the way that material reality affects or interacts with identities. In the norm of courtesy, for example, members of Congress place value on courtesy not exclusively because of the consequences to other objectives that being courteous delivers (which is how Sinclair explains it). Rather, members value courtesy as part of their identity as lawmakers. To be a lawmaker is to be courteous, a preference irrespective of material or consequential outcomes it delivers.

The strictly materialist interpretation of actors and actions—one in which the logic of consequences is the primary if not only determinant of behavior—is challenged by the constructivist approach in three key ways, whether in the international system or in Congress. First, beliefs and expectations that actors have of one another are constituted by "social rather than material structures" (Wendt 1996, 20). Second, "identities rather than just behavior are affected" (Ibid., 21) by the material system. That is, while the external system may affect behavior, identities affect what are perceived to be interests—and a logic of consequences is, in turn, determined by the strategic rationales of maximizing those ideational interests. Third, treating actors as "autistic" (which is to say ontologically independent, existing *a priori* to the system in which they exist (Ibid., 148)) ignores the process and the interactions by which identities and interests are determined at a systematic, holistic level—that is, shared beliefs among actors construct identities and interests. None of this is meant to suggest that material factors do not determine actor behavior or choice, or some far-flung notion that reality is comprised only of ideas. Rather the way in which both material or institutional constraints and ideas that construct identities and interests affect how actors know and behave in the material context they inhabit.[2]

As Wendt puts it, "interests are ideas" (Ibid., 98). Wendt's approach to international relations is reflected in a statement that closely approximates and helps us understand the role of ideas in determining interests in a social theory of Congress:

> [T]he meaning of the distribution of power in international politics is constituted in important part by the distribution of interests, and that the content of interests are in turn constituted in important part by ideas . . . The claim is *not* that ideas are more important than power and interests, or that they are autonomous from power and interest. Power and interest are just as important and determining as before. The claim is rather that power and interest have the effects they do in virtue of the ideas that make them up. Power and interest explanations *presuppose* ideas, and to that extent are not rivals to ideational explanations at all. (Wendt 1999, 135 *italics* in original)

Wendt continues, arguing that treating ideas in causal terms is not enough: "The issue of 'how' ideas matter is not limited to their causal effects. They also matter insofar as they constitute the 'material base' in the first place, that is, in so far as it is 'ideas all the way down'" (Ibid., 135). Put another way, people do not have a sense of what their material interests are without a set of ideas about what those interests are. Those interests are not determined by material factors alone; rather these ideas are socially constructed, constitutive, and normative.

Finnemore's account of the role of norms in the international system provides an effective model for applying constructivist theory to the U.S. Congress. The distinction between behavioralist and constructivist theories is a difference between the *logic of consequences* and the *logic of appropriateness*. The constructivist approach embodies both rational choice as well as the ideational origins of preferences themselves:

> Actors conform to . . . [norms of behavior and social institutions] in part for 'rational' reasons (for instance, because of the costs involved in 'bucking the system' and the resources that become available through conformity) but also because they become socialized to accept these values, rules, and roles. They internalize the roles and rules as scripts to which they conform, not out of conscious choice, but because they understand these behaviors to be appropriate. (Finnemore 1996, 29)

In this configuration, norm adherence or rejection can be based on the consequences of doing so or not. But norm adherence is not exclusively consequentialist, or instrumental, toward some other goal or interest. Norms are also *a priori* preferences—knowledge of what one wants such that a rational, strategic actor will behave logically toward getting it and understandings of what is appropriate or what is an interest given a particular institutional or social context. Maintaining the norm—these sense of appropriateness of certain ideas or behavior—is an interest in and of itself, irrespective of other strategic imperatives.

A constructivist approach to Congress speaks to how material interests (such as determined by institutions or the behavioral imperatives of acquiring power) become meaningful in individual and collective behaviors, such as norms. The material determinants of interests do not provide meaning to such interests, and inversely not everything that becomes an interest has a clear material basis. Finnemore explains this relationship in talking about states in the international system:

> State interests are defined in the context of internationally held norms and understandings about what is good and appropriate. That normative context influences the behavior of decision makers and of mass publics who may choose and constrain those decision makers. The normative context also changes over time, and as the internationally held norms and values change, they create coordinated shifts in state interests and behavior across the system . . . The cases presented here demonstrate that states' redefinitions of interests are often not the result of external threats or demands by domestic groups. Rather they are shaped by internationally shared norms and values that structure and give meaning to international political life." (Ibid., 2–3)

In other words, whereas material and ideational bases define social structures and the origin of interests, in the push and pull of these two bases, the ideational can strongly affect interests irrespective of changes or stability in the material base. Put succinctly, ideas can independently determine interests. In Finnemore's case, international norms can affect perceptions of interests that then may shape rational decisions about international conduct. In the congressional context, norms regarding the importance of cooperation versus conflict can affect congressional behavior irrespective of imperatives of strategic behavior toward ideological or electoral objectives.

CONSTRUCTIVISM AND CONGRESSIONAL NORMS

Norms, in the constructivist framework, are constitutive: they inform preferences and shape identities. In constructivism, interests are not exclusively determined by material or consequential factors—members of Congress determine interests in part based on the ideas they hold regarding what matters, what is important, and what is appropriate. Norms in this constructivist sense are ideas about what members hold as important—they are valued not just because of their material consequences or objectives they help members achieve, but because members believe in them as ideas that inform them of what is appropriate. They are preferences.

In the constitutive sense, therefore, congressional norms act as obligations on behavior upon which instrumental decisions can be based or justified: "Rules and norms are, therefore, guidance devices which are designed to simplify choices and impart 'rationality' to situations by delineating the factors that a decision-maker has to take into account" (Kratochwil 1989, 10). Norms can help establish "which preferences deserve priority over others, which ones ought to be changed, and which judgements deserve our assent" (Ibid., 12). Beyond a causal role alone, norms help inform the nature of preferences in the first place, and these preferences may then be strategically pursued. Norms inform and create shared understandings of what is rational and, in this sense, therefore, what we understand to be rational is socially constructed.

Norms exist as "social facts" "by virtue of all the relevant actors agreeing that they exist" (Ruggie 1998, 12). Such social facts differ from other "socially relevant" facts, such as material factors—which Ruggie calls 'brute' facts—including institutional rules, electoral laws that determine the legitimacy of membership as a Representative or Senator, or even the physical composition of the Capitol itself; and "'subjective facts,' so designated because their existence depends on being experienced by individual subjects, like an individual actor's perceptions of or preferences about the world" (Ibid., 12–13). In Congress norms include, for example, apprenticeship, reciprocity, courtesy, and others. These norms exist as "social facts"—things "which have no material reality but exist only because people collectively believe they exist and act accordingly" (Finnemore and Sikkink 2001, 393).

Ideas, such as norms, are "constitutive" because they form the ontological basis upon which identities, beliefs, and preferences are formed and by which related rational, strategic, or consequential decisions and actions may be made. Rational choice theories of Congress emphasize the causal relationship between preferences and behavior and assume that material, structural reality exists *a priori*, ontologically independent of agents. Congressional norms, however, inform identities and the understanding of what are preferences in the first place. Returning, again, to Wendt, "ideas also *constitute* social situations and the meaning of material forces. This is not a causal claim . . . social structures also constitute actors with certain identities and interests" (Wendt 1996, 79). A social theory of Congress focuses on constitutive nature of norms rather than their causal relationships, looking to how ideas inform interests as compared to how they affect behavior.

Even reelection, the interest held as primary among congressional scholars and foundational to rational choice studies of Congress, may be interpreted as a constituted interest. While it is a widely accepted empirical claim that members prioritize reelection above all other priorities (Mayhew 1974), this preference is premised on an *idea* that remaining in power is a superior choice to innumerable alternatives which range from taking positions unpopular to an electorate or opting to limit the length of service in Congress. Reelection is only as important as members of Congress think it is. And perhaps it is not important in all cases. John Kennedy's *Profiles in Courage* (1957) may be a short book, but it points to the possibility that some members may choose unpopular or electorally nonstrategic positions over the electoral imperative, for example. Reelection, in the constructivist view, may be widely pursued, but it nevertheless is a socially constructed interest. The electoral imperative is in this view, therefore, a norm, a preference upon which rational behavior is determined—as it happens, a widely shared norm and one that institutional rules make survival in Congress difficult if its rationality is not followed. But it is a norm nevertheless. A member does not have to value reelection; they may just be less likely to remain a member if they do not. Moreover, the electoral imperative need not imply any specific kind of behavior; paths to reelection are many and based on modern incumbency rates of 80 percent in the Senate and over 90 percent in the House, and it is evident that the actual risks to reelection are readily overcome (Kondik and Skelley 2016). There is no one way to behave "re-electorally"; that is, few ideas or behaviors can be considered as unqualified necessities in order for reelection to occur. It is in this extra-material space that ideas matter and norms take shape and affect the preferences and behaviors of members of Congress.

A constructivist account of the case of assassination in international relations provides an unlikely but otherwise good explanation of the dual material and ideational roles that norms play in a social theory of Congress. State leaders largely adhere to a prohibition on assassinating leaders of other countries, despite cases where a strategic or cost-benefit assessment would point to the value of killing one's foreign rivals. The explanation lies, at least in part, on international norms—the inappropriateness of engaging in such behavior. On the one hand, "norms can serve as systematic constraints on action. Simply put, there are costs associated with violating norms . . . [while] these costs by no means assure perfect compliance with all norms all the time, they do create considerable disincentives to norm violation that must be weighed against the immediate advantages that might be gained" (Thomas 2000, 133). On the other hand, as constructivists such as Wendt, Finnemore, and Katzenstein remind us, "norms not only may constrain states in how they pursue their interests but may play a more fundamental role in shaping those interests. Norms specify standards of behavior by reference to which states define their values, goals, and national purposes—in other words, their identities" (Ibid., 133). In other words, leaders don't assassinate other leaders because it is inappropriate to do so.

In a social theory of Congress, while assassination fortunately is not a relevant factor, the same logic of appropriateness applies. Members confront material constraints that drive interests (e.g., reelection) but behavior cannot be fully reduced to rational "means-ends" goal seeking toward an assumed "rational" objective. Where we see evidence of consistency among lawmaker behavior, such as in party unity scores, the presumption that such behavior is exclusively goal seeking or even ideologically driven misses the possibility that lawmakers are simply acting on a norm—for example, norms of cooperation or norms of conflict.

In approaching this topic, I examine how ideas and identities shape norms of cooperation and conflict and norms of a changing culture. In contrast to the rational choice approach to norms, rather than assuming norms exist *a priori* and function as one among many variables in forming strategic choices of individual, autonomous actors, the social theory of Congress looks to how norms shape understandings of the nature of being a lawmaker and help constitute preferences themselves. For example, as argued more fully in chapter 4, the norm of courtesy is not determined exclusively based on the formal rules—material constraints—of member behavior. The way in which members understand the rules in the context of their identities as lawmakers and the value they place on courtesy conditions the manner in which they adhere to or reject those rules. The norm of courtesy, in this example, is both materially determined by formal rules as well as socially constructed by the beliefs members have about what is appropriate behavior as a member of Congress. Members are courteous not just because of the consequential requirements of not being sanctioned for rule violations; they are courteous because they believe in courtesy and to behave courteously becomes an interest irrespective of other imperatives to do so.

In chapter 5, partisanship is examined as a norm and ideas pertaining to partisanship manifest themselves in the behavior that members of Congress accept as appropriate, irrespective of strategic or consequentialist motives. Partisan teamsmanship, for example, has been understood as a causal driver of congressional behavior where lawmakers seek strategic advantages of their party over another party (e.g., Lee 2009; Theriault 2008). In contrast, the approach argued here treats partisanship as constitutive—lawmakers are partisan because they share an idea of what it means to be partisan and what norms of behavior are appropriate to partisan identity. Partisanship in a social theory of Congress is a norm irrespective of ideological or strategic gains of partisan behavior. How members react to an institutional, strategic, or material context is not deterministic—it is based on what members believe is appropriate in such contexts; it is based on norms. This is not to say that the consequentialist logic of partisanship is not explanatory; it is just incomplete. Therefore, while a strategic material framework remains causally explanatory, to put a turn on Wendt's phrase regarding anarchy in the international system, partisanship is what lawmakers make of it. A similar dynamic is at play regarding norms of cooperation and norms of conflict, as addressed in the chapters ahead.

EPISTEMOLOGIES AND METHODOLOGIES

Do norms explain anything regarding Congress that electoral, strategic, or ideological explanations do not? Yes. Norms are ideas that inform the basis of preferences, provide a sense of appropriateness shared among members of Congress, and shape the interests upon which behavior is determined to be rational. Norms of cooperation and conflict affect the choices members make about their objectives and the outcomes they seek by informing preferences. Societal norms assimilated into Congress affect which behaviors are acceptable or not. Finnemore writes, "State interests are defined in the context of internationally held norms about what is good and appropriate" (Finnemore 1996, 2). This is also true in the context of Congress. Members prioritize cooperation or conflict not exclusively *because* of electoral, institutional, or ideological objectives. Rather, such priorities are *constitutive* of what members understand to be good and appropriate and thus form the bases of preferences themselves. Cooperative or conflictual behavior exists not only because they help achieve some other consequential end—cooperation and conflict are ends in and of themselves, intrinsic to the identities of members of Congress in the twenty-first century.

If congressional norms exist in the constitutive manner argued for here, it implies an ontology that is not exclusively causal and requires epistemologies methodologies that can uniquely identify the presence and constitutive effect of such norms. Epistemologically, a social theory of Congress does not exclusively seek to identify the causal relationship between a norm and an outcome, but rather includes the identification of a norm as a sense of appropriateness, preferences, or identities—irrespective of causal relationships between such norms and particular behaviors. It is not that outcomes do not matter or norms do not have causal consequences. Rather, the nature of the shared understanding and the manner in which norms are known among lawmakers is what gives the norm its social quality. If a social theory of Congress offers an ontologically distinct vantage point, it is not about cause and effect but about the manners in which members of Congress know their identities as members of Congress—it is about how members of Congress know what they want. Behavioralist epistemologies of understanding Congress are therefore insufficient to fully understanding the full scope of the role of norms play in the institution. In other words, in a social theory, we are not looking for cause-and-effect standards of evidence known in behavioralism, but for the existence of normative ways of knowing the world.

Consequentialist reasoning is exactly what a constructivist approach asks us to question—consequentialist reasoning assumes *a priori* that actors have particular interests toward which strategic behavior is directed. What a constructivist approach to the study of Congress proposes is that these interests are not given; interests are determined by the meanings actors impart onto their social environment. A constructivist approach to Congress is not focused on the strategic or rational pursuit of objectives, it is focused on the origins of preferences themselves—and those objectives, that is the interests that members hold, are not only or exclusively materially determined by factors such as the electoral imperative, obtaining power in Congress, partisan strategy, or public policy objectives. A social theory of Congress looks to this other nature of the origins of interests, in which preferences are determined by the shared ideas, meanings, and norms through which members of Congress understand various material or institutional constraints. The interests themselves exist as social facts, irrespective of material or strategic factors, based on shared understandings of what is appropriate in a social setting. Ideationally, norms are part of the identities of members of Congress, an end on their own, and a preference independent of the material consequences of their belief in upholding them. When Merry (*supra.*) speaks of a "cultural sensibility," he is not speaking of a rational imperative, but rather of a sense of the appropriateness, from which particular objectives may more readily follow than if that sense did not exist. But in a constructivist sense, in the Merry example courtesy is normative: it is an idea of what is desired. The strategic logic to behave courteously is not the norm; it is behavior geared toward maximizing an ideational preference.

Norms in Congress—whether of cooperation, conflict, or broader cultural values— exist not only because they facilitate the obtainment of desired outcomes by strategic actors. The underlying assumption in the identification of norms is that they exist as both causal and constitutive phenomena—exhibiting aspects of the logics of consequences and of appropriateness. If norms are "aspects of social structure that emerged from the actions and beliefs of actors in specific communities and in turns norms shaped those actions and beliefs by constituting actors' identities and interests" (Hoffman 2010, 3), unique methodological strategies are required to understand the existence and effects of such norms. Particular norms also exist for no other reason than members think it is appropriate to adhere to those norms. This is the important distinction that a social theory of Congress makes: behavior is not simply objective-oriented; not everything is instrumental or consequences-focused. Behavior is also undertaken for its own sake, based on a shared sense of appropriateness and meanings that members impart onto what they understand as their role as legislators. The logic of appropriateness, in a constructivist view of Congress and its members, requires us to question and probe the origins of interests. In a social theory of Congress, norms are not exclusively instrumental in that they exist to facilitate some other *a priori* objective. Rather, in the constructivist approach, members of Congress adhere to particular behaviors not as a means toward some other ends, but as ends in themselves. Epistemologically, therefore, efforts to identify norms do not just seek the outcomes such norms facilitate or provide; rather to identify a norm is to identify the ideas that inform the preferences themselves.

A seasoned congressional scholar once put it to me, "Everyone who studies Congress thinks norms matter, but nobody can explain why" (Conversation with Author, April 2017). Indeed, it is a central challenge of constructivism, which by its nature is not intrinsically a causal theory, to provide empirically valid evidence for the contentions it makes about norms (Finnemore and Sikkink 2001; Hoffman 2017, 8–11). Methodologically, the study of norms in Congress may be approached from several strategies from a constructivist perspective, virtually none of which have been explored in legislative studies. All of these approaches may be considered within the broader discussion in constructivism about epistemology and methodology. The present work is an opening call to engage this discussion in the study of the U.S. Congress.

The first approach presented in this book is rather more conventional—simply identifying specific norms of the modern Congress, through participant observation, semistructured interviews, and survey data. This approach allows us to observe, from the perspective of current and former members and staff, what they view as appropriate, what norms they understand to exist as shared among fellow members. By studying the community of actors we can identify shared norms from the perspective of that community, what they understand as appropriate, and how those norms function among members, staff, and active participants in the social community of the modern Congress. The study of ideas and their meaning in a social context favors qualitative assessment. Norms are ideas, so we may use interviews and surveys and textual data to derive from those who hold norms how such norms are viewed by those who hold them. Indeed, almost 95 percent of constructivist research employs a qualitative approach: "This makes sense; constructivism, at its core, is about capturing meaning and meaning-making processes. Ideational factors shaping international affairs pose methodological challenges more amenable to interpretative and inductive qualitative methodologies than do quantitative methods" (Bertucci, James, and Hayes 2018, 26). Interviews, surveys, and participant observation are one set of approaches to get at this making of meanings in Congress.

A second methodological approach entails capturing the behavioral effects of the logic of appropriateness. This is an imperfect science. A social theory of Congress is not fully confined to inferential logic or causal relationships. As Finnemore puts it, constructivists "emphasize the importance of intersubjective understandings in structuring the ways in which actors understand what kinds of actions are valuable, appropriate, and necessary" (Finnemore 1996, 15). By looking at the nature of preferences and identities, it is not necessary to isolate causal consequences to demonstrate that a norm exists. Wendt critiques behavioralism in international relations theory by stating "methodology can become tacit ontology" (Wendt 1999, 115). If we assume interests preexist and the behavior of individual actors is strategic, then we select methodologies that identify rational, strategic behavior toward preexisting preferences. In this way, we "backfill" rational explanations into whatever behavior we witness, superimposing economic optimization and strategic behavior where that is not the primary object that matters in normative forms of social behavior. In looking at the nature of preferences, identities, and norms it is not necessary to isolate causal consequences to demonstrate that a norm exists. If we allow for "ideas all the way down" (Wendt 1996, 96), which manifest as norms, we see new ways of thinking and knowing Congress and its members. We embrace an alternate ontology which requires an alternative epistemological framework and methodological approaches.

This said, methodological strategies do exist to inferentially determine the existence of norms. Behavioral indicators are presented in chapters 4 through 6 to demonstrate the existence of particular norms of cooperation and conflict and societal values, as reflected in the conduct and ideas of members of Congress. In chapter 4, courtesy is illustrated as a norm serving little other purpose other than to a reflect members' shared attitudes toward cooperation. If previous scholarship on congressional norms has focused in depth on the consequentialist manner in which the norm of courtesy works (e.g., Weingast 1979; Sinclair 1989; Rohde 1984), here, norms are examined from the perspective of the logic of appropriateness—cases where norms are adhered to even when other ideological, partisan, or strategic purposes for doing so are not evident, where norms are preferences in their own right (i.e., Finnemore 1996; Wendt 1999; Kratochwil 1989; Bertucci 2018). Finnemore illustrates the contrast between the logics of consequences and appropriateness can be used to determine the presence of norms among a set of social actors:

> The logic of appropriateness would predict similar behavior from dissimilar actors because rules and norms may make similar behavioral claims on dissimilar actors. The logic of consequences would predict dissimilar behavior from dissimilar actors because actors with different utility functions and capabilities will act differently. (Finnemore 1996, 30)

By this reasoning, methodologically, we can find evidence of normative behavior, for instance, when ideologically disparate members adhere to similar behaviors without apparent strategic purpose. In this regard, in a constructivist case for the courtesy norm, again, members are courteous not because it helps them achieve some broader objective—a means toward an end—rather members are courteous simply because being courteous is valued in its own right. Subsequent behavior may or *may not* be strategic or rational in pursuit of courteousness; courteous behavior will be witnessed simply because it is valued; that is, it is understood as appropriate to be courteous.

In chapter 5, the example of procedural disobedience illustrates how the emergence of nonconformity as a norm of conflict is derived from the identities of lawmakers in relationship to institutional functioning and the willingness of lawmakers to undermine the operation of the Congress itself. This norm is not instrumental or merely based on ideological goals, but exists as a sense that nonconformity is an appropriate attitude toward institutional rules and functionality. Partisanship is examined based on the nonideological sense of identity that accounts for its being valued in its own right, irrespective of strategic or rational objectives. It is increasingly understood as appropriate to be partisan.

Norms can be embedded in the institution of Congress in terms of formal rules as well as informal practices. If it is so that "[n]orms are merely nebulous ideas until we give them properties of rules" (Onuf 2018, xvii), then we see the formalization of norms in the formal rules of Congress. Where norms change, we see the rules change. In this manner, ideas become formally embodied in institutions and have a direct implication on the manner in which power in Congress can be achieved (or not) and the ways in which policy objectives can and cannot be pursued. We see norms of cooperation and conflict operating, simultaneously, in the modern Congress as not only ends in themselves but also irrespective of ideological or strategic objectives. Where societal values change we see where congressional rules on professional behavior change, as evidenced, for example, with cultural views on sexual propriety discussed in chapter 6. In such respects, we see how constitutive norms matter in consequential ways: as norms change, so does the institutions and how it functions. Moreover, strategies put forward here, while they help identify constitutive and causal nature of congressional norms, are not exhaustive. Just as international relations scholars have sought numerous strategies to understand norms (e.g., Klotz and Lynch 2007). Much good and innovative work on a social theory Congress is open to other scholars of American politics.

SUMMARY

It is not the purpose of the present work to explore every unexamined corner of congressional studies from the constructivist perspective. Rather by introducing a social theory of Congress, the purpose is to open the study of Congress to the constructivist paradigm and to show the promise that this new territory holds for our understanding of the American national legislature and, beyond this, American politics more broadly. From an academic perspective, the social theory of Congress opens up the field of congressional studies to the rich and provoking debates of constructivism which have occurred among scholars of international relations. To date, congressional studies (and much other academic research on American politics), seeks to explain political behavior and outcomes by assuming political actors hold fixed interests and behave in economic, strategic ways to maximize the value of outcomes against those interests. In a congressional context, these interests are ordered around ideological (Poole 2007), electoral (Mayhew 1974; Fenno 1977), and strategic (Theriault 2008; Lee 2009) outcomes. The constructivist field of inquiry is virtually untapped in the field of legislative studies in American political science, with no existing research applying the constructivist model to the study of Congress. Like international relations theory and comparative politics of the pre-1990s period, congressional studies continues to be dominated by rational choice and behavioralist models. Yet, beginning in the 1980s and 1990s, political scientists in the fields of international relations and comparative politics began examining the role of norms to explain international behavior in the ways for which national interests, rational choice, and strategic behavior seemed incomplete. This exploration on constructivism is dynamic, provoking, and ongoing.[3] It is time for congressional scholars to catch up.

Like its counterpart in international relations, a social theory of Congress will not replace rational choice models or behavioralism; rather a social theory provides a richer, more complete description of the social system that is the U.S. Congress. Norms, for instance, may or may not directly account for particular policy outcomes, but understanding norms helps understand the preferences of the individuals and the behavior of the institution that yields those outcomes. Not to mention, other theories have their own shortcomings in terms of adequately accounting for specific outcomes and the agenda of congressional studies is full of open question and unexamined avenues of research (Binder 2015). Like other theoretical approaches to the study of Congress, a social theory is not auxiliary or secondary—it is a necessary piece to understanding the behavior of Congress and its members.

Perhaps the easiest way of understanding, even resolving, the debate and controversy between positivism or rational choice and poststructuralism is not to actually to resolve the approaches, but to recognize the tension, to engage the conversation of the material *and* the ideational, to admit the dialectic into our study and knowledge of the U.S. Congress. It is dubious to suggest that all politics is ideas, and nor is that this author's intention. But neither should we be satisfied with exclusively economic or rational explanations of congressional behavior. Rather it is important to acknowledge and explore the interrelationship between materialism and idealism. Moreover, if ideology is a component of member behavior, a constructivist approach invites congressional scholars to greater consideration of the ideas that motivate ideology and, therefore, much of the strategic behavior in Congress specifically and American politics more broadly. Members of Congress are human, after all. And as such their behavior, like that of all of us, is a manifestation of the basest material calculations and the most abstract ideals and ambiguous whims of human imagination and caprice. A social theory of Congress acknowledges this interplay and sets about to understand what this tension means for the behavior, functioning, and policy outputs of the American national legislature.

NOTES

1. In this respect, norms are to institutions what architecture is to shelter. Just as a building meets particular structural ends and requirements, there are basic material requirements that institutions meet to serve their primary purpose. But what one values beyond these material needs is aesthetic—it is about values, culture, beliefs, and a sense of what is appropriate.

2. In this sense, where Wendt (1992) argues that "anarchy is what states make of it," in the context of Congress, a constructivist argument would be that the electoral imperative is what members of Congress make of it.

3. There are many excellent summaries of the state of debate in constructivism, including Finnemore and Sikkink (2001), Hoffman (2010), and Jung (2019). A political scientist can examine such work and imagine replacing phrases such as "state" and "international relations" with "member of Congress" or "the legislature" to see many conceptual parallels between both the topics and the parallel intellectual puzzles in these otherwise different fields of political study.

Chapter 3

Historical Norms and the Modern Congress

A Survey

We are told by scholars of Congresses past that there are "unwritten but generally accepted and informally enforced norms of conduct" (Matthews 1959, 1064). Conformity to norms of cooperation has been an important part of the way the Senate works and the "professional legislative conduct" of the House of Representatives (Polsby 1968, 166). In the twenty-first century, cooperation is still an important aspect of the norms—the modern folkways—of both the House and the Senate. Members of both chambers assent to numerous informal, unwritten rules, with both tacit and explicit consent; much like the twentieth century, many of these norms foster "respect and cooperation" among one another (Wahlke et al. 1962, 143). Gone—at least for the present—are the days violence on the floor, of pistols, and bowie knives of the pre-Civil War period, and the "guns and dogs, canings and fisticuffs, that occupied so much of the 19th century scene" (Freeman 2018; Polsby 1968, 168). Conformity to norms of cooperation is part of what makes possible the functioning and work of the institution of the U.S. Congress and of its individual members.

   Yet, the conformity and the cooperation it facilitates are not universally sought by all members. That is, not all Senators and Representatives seek the respect and cooperation of their fellow members. In fact, in the modern Congress, norms of conflict are visible, viable, and possibly growing among a subset of members who favor disagreement over cooperation. Nonconformists have always existed—members who made a name for themselves through disruptive behavior. In the 1950s Matthews wrote, "Nonconformity is met with moral condemnation . . . [and] the conformists tend to be the most influential and effective members of the Senate" (Matthews 1959, 1086). However, in the normative context of the twenty-first century, this can no longer be said with such confidence. In a Congress characterized by partisan polarization, nonconformity and partisanship itself have emerged as viable normative attitudes to membership. In the modern Congress, members can embrace conflict as a means of achieving success and norms fostering conflict have become routine qualities among those serving in Congress.

As presented in chapter 1, legislative norms are informal prescriptive rules, often unwritten or unspoken, about how lawmakers should or ought to behave in the functioning of the institution, violations of which may result in some form of reprobation or sanction. As a social theory of Congress contends, such norms may be constitutive, in that they form the basis of the identities or preferences that lawmakers hold with regard to their role as lawmakers. These informal prescriptive rules are inherently ambiguous social facts—the exact terms of the rule and the conditions upon which violations thereof may be met with sanction is intrinsically inexact, and not all norms are shared among all members. With this operational definition of norms and an ontological basis in hand for how norms affect congressional behavior both causally and constitutively, we can more carefully examine what norms exist in the modern Congress.

Previous scholarship has identified numerous legislative norms present in the U.S. Congress, primarily post–World War II and in the second half of the twentieth century. It is a relatively limited corpus which varies in the method and manner by which norms are identified—including wide variance in definitions, data gathering, and empirical testing. Early scholarship on the topic relied on personal observation, inference, and public documents (e.g., Truman 1951; Huitt 1957) or some form of *in situ* observation and interviews with lawmakers and congressional professionals, although the degree of structure of the interview protocol varied (Matthews 1959, 1960; Fenno 1962; Wahlke et al. 1962; Asher 1973; Hebert and McLemore 1973; Loomis and Bartlett 1981; Rohde, Peabody, and Ornstein 1985; Choate 2003). Other research assumed or took for granted the existence of norms identified by other scholars and examined the nature and function of norms on individual members or the institution as a whole, often employing rational choice or game theory approaches to account for norm adherence, rejection, and evolution (e.g., Fenno 1966; Weingast 1979; Rohde 1988; Sinclair 1989). Appendix E provides an index of norms identified in such previous work.

LEGISLATIVE NORMS OF THE
TWENTY-FIRST CENTURY

In a social theory of Congress, as presented in chapter 2, norms serve both material and ideational functions. In the material sense, norms serve a logic of consequences—members make strategic decisions about whether to adhere to unwritten rules based on a cost-benefit analysis of doing so. Such norms may be prescriptive or proscriptive—indicating behaviors that should be done or that should not be done. In the ideational sense, norms serve a logic of appropriateness—they are constitutive of what is considered acceptable or unacceptable in the first place; they are the basis of the ideas of what constitutes being a member of Congress and preferences of members are determined upon such ideas. In the ideational sense, the proof of the norm lies not in the other consequences it delivers but in the norm as an interest in and of itself.

The normative context of the twenty-first century Congress lies between cooperation and conflict. The modern Congress not only has changed substantially but also retains a notable degree of the character of the past. Norms are part of this continuity—they suggest ways in which Congress of today is far more similar to the "textbook" Congress of the mid-twentieth century than is evident in current controversies over partisan polarization and congressional dysfunction. The Congress of the opening years of the twenty-first century embodies norms of cooperation similar to those of previous times; but also in sharp contrast to that past, a normative context of conflict is simultaneously developing. Cooperation, as evident in existing contemporary norms such as apprenticeship, reciprocity, and courtesy, is a significant attribute of the Congress of the twenty-first century. Norms of cooperation are part of what prevents Congress from becoming even more contentious than it already appears to be. These norms have a consequential basis, but they also are ideational—members are incentivized to cooperate in some ways, but they also uphold norms of cooperation simply because they believe it is appropriate to do so. But norms are changing.[1]

Norms of cooperation in the modern Congress remain predominant but norms of conflict are emerging and widely held. Norms of conflict contribute to an already contentious political context dominated by ideological, partisan, and strategic competition. Such norms add an ideational basis to this already fraught political context, creating an underlying sense that conflict is appropriate to serving in the modern Congress, irrespective of its rational or strategic purposes—conflict informs norms, identities, and interests. If norms of conflict become the prevalent norms, or those of cooperation erode, a culture of conflict will pervade in the U.S. Congress in ways we have yet to see in the modern era. Norms may be part of what is holding the modern Congress together, but norms can also tear us apart. In other words, because the modern Congress continues to embody norms of cooperation, is not so bad after all. Or, at least, *it could be worse*.

In all, the findings of this research point to several prominent norms of the modern Congress, as evidenced by direct observation, semistructured interviews, and survey research, and recognized by a preponderance of members and staff and congressional observers: *apprenticeship*, *reciprocity*, and *courtesy* are prevalent norms of cooperation; *partisanship*, *nonconformity*, and *fundraising* are prevalent norms of conflict. These norms broadly facilitate cooperation or promote conflict among members and within the functioning of the Congress. In addition, evidence points to two norms of the modern Congress that have only recently emerged based on changes in society and which shape member behavior and attitudes, even though they are not directly tied to the legislative purpose: *sobriety* and *sexual propriety*.

By their very nature, norms are ambiguous social facts—they are unwritten rules or shared attitudes. Not everyone will understand each norm in the same way, and there is no guarantee of unanimity among everyone in perceiving the existence of the same norms. Primary norms of the modern Congress are described here based on their material or ideational characteristics and whether they are prevalent in either or both chambers. To hold true as a primary congressional norm, a norm must be perceived repeatedly across interviews and observations, including survey evidence, have clear and multiple examples, and be capable of being clearly and independently defined in terms distinct from other norms. Norms less widely recognized among members and staff would function in much the same manner as those more universally accepted or followed. Subsequent chapters more closely explore the empirical evidence of the existence and effects of particular norms of cooperation and conflict and of a changing society. It is not contended that these are the only norms of the modern Congress. It is unlikely that such an exhaustive account could be provided. Rather, these are primary shared norms for which there is substantial evidence and which shape the character of the Congress of the twenty-first century.

Building upon past work on legislative norms, the present chapter utilizes survey evidence to capture normative attitudes of the modern Congress, while the chapters ahead combine this with additional quantitative data, semistructured interviews, and direct observation in the first systematic study of contemporary congressional norms in over two decades, since Judd Choate analyzed the norms of the 104th Congress (1995–1997). One of the purposes of the present study is to establish a standard, reliable, and reproducible approach to identifying legislative norms upon which future scholars can refer and build. In so doing, this chapter presents a survey approach to assess norms in the modern Congress, allowing comparison with previous such work, and setting a baseline for future longitudinal exploration of the presence and evolution of congressional norms. Subsequent chapters examine where norms of cooperation, conflict, and of a changing culture have empirically demonstrable effects or meaning in the U.S. Congress.

A SURVEY OF CONGRESSIONAL PROFESSIONALS

What do current and former members of Congress and staff perceive as the norms of the modern Congress? Since the 1950s researchers have been asking questions of congressional professionals about what legislative norms exist. Generally speaking, methodologies and research approaches of previous work was not done with the goal of being a repeatable effort. For instance, Matthews's folkways are often the topic of subsequent study, but there is not a methodologically consistent manner by which these folkways have been identified or validated across studies. Matthews himself used a method of personal observation and largely unstructured interviews (Matthews 1960, 271), an approach that does not lend itself to reproducing the results. In only a few cases was a systematic effort at norm identification put forward, where interview or survey questions were repeated or closely followed, such as when Wahlke's (1962) question reappeared in the research of Hebert and McLemore (1973). Surveys and interview protocols have been used by previous scholars (e.g., Loomis and Fischel 1981), but little effort before the present study has been made to systematically incorporate these questions into new research.

In a survey of twenty-first century norms, in addition to revisiting what has been previously asked, new questions are warranted based on a contemporary understanding of the U.S. Congress. The contemporary Congress is different in many significant respects from that when previous research on congressional norms was conducted. Norms research of the 1950s and 1960s, prior to the reforms of the 1970s, emerged in a Congress of a strong committee system and weaker parties. Reforms of the 1990s contributed to a growth in the strength of parties and warrant questions regarding about the extent to which the partisanship affects norms held by lawmakers (Polsby 2004; Cox and McCubbins 2005; Smith 2007). Other changes in the Congress and in American politics, such as the rise of partisan polarization not only in Congress itself (Voteview 2016; Kaushal 2014) but also among the electorate (Abramowitz 2018) or the elected and political elites (Fiorina 2017), affect the context of congressional norms and must be considered in a modern look at the topic.

The Survey Questionnaire

To update this line of inquiry and to build our understanding of what congressional professionals understand as the norms of the modern Congress, a new survey questionnaire was developed, building upon the research of the past, integrating relevant questions of previous surveys or interviews where they are available, and adding new questions that reflect research

on the modern Congress and a theoretical framework—a social theory—
for understanding the dynamics of norms in the U.S. Congress. The
survey instrument combined a series of Likert responses on a 1-to-5 scale
and open-ended questions designed to elicit attitudes regarding particular
congressional norms, based on questions asked in previous research on
legislative norms, new questions derived from contemporary congressional
scholarship, separate semistructured in-depth interviews, and the author's
direct observation. In the questionnaire, a battery of thirteen prompts are
presented to respondents and particular behaviors are rated along a five-point
Likert scale of appropriateness, wherein "1" indicates a behavior is "highly
inappropriate" and a 5 indicates it is "highly appropriate," with 3 indicating
"neither appropriate nor inappropriate."

The selection of topics and wording of questions is drawn from evidence
of what norms are present in the modern Congress based on current literature,
direct observation, and semistructured interviews conducted with current
and former members of Congress and staff conducted over the period
2016–2019. For longitudinal, comparative purposes, it makes sense to
include some survey questions on norms previously identified in the research
on legislative norms, but more recent scholarship demands other additional
questions be included that reflect the newer dynamics of the contemporary
Congress. Thus, for example, Hebert and McLemore's (1973) question on
the apprenticeship norm, about "being more of an observer than a participant
when you first enter the legislature" is included, verbatim, because interviews
with current and former members of staff as well as recent Congressional
publications (U.S. Senate 2005), points to the apparent existence of
apprenticeship. Other questions from previous research are presented as close
to verbatim as possible but modified to elicit needed responses on the scale
of appropriateness, such as several questions from Asher (1973) on House
norms, which are modified to fit the 1-to-5 scale format.

New questions, original to the present research, are asked based on evidence of new norms existent in the modern Congress. For example, partisanship as a norm is addressed through questions on voting with the opposition
and supporting bipartisan compromise and specifically in the House regarding the so-called "Hastert rule," "requiring the support of a majority of the
majority party for legislation to advance." Norms that were perceived in the
past but not identified via interview or survey questions are addressed through
original questions in the present survey, such as when the specialization
norm, first identified by Matthews's observations, is queried with the prompt,
"Specializing in a field or policy area as compared to being a generalist."

A total of thirteen norms or variations on individual norms are directly
queried in the survey: (a) apprenticeship as measured by an observer period;
(b) apprenticeship as measured by the value of learning the chamber rules; (c)

courtesy as measured by criticism of other members on the floor; (d) courtesy as measured by maintaining friendly relations with members of one's own party; (e) courtesy as measured by friendly relations with the opposite party; (f) reciprocity as measured by vote trading; (g) specialization; (h) partisanship as measured by support for voting with the opposition; (i) partisanship as measured by support for bipartisan compromise; (j) partisanship as measured by supermajoritarianism in the Senate; (k) partisanship as measured by the Hastert Rule—requiring a majority of the majority for major legislation passage—in the House; (l) fundraising and raising money for fellow party members; and (m) relations with special interests to understand reciprocity. Table 3.1 provides the question prompts from the survey and the complete survey instrument is reproduced in Appendix III.

Other norms are not queried in the survey due to a lack of compelling evidence for their modern existence. For example, institutional patriotism, the expectation that "Senators are expected to believe that they belong to the greatest legislative and deliberative body in the world," (Matthews 1960, 101) holds little weight in the contemporary experience of Congress, especially in a context where, as I later argue, nonconformity is becoming more prevalent. In the interests of holding the attention of busy respondents, it does not seem worth it to ask superfluous questions that may be of curiosity to political scientists but burdensome or distracting to contemporary congressional professionals. Where direct questions about a norm seem unlikely to elicit a measurement of the attitude regarding a norm, behavioral questions are asked; for example, like Asher (1973, 501), reciprocity is measured in a question about the appropriateness of vote trading. The survey also includes open-ended questions to elicit qualitative responses on the presence of other norms in the modern Congress; these responses are examined in later chapters. To aid scholars who may wish to replicate or design their own surveys on congressional norms, Appendix IV includes an index of both interview and survey questions of previous scholars of legislative norms; through these the reader also can consider the original wording of previously asked questions on the topic.

Survey Methodology

The survey was conducted during the period April through November 2019, via anonymous paper survey, confidential in-person questioning, and an anonymous online electronic survey tool. A total of 319 respondents were drawn among a population limited to current and former members of Congress and staff, as well as long-serving congressional journalists and think tank analysts with extensive direct experience on the Hill; the sample was restricted to those with active and ongoing professional engagement with Capitol Hill as of the period of the survey.[2]

Table 3.1   Anonymous Social Science Survey on Congressional Norms (April–November 2019)

Question Prompt (Likert Scale Responses)
Please read the following series of statements about the appropriateness of certain behaviors by members in the House/Senate of TODAY and rate each of them on a scale of 1 to 5. In this case, a one (1) would denote something which is highly inappropriate, three (3) neither appropriate nor inappropriate, and a five (5) would denote a highly appropriate type of activity.

	Norm Being Queried
a. *Serving an apprenticeship period—that is being more of an observer than a participant when you first enter the legislature.*	Apprenticeship
b. *Learning the House or Senate procedural rules.*	Apprenticeship
c. *Never personally criticize a fellow Member on the floor of the chamber.*	Courtesy
d. *Maintaining friendly relationships with members of your own party.*	Courtesy
e. *Maintaining friendly relations with members of the opposing party.*	Courtesy
f. *Voting in a certain way on a bill that you cared little about in order to gain the vote of a fellow member on a bill that you did care about.*	Reciprocity
g. *Specializing in a field or policy area as compared to being a generalist.*	Specialization
h. *Voting with the opposition party.*	Partisanship
i. *Reaching bipartisan compromise in order to pass legislation.*	Partisanship
j. *Supporting cloture even when one opposes a bill.*	Partisanship—Supermajoritarianism (Senate Only)
k. *Requiring the support of a majority of the majority party for legislation to advance.*	Partisanship—Hastert Rule (House Only)
l. *Raising money on behalf of fellow party members.*	Fundraising
m. *Meeting with interest groups or lobbyists representing multiple sides of an issue.*	Relations with Special Interests / Reciprocity

Open-ended question:

Norms of Today: What are some of the norms—the "unwritten rules" or informal "rules of the game" —of today's Congress? Consider types of behavior that are acceptable or those that are not acceptable in the behavior of members and the functioning of the chamber. Please list or describe as many examples that come to mind in the space below.

Open-ended question:

Changing Norms: Are there norms that have changed since you started working on the Hill or in your career pertaining to Congress?

Source: Brian Alexander. Questionnaire for survey, "Anonymous Social Science Survey on Congressional Norms," designed and conducted by Brian Alexander (April-November 2019); table by the author.

The Likert scale measures the respondent's perceived level of appro-priateness of particular behavior, with a response of 1 indicating highly inappropriate, 3 neither inappropriate nor appropriate, and a 5 indicating highly appropriate. Likert responses are categorical, therefore a one-sample proportion analysis for values greater than 3 is used to determine the strength of the presence of each norm—that is, the percentage of respondents who indicate a norm is appropriate or highly appropriate provides a measure for the strength of a norm. There is no standard proportion that would conclu-sively determine the presence of a norm or not. Therefore, survey data is also weighed, in chapters ahead, against other qualitative data from open-ended questions, interviews, direct observation, and other quantitative analysis, to present a more robust case for the presence of particular norms in the modern Congress. Two-sample proportion tests are used to determine whether there are statistically significant differences in the strength of each norm among respondents in the House and the Senate as well as among Republicans and Democrats.

Respondent Characteristics

Survey respondents were queried to make sure they meet the criteria of being current or former members and staff; if former, then they must be an active congressional professional (working in an ongoing capacity in legislative affairs with regular Hill contact, such as lobbyist, journalist, among others), as well as to elicit basic demographic data relevant to the study, yielding a total of 319 valid survey responses. Respondents were asked to identify their current or most recent position on Capitol Hill: 30.45 percent ($n = 95$) said the Senate, 64.42 percent ($n = 201$) the House, 1 percent ($n = 3$) as nonpartisan congressional staff, and 4.17 percent ($n = 13$) as working in Hill-focused journalism or think tanks. Party identification included 47.13 percent (n=148) Republicans, 46.82 percent (n=147) Democrats, 5.1 percent independents ($n = 16$), and only 0.96 percent chose Other ($n = 3$). The gender of respondents was 72.52 percent ($n = 227$) male, 25.56 percent ($n = 80$) female, and 1.92 percent (6) other/prefer not to answer. Age of respondents is broken into four response choices: 18–29 years at 15.92 percent ($n = 50$); 30–44 years at 29.94 percent ($n = 94$); 45–59 years at 33.12 percent ($n = 104$); and 60 or older at 21.02 percent ($n = 66$). An effort was made to gain gender parity in the responses, but unfortunately it was not achieved. The proportion of women respondents does correspond to the ratio of women to men in the modern congress, where 127 of 535 seats (23.7 percent) are women, which includes 26 of 100 in the Senate, and 101 of 435 in the House (Center for Women and Politics 2020). There is greater gender parity of women staff on Capitol Hill, with women occupying 45 percent of staff positions but research suggests that women are more likely to occupy administrative rolls than men, and they occupy leadership and most policy positions at lower rates than men (Burgat 2017).

Survey Results

Survey findings point to a large degree of consensus across chambers and across parties about congressional norms. The overall findings point to evidence of norms of both cooperation and conflict existing simultaneously in the modern Congress. However, unique exceptions point to a stronger norm of partisanship in the House and an overall a higher propensity among Republicans than Democrats in favoring conflict over cooperation. Table 3.2 presents findings at the chamber- and party-levels indicating the proportion of survey respondents who indicate a particular norm is perceived as appropriate or highly appropriate (i.e., responses greater than three).

A key finding from the survey is that there is broad statistical agreement among responses in the House and Senate on congressional norms. The strength of each norm surveyed is evident based on percentiles of respondents who indicated the appropriateness of particular behaviors. Norms for which over 90 percent of respondents indicated as appropriate are: apprenticeship as measured by learning chamber rules; courtesy toward fellow party members; and reciprocity as measured receptiveness to meeting with special interests. Over 80 percent of respondents view courtesy toward the opposition party, bipartisan compromise, and fundraising as appropriate; over 70 percent of respondents view courtesy on the floor as appropriate; reciprocity as measured by vote trading and specialization are rated as appropriate by over 60 percent of respondents; partisanship as measured by voting with the opposing party is rated as appropriate by over 50 percent of respondents. Partisanship in the Senate as measured by support for cloture is rated as appropriate by 40 percent of respondents; finally, partisanship in the House as measured by support for the so-called "Hastert rule" is rated as appropriate by over 20 percent of respondents.

Despite much agreement, there are two important distinctions about congressional norms with statistically significant differences among respondents. First, partisanship as a norm, measured by the appropriateness of reaching bipartisan compromise in order to pass legislation, is rated significantly higher in the Senate, at 97.5 percent, compared to the House, at 86.0 percent ($p = 0.005$). That is, respondents from the Senate more strongly see bipartisan compromise as more appropriate than their House counterparts. Second, courtesy, measured by the appropriateness of maintaining friendly relations with members of one's own party, is modestly more highly rated in the Senate, at 97.87 percent to 92.53 percent ($p = 0.067$). These results

Table 3.2 Survey of Congressional Norms, 2019

Norm	Results by Chamber				Republicans R>3	p Score R-D	Results by Party		
	House R>3	p Score H-S	Senate R>3	Chambers All >3			Democrats R>3	Independents R>3	Party All >3
Apprenticeship (Observer Period)	42.29% 85/201	0.755	44.21% 42/95	43.31% 136/314	44.60% 66/148	0.7128	42.46% 62/146	37.50% 6/16	43.13% 135/313
Apprenticeship (Learning Rules)	92.04% 185/201	0.662	90.52% 86/95	92.04% 289/314	90.48% 133/147	0.2775	93.88% 138/147	93.75% 15/16	92.34% 289/313
Courtesy (Floor)	73.00% 146/200	0.61	75.79% 72/95	74.12% 232/312	77.71% 115/148	0.2389	71.73% 104/105	62.5% 10/16	74.04% 231/312
Courtesy (Intra-party)	92.53% 186/201	0.067+	97.87% 92/94	94.25% 295/313	94.6% 140/148	0.7804	93.83% 137/146	93.75% 15/16	94.25% 295/313
Courtesy (Opposition Party)	90.29% 121/134	0.586	87.5% 42/48	89.95% 170/189	91.78% 67/73	0.4212	88% 88/100	91.67% 11/12	89.9% 169/188
Reciprocity (Vote Trading)	68.50% 137/200	0.814	69.90% 65/93	68.16% 212/311	63.02% 92/146	0.065+	73.11% 106/145	68.75% 11/16	68.06% 211/310
Specialization	57.92% 117/202	0.1196	67.37% 64/95	61.27% 193/315	59.46% 88/148	0.4281	63.95% 94/147	56.25% 9/16	61.15% 192/314
Partisanship (Voting with Opposition)	52.50% 105/200	0.256	59.58% 56/94	55.13% 172/312	49.32% 72/146	0.034*	61.64% 90/146	56.25% 9/16	55.3% 172/311
Partisanship (Bipartisan Compromise)	86.00% 172/200	0.0049**	97.50% 78/80	89.26% 266/298	90.71% 127/140	0.2417	86.23% 119/138	100.00% 16/16	89.23% 265/297
Partisanship (Cloture)	47.30% 70/148	0.691	44.68% 42/94	46.92% 122/260	46.10% 59/128	0.9586	46.43% 52/112	62.50% 10/16	46.72% 121/259
Partisanship (Hastert Rule)	28.00% 56/200	0.663	30.66% 23/75	28.33% 83/293	37.50% 51/136	0.0017**	20.29% 28/138	18.75% 3/16	28.33% 83/293
Fundraising	89.34% 176/197	0.299	85.10% 80/94	88.03% 272/309	91.73% 133/145	0.1767	86.81% 125/144	75.00% 12/16	88.31% 272/308
Special Interests	92.58% 187/202	0.7455	91.49% 86/94	92.67% 291/314	93.88% 138/147	0.2775	90.48% 133/147	100.00% 16/16	92.65% 290/313

Source: Brian Alexander. Survey data. "Anonymous Social Science Survey on Congressional Norms," (April-November 2019); table by the author.

point to important differences in the norms of each chamber: the Senate values bipartisan compromise with the opposite party as more appropriate than the House, and Senators value friendly relations within their own party more so than their House counterparts. In sum, respondents from the House and Senate are largely in agreement about the strength of norms in their respective chambers but the Senate slightly more favors norms of bipartisan cooperation and intra-party courtesy than the House.

However, Republicans more strongly favor conflict over their Democratic counterparts. Where there are significant differences between the parties, it is consistently the Republicans who are more supportive of norms of conflict, as measured by questions on the Hastert rule, reciprocity, and voting with the opposition. The Hastert rule is among the least favored norms—registering as appropriate among on 28.33 percent of all respondents. However, among those who do support it, significantly more Republicans do so than Democrats. Republicans see the Hastert rule as appropriate at 37.5 percent as compared to Democrats at 20.29 percent ($p = 0.002$). The norm of reciprocity, as measured by trading votes on legislation, is viewed as appropriate by fewer Republicans (63.02 percent) than Democrats (73.11 percent), a modestly statistically significant difference ($p = 0.065$). Partisanship, as measured in terms of the appropriateness of voting with the opposition party, is viewed by 49.32 percent Republicans as appropriate as compared to 61.64 percent Democrats ($p = 0.034$). In sum, these findings suggest that Republicans see conflict as more appropriate than Democrats. This finding is consistent with other observations among political scientists that the rightward tilt among Republicans is greater than that of the Democrats to the left and the argument of political scientists David Mann and Norm Ornstein which places greater blame for conflict in American politics in the hands of the Republican Party (Dionne, Ornstein, and Mann 2017).

Because the responses are based on a sense of appropriateness—a subjective, qualitative measure—it does not make sense to rank the strength of each response as if it were an integer or quantitative value. However, we can see that some norms are viewed as appropriate at substantially higher levels than others. For instance, courtesy toward fellow party members is viewed as appropriate among 94 percent of respondents, for example, while the partisanship norm, evidenced by the sense that the Hastert rule requiring a majority of the majority to pass legislation, is viewed as appropriate among only 28 percent of respondents. Overall, therefore, it appears that norms of cooperation are more broadly valued than those of conflict in the U.S. Congress. Perhaps it is surprising that, in an era where there is little ideological overlap between the two political parties, there is overall agreement between the parties on congressional norms. This suggests an important undercurrent in Congress, which is that norms help control an otherwise increasingly partisan and polarized institution from becoming even more so. The broad bipartisan, bicameral support for norms of cooperation is an area where Congress is not as dysfunctional as often portrayed. Agreement on norms of cooperation prevent Congress from being even more fraught with partisan tension.

Contributing to the context of conflict, although on its own not necessarily a norm of conflict, is the emergence of fundraising as a norm among lawmakers in Congress. In survey results, 88.3 percent of all respondents indicated the appropriateness of raising money on behalf of fellow party members, with no statistical differences between Republicans and Democrats or the House and Senate. Fundraising is an imperative in the modern Congress, where elections cost more than ever and party pressures to raise money leave members little choice other than to do so. But what the responses to this question also point to is the sense of propriety of this practice, whether members like fundraising or not. This support for fundraising has perhaps contributed to conflict in the institution, even at the expense of other norms like apprenticeship. A seasoned congressional observer and former Hill staffer noted,

"I think apprenticeship is still a norm, but I think money has changed it. It is rooted more on money nowadays. A newer member often seeks an older member as a mentor. But older members often seek as their protégés people who they think can help them financially, whom they think can help raise the money . . . A lot more of the apprenticeship-mentorship thing and more of the new guy-old guy relationships are built on money than they were when I got here in the 1980s" (Interview 2016).

Fundraising on a partisan basis has become part of lawmakers' identities and senses of what is appropriate. To be a modern lawmaker is to be a partisan fundraiser, and in so doing contributes to the overall context of conflict.

The survey also helps to illustrate how some norms, evident in the past, are less prevalent today. For instance, specialization is an historic norm regularly addressed by previous scholars (Matthews 1960; Asher 1973; Loomis and Fishel 1981; Choate 2003), and therefore was included in the survey. Statistically, 61 percent of respondents indicated it is appropriate to specialize in a field or policy area as compared to being a generalist. But there was no statistical difference between parties or, more importantly, chambers, where it had previously been thought that Representatives tended to specialize more than Senators (Asher 1974; Shepsle 1989). However, beyond the responses to the specific survey question, there is little additional evidence for it—specialization was not spoken of in open-ended questions or semistructured interviews. In a period of greater legislative activism and the passing of the era of strong committees, it is perhaps not surprising that modern congressional observers do not speak of a specialization norm. If specialization is a norm of the modern Congress, it is not one that seems particularly strongly held.

SUMMARY

Survey evidence provides insights into the nature of norms in the modern Congress. The perceptions of active congressional players—current and former members and staff—points to broad consensus on particular norms, especially those of cooperation, with variations between parties and chambers on norms of conflict. Differences point to a more partisan Republican party compared to Democrats and a more conflictual House compared to the Senate. A more detailed analysis in the chapters ahead incorporates survey data with open-ended question responses, qualitative interviews, other statistical measures, and direct observation to paint a fuller picture of congressional norms in the twenty-first century. The combined survey data and other evidence reveal the prevalence of norms of cooperation that include apprenticeship, reciprocity, and courtesy; norms of conflict that include nonconformity and partisanship; and norms of a changing culture including sobriety and sexual propriety.

As this combined evidence suggests, the modern Congress exists between two apparent contexts: one rooted in an older era of compromise and cooperation and a newer era of disagreement and conflict, in addition to a broader context of a changing culture, where norms of a changing society have emerged on Capitol Hill. The capacity of the institution to ameliorate broader American ideological and political conflict will be shaped by the manner in which these normative predispositions play themselves out. To date, cooperation remains the prevalent ideal, but as the broader partisan context and emerging norms of conflict attest, it should not be taken for granted that this will always remain the case. Moreover, in a social theory of Congress, where norms act as the bases for preferences, normative attitudes of cooperation, conflict, or social attitudes are not exclusively instrumental or strategic. From the perspective of constructivist theory, norms are part of the identities and the sense of what is appropriate among members of Congress. For some, for instance, conflict is a preference, independent of other ideological or strategic considerations or consequences, which affects not just the capacity to achieve agreement, but the willingness to do so. The future of the interplay of these normative contexts has important implications for the manner in which the Congress manages political and ideological conflict in American politics.

NOTES

1. A reader may ask, what explains why norms are changing? It is not a coincidence that norms of conflict are emerging at the same time conflict is prevalent in other areas of American politics and within Congress itself. If norms inform a sense of what is appropriate, as other conflicts emerge the sense that conflict is appropriate would also emerge among social actors. But not all conflict is ideological, electoral, or strategic. As with cooperation so too with conflict, norms inform identities and a shared sense of what is appropriate among actors on Capitol Hill. Additional research would be fruitful that further explores the relationship between changes in material and political contexts and the normative logics of consequences and appropriateness. Earlier research in congressional studies on the evolution of norms (Rohde, Peabody, and Ornstein 1985; Choate 2003) looked at this question from a rational choice or behavioralist perspective. To add a constructivist dimension to this query in an updated context would contribute to our understanding of the ideational basis of members' senses of appropriateness and to broader dynamics of normative change.

2. The survey commenced in Spring 2019 when Luke Basham, who served as my research assistant, and I hand-delivered paper copies of the survey to every congressional office in the House and the Senate. No minor feat of gumshoe social science, by walking several combined miles in the halls and campuses of the House and Senate office buildings, Luke and I visited nearly every member office, hand-delivering a paper copy of the anonymous survey with a self-addressed stamped return envelope. At the time of the office visit, we also gathered an e-mail address to which I could personally follow-up with an anonymous online version of the survey. In preparing to conduct the survey, I was cautioned by fellow congressional scholars that acquiring a productive response rate would be difficult. In decades past, scholars would hand-deliver surveys to Capitol Hill and receive a reasonable number of responses. For example, Burdett Loomis generously drew from his archives to provide me a copy of the paper survey he and Jeff Fishel successfully implemented in among forty-five of seventy freshman offices of the class of 1974 (published in Loomis and Fishel 1981). However, warnings about low response rates for hand-delivered surveys proved valid—fewer than a dozen hand-delivered surveys were returned among hundreds delivered. The electronic follow-up, however, was successful. A combination of e-mail addresses from the in-person visits and contact information of current and former members and staff from Leadership Directories and other electronic sources yielded the broad sample of current and former members and staff who ultimately responded to the electronic survey.

Chapter 4

It Could Be Worse

Enduring Norms of Cooperation

This chapter makes a constructivist case for how norms function in the U.S. Congress, highlighting a key normative paradigm of the twenty-first century: cooperation. In so doing, the case is made that norms function not only in the materialist or consequentialist manner by which they have been described in research of the past, but that they also function ideationally. Chapter 3 presented survey evidence about the prevailing norms of the contemporary Congress, which includes those of cooperation and conflict. Here, the purpose is not to address every norm that has been identified or that could be identified. Rather, the argument focuses on the prevalent norms of cooperation, which include *apprenticeship*, *reciprocity*, and *courtesy*, in order to demonstrate in a constructivist manner the role of norms in the Congress as well as to provide better understanding of how these norms of cooperation exist and operate.

The enduring presence of norms of cooperation is an important aspect of the functioning of the modern Congress. Norms of cooperation are certainly under attack from many quarters of American politics, including among members of Congress themselves. But that norms of cooperation are adhered to even in limited form helps account for why coarseness and dysfunction in American politics are not worse than they already are. Norms of apprenticeship, reciprocity, and courtesy hold in common an understanding that cooperation is appropriate. Part of the identities of members of Congress is to understand and assume cooperation in their role as lawmakers in ways that mitigate conflict and facilitate legislative business. That members value cooperation in resolution of policy disputes and the development of legislation is reflected in the presence of norms such as apprenticeship, reciprocity, and cooperation examined here. In a social theory of Congress, this sense of the appropriateness of cooperation is not inevitable nor exclusively a function of strategic or ideological objectives. Rather, cooperation is understood as an end in itself and what members of Congress view as appropriate in their role as lawmakers, irrespective of other considerations.

Building a constructivist case for norms of cooperation in the U.S. Congress raises empirical challenges, including norm identification and distinguishing consequential and constitutive nature of norms. These will be met with a combination of several strategies, including survey responses, inferential statistical analysis, and the words of current and former members and staff. Any of these approaches can be built upon by future researchers to more fully flush out the existence and dynamics of these norms, as well as others, in the modern Congress. Although causal effects of constitutive norms is a subject worthy of further consideration, it is not the focus of the present chapter. Causal arguments are not necessary for a sufficient constructivist argument—if a norm serves as a preference or informs the shared identities of social actors, its presence need not be demonstrated by consequential or behavioral outcomes, although these outcomes do exist.

APPRENTICESHIP

Writing in the 1950s, Donald Matthews called apprenticeship "the first rule of Senate behavior." Under the apprenticeship norm "the new senator is expected to keep his mouth shut, not to take the lead in floor fights, to listen and to learn" (Matthews 1960, 92–93). Apprenticeship is an understanding that new members are to undertake a period of learning, keeping a lower profile, and deferring to more senior members during some period of time before they take a more active role in chamber proceedings. Close examination of the evidence suggests the apprenticeship norm is present in the modern Senate, but less clearly so in the House of today.

Matthews first pointed to apprenticeship as a folkway of the Senate. But Matthews observed even in the 1950s that "the practice of serving an apprenticeship may be on the way out," (Matthews 1960, 94). Indeed, modern observers speak to the decline of apprenticeship. A typical comment reflecting the demise of the maiden speech is offered in this observation by a former senior Republican staff member: "It used to be that you didn't speak until you were spoken to as a freshman member. You did a maiden speech, but you waited . . . I think that's certainly less the case today" (Interview 2019).

In the present age, apprenticeship is viewed as a period of restraint and learning, a sign of both respect toward more senior members, as well as an attitude of humility among junior members toward the rules and rituals of the institution. As one Republican Senate staffer said: "You respect leadership, you respect people who have seniority, people who have experience, and you defer when you first get there. You're there to learn, you are elected the same as they are elected, but they know things you don't know" (Interview 2019). Another long-serving Republican Senate staffer put it with colloquial flair, "Most new senators know you need to put in some time before you can drive the Jeep" (Interview 2019).

The Senate even has had a freshman senator mentorship program to provide new members "with advice-givers as they get situated in their new roles" (Libit 2009). In this vein, freshman Democratic Senator Barack Obama counted Indiana Republican Richard Lugar as a mentor when the junior senator landed a spot on the Foreign Relations Committee, which Lugar chaired (Libit 2009; Interview 2016; Kaplan 2019). Hilary Clinton is frequently mentioned as a good example of following the apprenticeship norm: "When there was a press conference, she didn't run to the microphone. She stood behind the senior senators. She spoke third or fourth. Overall, she sought advice from other members. There is a lot to be said for not coming in and thinking you are king of the hill, of showing that you are going to learn the system" (Interview 2016). Although not everybody seeks a mentor, a senior professional staffer stated, "When new members come in it's not unusual for an older, more senior Senator to serve as a sort of mentor. It's not as prominent as it once was, but I think we still do it" (Interview 2016). Other hardships of junior members of the House and Senate during an apprenticeship period include, as they did in Matthews's day, the struggle for plum committee assignments, the lottery for well-placed offices on Capitol Hill, and the expectation of fulfilling routine tasks like serving as presiding officer (Cochrane 2018; Hawkings 2016a).

Members continue to view apprenticeship as appropriate and part of what newer members should experience. Empirical evidence suggests that the apprenticeship norm remains active in the modern Congress. Some indicators are stronger than others. For instance, on the proxy measure for the apprenticeship norm, first queried by Asher (1973) and replicated in the present survey, fully 92.04 percent of all respondents, an equal number from the House and Senate, recognize the appropriateness of "learning the House or Senate procedural rules." Survey evidence points to slightly less than half of respondents as recognizing the classic definition of apprenticeship. On the question of the appropriateness of being more of an observer than a participant when one first enters the legislature, 42.29 percent of House respondents said it is appropriate as did 44.21 percent of those from the Senate.

We also witness adherence to the apprenticeship norm in the Senate through the tradition of the maiden speech—a waiting period whereby new Senators are not to speak on the Senate floor until after the passage of some indeterminate period of learning and observing Senate practice. Some observers allege a decline of the maiden speech tradition. For instance, in 2003,

Senator Bill Frist observed the maiden speech is "something we have gotten away from in the last several Congresses," in a special Senate publication of maiden speeches by new Senators of the 108th Congress (United States Senate 2003). However, examination of new evidence on maiden speeches gathered for this book suggests two interesting findings. First, the tradition was never quite as strong as commonly thought. Second, rather than being in decline, evidence indicates that the waiting period for maiden speeches, after having dipped, is actually on the rebound in recent Congresses.

New Senators, as the tradition goes, are to keep their mouths shut and are to engage in this "ritual of remaining silent during floor debates . . . [and] by waiting a respectful amount of time before giving their so-called maiden speech, their more senior colleagues would respect them for their humility" (U.S. Senate Historical Office 2019). As a former twenty-first century Senate Majority Leader described it, "you don't jump out on the floor of the Senate and start making a speech on your first day, your first week, or even your first month . . . you should wait maybe three months" (Interview 2019.) Matthews wrote, "Just how long this often painful silence must be maintained is not clear" (Matthews 1960, 93). Interviewees in the present research suggested "months," although there is not wide agreement on the actual duration. The Senate historian's website suggests the wait time is "from several months to several years" (U.S. Senate Historical Office, 2019).

In fact, the waiting period for the Senate maiden speech has never been as long as most observers have suggested. Analysis of data from the 80th through the 115th Congresses, newly gathered for this study, allows us to fix the average time a new Senator waits to give his or her maiden speech at a mere 48.2 calendar days (see table 4.1).[1] There are a total of 532 new Senators during the period 1947–2017, with an average of 14.75 new Senators per Congress (Senators who left and then returned to the Senate are counted as new only

Table 4.1   Average Calendar Days Waited Before Senate Maiden Speech from Date of Taking Office, 80th–115th Congresses (1947–2019)

	New Senators per Congress	Average Days to Speech per Congress	Average Days to Speech per Congress (Republicans)	Average Days to Speech per Congress (Democrats)
Mean	14.06	45.42	45.41	45.89
Max	27	89.06	93.00	119.50
	(83rd Cong.)	(113th Cong.)	(115th Cong.)	(112th Cong.)
Min	5	20.85	7.67	5.67
	(98th Cong.)	(104th Cong.)	(102nd Cong.)	(109th Cong.)

Source: Luke Basham. 2020. "Maiden Speeches and Apprenticeship: Continuity and Change in the U.S. Senate," Senior Honors Thesis, in requirement for completion of the Bachelor of Arts degree. Washington and Lee University, Lexington, Virginia. Thesis Committee Chair: Brian Alexander. Table by the author.

during their first term). The range of average wait times per Congress is from 20.9 calendar days (104th Congress) to 89.1 days (113th Congress). There is no significant difference in the wait time among Republicans (avg. 45.9 days) and Democrats (avg. 45.4 days). To assess this wait period, the number of calendar days is calculated between when a new Senator takes office and the date of their first major statement on the Senate floor. Importantly, the figure of 48.2 days is more complete and accurate than estimating the wait-time based on the time at which a ceremonial maiden speech was announced or made. For instance, Senator Ben Sasse (R-Nebraska) made a ceremonial maiden speech to much fanfare on November 3, 2015, during the 114th Congress. Fred Barnes of the *Weekly Standard* reported that Sasse, "revived a long-forgotten Senate tradition by waiting a year from his election before uttering a single word on the Senate floor" (Barnes 2015). In actuality, Sasse, who assumed office on January 3, 2015, made lengthy and substantive comments in the Senate chamber on September 15, 2015, while speaking in opposition to the nuclear accord with Iran negotiated by President Barak Obama (United States Senate 2015a) and in again on October 1 in regard to the Affordable Care Act (Obamacare) (United States Senate 2015b). When Sasse delivered his so-called "maiden speech" six weeks later, it cannot be considered his first notable remarks in Senate debate. While a self-described ceremonial speech may be an important or interesting event, it is not consistently the case that such self-described maiden speeches reflect a deference to the spirit of the norm of apprenticeship or of Senators remaining silent on the Senate floor.

This short average duration of 48.2 calendar days to a maiden speech means that the period of waiting to undertake a maiden speech is hardly "months" and definitely not "years" as some observers have claimed. However, contrary to those who lament the tradition is on the wane, evidence suggests that in the most recent decade, the waiting period for the maiden speech is actually on the rise. In the period 1947–2019, maiden speech wait-times peaked in the 1950s, fluctuated downward through the early 2000s, but increased in the last decade (see Table 4.2). A decade-by-decade analysis indicates that the "halcyon days" of the maiden speech about which Matthews wrote—the

Table 4.2 Mean Senate Maiden Speech Wait-times by Decade

80th to 85th Congress (1947–1959)	65.40 Mean Days
86th to 90th Congress (1959–1969)	46.72
91st to 95th Congress (1969–1979)	41.53
96th to 100th Congress (1979–1989)	40.85
101st to 105th Congress (1989–1999)	27.31
106th to 110th Congress (1999–2009)	37.72
111th to 115th Congress (2009-2019)	64.04

Source: Basham. 2020. Ibid. Table by the author.

period of 1947–1959, comprising the 80th to 85th Congresses, had an average of 65.4 days waiting period before new Senators made substantive speeches on the Senate floor. This figure dropped to an average 46.7 days during the period of 1959–1969 of the 86th through 90th Congresses. Lower than average figures are present during 1969–1979 of the 91st–95th Congresses, with 41.5 average days. This latter period included the infamous post-Watergate class of 1974, about which older, more senior members were aghast as new legislators spoke up and even introduced legislation (Schmitt 2019). From 1979 to 1989, during the 96th to 100th Congresses, the average wait time for a maiden speech is 40.9 days. The number dropped substantially in the period of 1989–1999 to 27.3 average days in the 101st–105th Congresses, and remained lower at 37.7 days in the 106th–110th Congresses, covering the period 1999–2009. These low points of the 1990s and 2000s may account for expressions of the sentiment, such as stated by Senator Frist, that the maiden speech tradition was in decline among those whose Senate experience includes these periods into the early twenty-first century.

Notably, there has been a marked increase in the tradition in the most recent decade, with an average 64.0 days waiting period in the 111th through 115th Congresses, from 2009 to 2019. This suggests that, in the modern Congress, the tradition of the maiden speech is stronger than it has ever been since the decade of the 1950s. While the maiden speech tradition has varied, it is as evident in the modern Congress as it was in the mid-twentieth century. If we allow the maiden speech to stand as a proxy for the apprenticeship norm, in combination with supporting evidence provided by the survey, we see that the apprenticeship norm is a feature of the modern Senate.

Evidence is less firm, though not absent, regarding a norm of apprenticeship in the House. This is true of the past as well as the present. In his 1973 examination of the presence of Senatorial norms in the House, Asher found that "the very existence of a norm of apprenticeship . . . must be called into question" (Asher 1973, 509). A thirty-year veteran House Republican committee staff member went so far as to indicate that "being unwilling to learn process and procedure" is one of the informal rules of today's House (Survey 2019). An eighteen-year House Republican staffer stated, "Freshman members of both parties are talking way too much . . . They literally don't know how a bill becomes a law and they're talking like their old hands" (Survey 2019).

However, not everyone agrees that apprenticeship is absent in the House. A senior House administrative staffer said among the informal rules of engagement in the House is "deference to folks with seniority—when you are a freshman you come in and observe and generally tend to keep quiet and learn the ropes and you work your way up, you gain the experience that allows you to speak out" (Interview 2016) and a Democratic congressman who served for ten years, said, "there is still respect for more senior Members and their experience and insight and respect for the knowledge of knowledge-able members" (Survey 2019). Other efforts to measure apprenticeship in the House provide mixed proof of its existence. Some research, for instance, points to apprenticeship in the length of time members serve before gaining positions of seniority (Polsby 1968; Canon 1989). Other evidence on whether an apprenticeship period affected committee assignments in the 80th through 91th Congresses (Bullock 1970), the purportedly halcyon days of apprentice-ship, is inconclusive.[2] Combined with the 2019 survey responses that suggest about equal support in the House (42.3 percent) as the Senate (43.1 percent) for indicators of apprenticeship, there is at least some limited sense that an apprenticeship period is understood as appropriate. Apprenticeship may not be a hallmark of service in the House of Representatives, but it is not absent as a norm altogether.

RECIPROCITY

Much as Donald Matthews wrote of the Senate of the 1950s and Herbert Asher wrote of the House in the 1970s, reciprocity is widely recognized as a norm of today's Congress. Reciprocity is the implicit sense that members should help each other on legislative efforts—or at least not unnecessarily hinder one another—in exchange for being repaid in kind by their fellow members (Matthews 1960, 99; Asher 1973, 503).

One of the more explicit form of reciprocity is vote trading, sometimes called logrolling, which is voting in a certain way on a measure in order to gain the support of a fellow member on another measure. Both Matthews (1959; 1960) and Asher (1973) observed this behavior in the Senate and House of the 1950s and 1970s, respectively. Survey evidence from the modern Congress points to the existence of reciprocity norm across both chambers, with 68.1 percent of all respondents viewing vote-trading as appropriate. The norm is held by Democrats (73.11 percent) slightly more so than Republicans (63.02 percent, $p = 0.065$). There is little statistical difference between House and Senate respondents (68.5 percent and 69.9 percent, respectively). What is important in the constructivist sense about reciprocity is not the behavioral component—members may find it difficult to vote trade in an era where party leadership wields a high degree of con-trol over members (Weingast and Marshall 1988), especially in the House, or when earmark bans in both chambers make it harder to craft widely appealing legislation (Hudak 2013). What adds to the constructivist aspect of the norm of reciprocity is not just that it helps members ideologically or strategically, but that it is widely regarded as appropriate behavior, part of the bargaining culture that makes cooperation a key aspect of life on Capitol Hill.

Other evidence of the reciprocity norm comes across in attitudes expressed by members and staff from the House and Senate about other behaviors, such as procedural restraint, honesty, predictability, and "turf," the latter of which includes respect for other member's legislative purviews and the prerogative of constituent responsiveness. Not only are these common practices on Capitol Hill, there is a general sense of appropriateness attributed to these behaviors. Procedural restraint—the sentiment that one should not delay, complicate, or interfere with chamber action or when particular outcomes are inevitable—is a widely adhered to aspect of the reciprocity norm. This ranges from not being long-winded on the floor of the Senate, to not unnecessarily abusing the rules of each chamber, to avoiding dilatory practices which in the Senate may include objecting to routine unanimous consent requests or in the House offering nongermane amendments forbidden by rules agreements (Matthews 1959, 1071–1072). In another way of expressing it, procedural restraint entails "a willingness to let the business of Congress proceed" (Schneier 1988, 126).

The American public ranks the honesty and ethical standards of Senators and Members of Congress among the lowest of all professions. A 2019 Gallup survey places Senators and Members of Congress just below insurance sales people and just above the last-place car salespeople in list of twenty-two professions. Only 13 percent of respondents rated the honesty and ethical standards of Senators as high or very high, and members of the House came in at only 12 percent of respondents on the same scale (Jones 2019). However, while the general public may think of politicians as dishonest, in the currency of Capitol Hill honesty is among the most highly valued traits and a quality intrinsic to the reciprocity norm. As a Republican congressman with thirty years of service put it, "Being true to your word is critically important" (Survey 2019). Phrases like "be honest," "stay true to your word," "don't lie," and "don't misrepresent a bill or its effects" are regularly voiced by Republican and Democratic House and Senate members alike (Interviews 2019).

Predictability is another unwritten maxim that underlies the norm of reciprocity. Followed among political allies and coalitions, it is the sense that one should be predictable in policy and legislative positions and not undertake radical departures from expected courses without giving notice to leadership, partners, or fellow partisans. A House Democratic committee staffer stated, "Among partisan committee and leadership staff: no surprises. Share what you are doing. You don't have to reveal specifics, but they need to know that something is coming. This is applicable to committee markups, hearings, interactions with the press, and especially on the Floor" (Survey 2019).

Predictability does not apply to one's political adversaries—where surprise may be good strategy—but among one's colleagues, it is inappropriate to spring on them unanticipated pronouncements and courses of action.

Another aspect of the norm of reciprocity is what may be thought of as "turf"—the sense that certain members take ownership or have rights of priority on particular issues or legislative items and that one should be careful not to encroach on another member's electoral needs particularly among, although not limited to, fellow party members. Turf extends to fundraising and campaign behavior in other member's districts or states. A Republican staffer with twenty years-experience in the House captured turf like this: "Inappropriate: raising money in another Member of the same party's district. Inappropriate: file a bill that is virtually the same as another current Member's bill" (Survey 2019). A currently serving Democratic Senator stated a norm of "not campaigning against the other Senator from your state" (Survey 2019). Turf also means "not stealing" another member's claim to or jurisdiction over legislation, whether bills or amendments, that another member has a record of trying to advance. A Democratic House staffer with twenty-five years of experience put it this way: "Do not encroach on a colleague's issue, as in do not steal a legislative issue owned by a colleague" (Survey 2019).

A final and related aspect of the reciprocity norm is the sense that it is appropriate to allow members to act in ways contrary or partisan or coalitional needs if they are responding to constituent demands. This is, of course, tied to the electoral imperative and the need for members to effectively respond to constituents if they wish to be reelected (Mayhew 1974). But in the normative sense, it is considered highly appropriate for members to do things their colleagues may not like if it is in the name of voters. Members of the House and Senate provide each other great latitude in being responsive to the demands placed on them by their constituents, such as "voting their conscious" on tough votes, nonsponsorship of controversial bills, or withholding participation in coalitions on matters unfavorable to their electorate. One of the most widely respected refrains in bargaining and negotiating among offices for support on particular legislative or policy efforts is "my constituents won't allow it."

While being responsive to constituents may seem like obvious behavior for elected officials, it warrants recognizing that members not only prioritize the demands of their electoral coalition, and thereby see as part of their identity to serve in a representative role, but that their peers respect such behavior in one another. Additional evidence of this openness is in more than 92 percent of all survey respondents who agreed it is appropriate to meet with interest groups or lobbyists representing multiple sides of an issue (table 1.2). Even in a highly partisan climate, exceptions are made for fellow partisans to serve constituents over party demands. This aspect of reciprocity should not be taken for granted—hypothetically, members could identify alternate means to limit and vet their encounters with the general public, nonresidents, or nonsupporters, to their possible advantage. That they do not is a vestige of the spirit of cooperation that facilitates a more pluralistic representative system. This is especially notable in an era where partisan disagreement underlies so much other behavior.

COURTESY

Courtesy is another of the "folkways" identified by Matthews in the U.S. Senate at the middle of the twentieth century. As he states it, courtesy means "avoiding personal attacks on colleagues, striving for impersonality by divorcing the self from the office, 'buttering-up' the opposition by extending unsolicited compliments" (Mayhew 1974, 1070). The norm has been observed by scholars and practitioners alike in the House and the Senate, as well as in state legislatures (Wahlke et al. 1963; Hebert and McLemore 1973).

Courtesy in the House has been explained as maintaining friendly relationships (Asher 1973, 502). Sometimes, the term "comity" is used to mean courtesy, other times to mean, simultaneously, courtesy and reciprocity (Uslaner 1993).[3] In other cases, the term "civility" is used in reference to "the presumption of mutual respect" which restricts the rhetoric that may be used on the floor and facilitates the ability to deliberate (Annenberg 2011, 2). In the Senate of the 1970s, courtesy was described as being much like that of the 1950s: "One hears the same flowery language, the same deliberate civility, the same praises of colleagues" (Rohde, Peabody, and Ornstein 1985, 167). Even though the clubby atmosphere of mid-century Congress was on the wane, the 1980s Senate was described as one of "trust and reciprocity" (Baker 1989, 180).[4] Thomas Jefferson may have been an early observer of the norm of courtesy in the Senate. In his final act as president of the Senate, he delivered an address in which he observed, "the habits of order & decorum which so strongly characterize the proceedings of the Senate, have rendered the umpirage of their President an office of little difficulty: that in times, & on questions which have severely tried the sensibilities of the house, calm and temperate discussion has rarely been disturbed by departures from order" (TJ to the Senate 28 February 1801).

Each of these understandings embody what we can see as a norm of courtesy in the U.S. Congress: the practice of members of the House and Senate treating one another with deference and respect, avoiding personal attacks or making political disagreements personal, offering excessive compliments, and behaving with general politeness in their interactions with peers. Another

way of thinking about it is that, regardless of whatever political or policy
conflict may be going on, members are generally friendly toward one another.

Courtesy Is Alive and (Relatively) Well
in the Modern Congress

It often draws a skeptical glance when a scholar, such as yours truly, suggests
to audiences that courtesy is a widely observed norm of the modern Congress.
The opposite is more commonly believed to be the case. Courtesy is regularly
spoken of as being on the decline by all manner of congressional observers.
Terms such as "eroding" or phrases such as "not like in the past" and other
such sentiments are frequently mentioned in relation to courtesy. A recently
retired Republican Senator laments, "Comity and courtesy, which have been
a hallmark of the Senate in the past, seem to be less so today" (Interview
2019). A former long-serving Democratic Senate staffer expresses a similar
sentiment: "There's a saying that this is the most exclusive club in the world
here, and there's a certain collegiality among the members here, even with
those in different party . . . I think that's a norm you see slowly eroding . . .
You see personal attacks on members that are part of the body somewhat
increasing" (Interview 2019). A Democratic Representative noted, "You try
to be decent, but there less respect up here. Even in the most heated disputes,
members used to treat each other decently. I'm not seeing as much of that"
(Interview 2016). Scholars as well have pointed to a decline in norms of courtesy, civility, and comity (Uslaner 1993; Smock 2011; Davidson, Oleszek,
and Lee 2012, 117).

Relying upon anecdotal or "impressionistic" (Uslaner 1993, 32) evidence,
it is easy to understand why courtesy is thought to be absent or on the wane
in the modern Congress. Media attention readily focuses upon particularly
dramatic breaches of decorum on the floors of each chamber (Stone and
Green 2017). Several cases in the last decade are often pointed to as signs of
a deterioration of the norm such as when South Carolina Representative Joe
Wilson shouted "You lie!" at President Barak Obama during an address to a
joint session of the Congress in September 2009 (CNN 2009); an unknown
Republican calling Michigan Democrat Bart Stupak a "baby killer" during
a March 2011 debate on health care (Sherman 2010); Senator Elizabeth
Warren, during testimony before a House committee, admonishing the
conduct of Representative Patrick T. McHenry with a resulting exchange
of terse words in May 2011; Senator Ted Cruz (R-TX) accusing Majority
Leader Mitch McConnell of a "flat out lie" during a floor statement in 2015
(Raju 2015); and Republican Senator Tom Cotton of Arkansas shouting
"bullshit" on the Senate floor during the Coronavirus debate in March of 2020
(Desiderio 2020). These stories are also passed around like lore on Capitol

Hill as evidence for the decline of norms in general, or courtesy specifically. In decades past, unsupported allegations of communist beliefs by Senator Joseph McCarthy in the 1950s, the obstreperous tactics of Newt Gingrich in the House of the1980s and 1990s, and even bipartisan civility retreats have been pointed to as evidence for the demise of courtesy in the Congress (Stolberg 2003). Meantime, outside the confines of the hearing room or the floors of the House and Senate, there are innumerable instances of members speaking in less than decorous terms of their colleagues on cable TV and in social media (Chergosky 2018).

Such perceptions of the decline of courtesy in the modern Congress reflect the general tone of conflict in American politics, tensions relating to the partisan polarization in Congress, and among the political class and general public at large (Voteview 2016; Kraushaar 2014; Fiorina 2017; Abramowitz 2018). During the presidency of Donald Trump, acrimony among members of the political class has seemed both daily and unprecedented (Bresnan, Caygle, and Ferris 2019). Meantime, Congress is chronically held in low-regard by the American public (Whittington 2019). In their 1997 study on civility in the House of Representatives, the Annenberg Public Policy Center wrote, "The discussion of civility and Congress occurs in a climate in which the public perceives that incivility is a pervasive social problem, trust in institutions is low, and Congress is not held in high regard" (Jamieson 1997). These sentiments have not abated in the two decades since. Gallup data puts overall Congressional approval at an average of 30 percent since 1974, while a 2019 Pew study finds overall trust in government "is near historic lows today." Members themselves are not immune to negative perceptions of their home institution, as evidenced in the long-held tradition of running against Congress (Smith, Roberts, and Vander Wielen 2013, 5) or the modern airing of grievances about life as a member today. Adding to all of this is a tendency among those with experience to perceive the norms of the past as better than those of the present (Luce 1935 cited in Schneier 1988, 664). As Montaigne famously said, "Whoever saw old age that did not applaud the past, and condemn the present time?" All of this considered, skepticism about the persistence of the courtesy norm in the modern Congress seems reasonable.

But courtesy is, in fact, alive and relatively well in the modern Congress. This is born, in no small part, of the fact that, irrespective of ideological, partisan, and strategic conflict that dominate contemporary political experience, members continue to believe it is appropriate to be courteous. This should not be mistaken for a love fest. Legislators do say nasty things about one another in the media and on social media, and committee hearings and after-hours floor speeches before C-SPAN cameras can be bruising. But while many perceive an overall decline in courtesy on Capitol Hill, it is just as easy to find those who speak to its enduring presence. What is striking—and important from the perspective of the functioning of the institution—is that in floor proceedings, in less public-facing business, and informal member-to-member and office-to-office relations, courtesy remains a prevalent norm. The preponderance of systematic evidence points to the presence of the courtesy norm in the modern Congress and an underlying logic of appropriateness by which it is maintained.

Courtesy in the Words of the Participants

Contrary to skeptics, the words of many current and former members and staff point to the strong degree courtesy norm is not only present but also valued on Capitol Hill. People who have served in Congress or worked on the Hill, in both House and Senate, repeatedly indicate that, in fact, the place is quite courteous. A veteran Capitol Hill journalist puts it like this: "The notion that it's got to be about business and not personal is a norm that is still hanging on. You make your anger about policy, not about personality" (Interview 2016). A recently retired Republican Senator noted, "Generally, from Congress to Congress, the norms in both the House and the Senate include a respect for each other, especially during the proceedings of the House and Senate, whether you're in committee or on the floor. And a degree of courtesy that demonstrates to the public as well as the people in the body that you have that respect" (Interview 2019). A senior Senate administrative staffer said, "There is an unwritten agreement in the Senate that when you go into the chamber there is a certain behavioral norm that includes following basic rules but it also includes being respectful" (Interview 2016). The sentiment of courtesy is neatly summarized in the exclamation of a staff member of one of the Senate's most liberal members: "Members are really nice to each other, despite what you might see on TV. I think there's a general norm of civility and deference" (Interview 2019). These comments are echoed by a Republican Senate staff member: "I think courtesy is something in the Senate . . . you're respectful to your fellow members, you're collegial with the members. If you look at people who are not good at that they're disdained, they're not liked" (Interview 2019).

Like the Senate, courtesy in the House is chronically thought of in terms of not being what it used to be. However, numerous comments indicate the norm, however "torn and frayed" it may be, is still understood as appropriate in that chamber. Statements from the House about courtesy include that of "be respectful of all members" according to a recently retired Republican congressman (Survey 2019), "avoid disparaging other members of Congress personally," noted a twenty-five-year Democratic staffer, and "publicly questioning the motives or patriotism of a member is inappropriate," according to a fifteen-year former Democratic congressman (Survey 2019). A House administrative staffer observed, "Conflict is the stuff that gets the attention in the media environment that were in. But it's overplayed. The vast majority of members still adhere to that norm that you need to show a certain amount of respect and it can't get personal" (Interview 2016). Courtesy is also captured in this upbeat expression of a sitting Republican congressman, "I believe that being kind and friendly to everyone no matter who they are, Democrat or Republican, member or staff, is a good way to live life and a good way to foster cordial relationships, and to help the body function more effectively" (Survey 2019). Obviously, neither the most sanguine nor the most cynical expressions reflect the general status of the courtesy norm in the House or Senate—and outside the Capitol in partisan media and on the campaign, courtesy may be harder to spot. But the prevailing sense is that courtesy is a norm in the Congress of the early twenty-first century.

Survey Evidence of the Courtesy Norm

If we go beyond just the words of current and former members and staff, where we see some lamenting courtesy's decline but others speaking to its enduring presence, we can look to a more statistical measure of the endurance of the courtesy found in survey evidence. In the 2019 survey, current and former members and staff, House and Senate, Republican and Democrat alike, report that courtesy is a norm and widely considered appropriate on Capitol Hill. As presented in chapter 3, survey findings point to strong support in the Senate and the House, among Republicans and Democrats alike for courtesy, with no statistical differences. Solid majorities of respondents—77.1 percent of Republicans and 71 percent of Democrats—indicate it is appropriate or highly appropriate to never personally criticize a fellow member on the floor of the chamber. Maintaining friendly relations with members of one's own party is viewed favorably by 94.6 percent of Republicans and 93.8 percent of Democrats, while maintaining friendliness toward the opposite party is also strongly viewed as appropriate, at 91.8 percent of Republicans and 88.0 percent of Democrats.[5] Such sentiments, directly capturing whether members and staff perceive such behavior as appropriate, point solidly in favor of courtesy as a prevailing norm.

Courtesy on the House Floor: Words Taken Down

Debate on the House floor heated up in July 2019 over comments by Speaker of the House Nancy Pelosi (D-CA) regarding controversial postings on Twitter by President Trump (Trump 2019).[6] During consideration of a Democratic resolution to condemn the president's tweets as racist, Speaker Pelosi said on the House Floor, "Every single Member of this institution,

Democratic and Republican, should join us in condemning the President's racist tweets. To do anything less would be a shocking rejection of our values and a shameful abdication of our oath of office" (U.S. House of Representatives 2019, H5851-2).

This led Georgia Republican Doug Collins to invoke the procedural step of "words taken down," against Speaker Pelosi for violation of a House rule in which "[p]ersonal abuse, innuendo, or ridicule of the President is not permitted" and whereby "[r]eferences to racial or other discrimination on the part of the President are not in order" (Wickham 2017, Sec. 370, 187-190). The House parliamentarian then sided with Representative Collins. What followed was a tense and procedurally intricate stand-off, with moments of unprecedented melodrama such as when the presiding officer Emanuel Cleaver II (D-Missouri) abandoned the chair (Tully-McManus and McPherson 2019). Then, however, the House voted in a 190–232 party-line vote to reject the motion to strike the Speaker's remarks and no penalty was delivered. Despite the precedent in House Rules prohibiting such speech, the House Democratic majority stood behind the Speaker in rejecting the Republican Collins's motion.

The tensions expressed in this House interchange, and the first demand in thirty-five years that the Speaker of the House's words be taken down, may seem a sign of the broader coarseness present in American politics these days (Pergram 2019a). Yet a closer examination of the history of the "words-taken-down" rule suggests a more complicated reality in which courtesy is the predominant norm, despite high-profile episodes such as the one with Speaker Pelosi.

Formal enforcement of the courtesy norm in the House can be analyzed through Rule XVII and the words taken down process. Under House Rule XVII, clause 4, members may call other members to order for use of disorderly or unparliamentary language during debate on the House floor or in committees. The process follows specific guidelines, initiated when a member invokes a privileged motion that another member's word "be taken down." The phrase refers to writing down the words, reading them back to the House by the Clerk, and a determination by the Speaker of the House, Speaker Pro Tem, or the Chair in committee, to determine if the words are in order (Baitinger 2019). The call must occur more or less at the time of the allegedly offending remarks, before other business or debate transpires. The Congressional Research Service (CRS) explains:

> The standing rules of the House do not state explicitly what language is considered to be disorderly, although clause 1(b) of Rule XVII prohibits Members from engaging in "personalities" in debate. House precedents catalog words and phrases previously deemed to be in order and those that were ruled out of order,

or unparliamentary. When ruling on the words objected to, the presiding officer considers the words themselves, as well as the context in which they were used, and bases the ruling on these precedents. On the floor, the Parliamentarian advises the Speaker based on precedents. (Baitinger 2019, 2)

Once a demand is made, debate suspends while the Chair reviews the words and makes a ruling. The Member accused of the offending words may offer explanation "only if prompted by the presiding officer or if another Member makes a motion to allow an explanation and the motion is agreed to by the House" (Ibid., 3). Typically, the words are read aloud by the Clerk. Prior to a ruling by the presiding officer, the member who spoke the words may request unanimous consent to withdraw them or the member who made the demand may independently withdraw it. The ruling, subject to appeal, can be either that the words are not unparliamentary or that they are out of order. Typically, but not always, words ruled out of order are stricken from the *Record* (Ibid., 3, fn.13).

If the member's words are ruled to be out of order, the sanction imposed is "that Member may not be recognized to speak for the rest of the day (even on yielded time) or insert undelivered remarks into the *Record* unless the Member is allowed to proceed in order by the House" (Ibid., 4) by unanimous consent or, on appeal, a voice vote. In short, the maximum penalty for using unparliamentary language is to be prohibited from speaking in the Congress for the remainder of a day.[7]

Measuring Courtesy with Words Taken Down

The words taken down process is used here as a measurement of courtesy over time on the House floor.[8] Specifically, courtesy norm violations are identified as individual instances where a member is accused of violating House Rule XVII, by another member of the House, including demands that a member's words be taken down, accusations of unparliamentary language or engaging in personalities, and admonitions from the chair. A dataset, compiled by systematically reviewing the *Congressional Record* for the period of the 80th (1947–1948) to 115th (2017–2019) Congresses and capturing each case that meets one of the following five criteria relating to the words taken down process and unparliamentary language under House rules governing decorum: (1) a demand that words be taken down is made and then withdrawn by the accuser prior to a ruling by the chair; (2) a demand that words be taken down is upheld (words are ruled out of order); (3) a demand that words be taken down is overruled; (4) a member accused of words taken down withdraws those words by unanimous consent; and (5) no formal demand is made but the chair issues an admonishment to members to adhere to rules of decorum.[9] A unique feature of the data presented here is that each breach of decorum is attributed to a perpetrator and an accuser, enabling each observation to include data on particular lawmakers, such as ideology scores, tenure, party, and others. The result is a binary categorical variable indicating when an individual member is accused of a formal violation of the norm of courtesy on the floor of the House. Table 4.3 summarizes the findings.

The words taken down measure does not capture all aspects of courtesy or discourtesy and represents only those instances in which one member called out another for violations of decorum rules on the chamber floor. It does not capture incivility that may exist elsewhere in Congress, and it is not the only way of measuring courtesy among members (Smock 2011; Dodd and Schraufnagel 2013, 81) or to speak to the possible decline of comity in other corners of American political life (Uslaner 1993). Annenberg admits, "Relying on the taking down process as our yardstick underestimates incivility" (Annenberg 2011, 2). Yet words-taken-down is a reliable, encompassing measure of courtesy on the floor and in relations among members that goes beyond anecdotal or impressionistic accounts. Data on the words taken down process represent decades of discourteous behavior where it perhaps matters most—on the floor of the House of Representatives.

Evidence of the Courtesy Norm and the Logic of Appropriateness

Analysis of the words taken down process reveals that whatever what we may think about congressional dysfunction and partisan bickering, the norm of courtesy is widely adhered to in the modern Congress. In the period of the 80th through the 115th Congresses, we see a total of 275 demands for words taken down; an average of 7.72 cases per Congress and a range from a low of zero cases in the 90th Congress to twenty-eight cases in the 104th (see Figure 4.1). During this period, there were a total of 2,958 individual members of

Table 4.3   Outcomes of Accusations for Demand of Words Taken Down, 80th–115th Congresses

Outcome of Accusation	Freq.	Percent
Accuser Withdraws Demand	45	16.36%
Demand Upheld—Words Ruled Out of Order *(Member Seated for Legislative Day)*	41 *(6)*	14.91 *(2.18)*
Demand Overruled *(Untimely Demand)*	62 *(16)*	22.55 *(5.81)*
Perpetrator withdraws Words	91	33.09
Chair Admonishes	36	13.09
Total	275	100

Source: Brian Alexander. Original data set. Table by the author.

Chapter 4

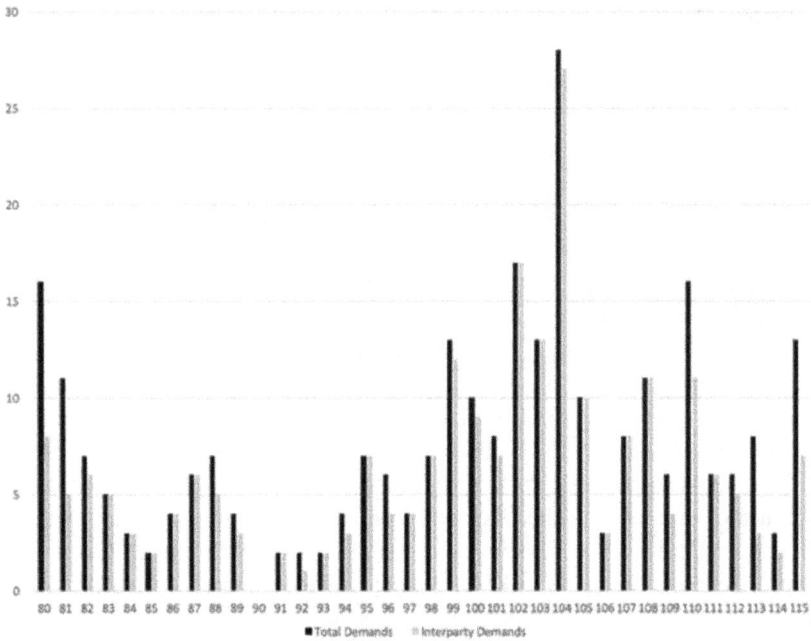

Figure 4.1   Demands of Words Taken Down, with Inter-party Data, House of Representatives, 80th–115th Congresses. Total Demands for Words Taken Down = 275, Total Inter-party Demands = 232 (84.36 percent), Total Intra-party Demands = 43 (15.63 percent), Binomial Test: p < 0.000** (Expected k: 125.5, Observed k: 232). *Source*: Brian Alexander. Original data set. Table by the author.

Congress and only 248 whose words were ever so challenged, a rate of 8.38 percent of members faced with a demand of words taken down over thirty-six Congresses (the rate based on the total 15,886 individual congressional terms served, the rate is 1.56 percent). This suggests that breaches of the norm of courtesy in the House of Representatives are extremely rare. The data support another notable insight. Inter-party norm violations—those cases where a demand for words taken down is made by a member of the other party—account for 84.36 percent (232 out of 275) of all cases in the 80th through 115th Congresses. Only forty-three (15.63 percent) are within the same party. The low number of intra-party accusations suggests that members have always been more courteous to those of their own party.

The evidence also supports a case for the logic of appropriateness in the adherence to the courtesy norm in the House. At minimum, the low occurrence of words-taken-down being invoked points to a general sense that members fundamentally believe it is appropriate to be courteous toward one another. More significantly, we may borrow from the approach of Finnemore, in which we expect "similar behavior from dissimilar actors" (Finnemore

1996, 30) to identify where competing strategic explanations are inadequate to account for the given outcomes. Specifically, in a statistical analysis of the characteristics of members who were accused of violating decorum, based on the words taken down process, common predictive factors such as ideology and party do not predict norm violations.[10] That is, the most ideologically conservative and ideologically liberal members are *no more likely* to violate the courtesy norm. If ideology were predictive of violations of the courtesy norm, it would point to partisan, electoral, or other strategic factors as contributing to nonconforming behavior. But this is not the case. In other words, courtesy prevails irrespective of competing factors that typically account for member behavior in the modern U.S. Congress.

Of course, to say that other explanations are inadequate is not irrefutable evidence that a sense of the appropriateness of courtesy is the cause of a lack of violations of decorum rules. As in much constructivist research, it remains a difficult and often an open challenge to establish causal inferential links between social phenomena such as norms and behavioral outcomes (Hopf 1998; Klotz and Lynch 2007; Bertucci, Hayes, and James 2018, chapter 2). Perhaps a future scholar will find a more direct means of operationalizing the courtesy norm and discovering its effects on member behavior. However, the preponderance of evidence—qualitative, survey, and behavioral—points to the sense that lawmakers see courtesy as appropriate and adhere to the courtesy norm as a shared preference, based on the logic of appropriateness, irrespective of other consequences. A similar case can be made for the Senate based on calls to order.

Courtesy on the Senate Floor: Calls to Order

Senate Rule XIX, "Debate," was at the center of a media maelstrom on February 7, 2017, when Republican Majority Leader Mitch McConnell of Kentucky invoked it against Massachusetts Democratic Elizabeth Warren— the first such occasion in two decades. Senator Warren was speaking on the Senate floor about the confirmation of Republican Senator Jeff Sessions of Alabama to be President Trump's attorney general. She referred to remarks about Sessions made in a letter written by Coretta Scott King, dating to 1986 when the Senate was then considering Sessions for a federal court appointment. Warren was first warned by the presiding officer about violating Rule XIX prohibitions on impugning another senator. When she continued to read from King's letter, Majority Leader McConnell formally accused Warren under Rule XIX: "The senator has impugned the motives and conduct of our colleague from Alabama" (United States Senate 2017, S854). A terse interchange ensued that included McConnell's reprobation, "Nevertheless, she persisted," which afterward became a battle cry among progressives (Wang

2017). A party-line vote upheld McConnell's accusation to seat Senator Warren, which prohibited her from speaking on the floor for the remainder of the debate on the Sessions nomination (Kane and O'Keefe 2017).

The Warren-McConnell confrontation stands as an example of the breaching of courtesy norms on the Senate floor—one made all the more controversial by the fact that partisan observers disagree over who was in greater violation of the norm: "The suggestion that reciting the words of the great Coretta Scott King would invoke Rule 19 and force Senator Warren to sit down and be silenced is outrageous," stated Democratic Senator Kamala Harris of California (Kim 2017). Indeed, such a case is dramatic and suggestive of the extent to which incivility can erupt in the modern Congress. But, just as in the House, a more systematic examination of the evidence points to the strength of the courtesy norm in the Senate.

Senate Rule XIX prohibits disorderly language in debate on the Senate floor. CRS summarizes the scope of the rule:

> Senate Rule XIX identifies specific language that is considered disorderly. This includes language directly or indirectly imputing to another Senator or Senators "any conduct or motive unworthy or unbecoming a Senator" (paragraph 2) and referring "offensively to any State of the Union" (paragraph 3). Rule XIX prohibits imputing conduct or motive "by any form of words" to a sitting Senator, which includes not just original words spoken in debate but quotes, news articles, and other materials . . . Senators have at times also been called to order for making disparaging references in debate to the House of Representatives or its Members. (CRS 2018, ii)

Rule XIX is the main mechanism by which the courtesy norm may be formally enforced in the Senate.

Like the House, analysis of the patterns of violations of the rules of decorum in the Senate indicates that the courtesy norm is widely upheld. Systematic analysis of calls to order under Senate Rule XIX finds the rule infrequently invoked. In the period 1962 to 2018, only seventeen formal calls to order under Rule XIX were made (U.S. Senate Historian 2019).[11] A gap from October 1, 1996, to February 7, 2017, exists in which no cases of a formal call to order occurred at all. Among all seventeen cases, only in the single case with Senator Warren in 2017 was a Senator actually met with the full sanction of the rule, wherein the accused Senator was prohibited from being allowed to proceed in order in debate. In the remaining cases, the issue was typically resolved in other ways: a finding of no violation of the Rule by the Chair; a voluntary withdrawal of the accusation; a voluntary withdrawal of the offending words; a motion to strike offending words; or the matter is overcome by other Senate business. Also like the House, accusations are mostly partisan, with thirteen cases being between members of opposite parties. Republicans have invoked the tactic most, acting as the accuser in thirteen of seventeen cases, including the only three intra-party accusations. In seven cases, the rule was invoked by a member of the majority, indicating calls to order are not a tactic exclusive to the minority party.[12] The CRS finding of fewer than four dozen cases where Rule XIX was invoked over a period of five decades suggests, if anything, that Senators are consistently courteous toward one another, even as partisanship and ideological conflict increasingly creeped into Senate behavior during the same period of time.[13]

On the one hand, data from House words-taken-down and Senate calls-to-order do suggest, overall, that courtesy is an actively upheld norm in the U.S. Congress. Other analyses using words taken down and an analysis of news articles on incivility also support this assessment (Annenberg 2011; Dodd and Schraufnagel 2013). But a second and perhaps more important point is that courtesy on the floor of the House and Senate remains significant in terms of the manner in which lawmakers interact with one another—irrespective of the rancor and tone in the rest of American politics. Adhering to a norm of courtesy in official floor interactions is a distinguishing and policy consequential feature of the U.S. Congress. Were members to behave less decorously or the courtesy norm were dispensed with in formal interactions during legislative business, it could result in even more rancor and even less legislative productivity. If there is a broader breakdown of courtesy in American politics in general, the fact that courtesy remains prevalent in members' behavior of the floor may be a saving grace of American politics—procedural decorum may not provide the broadest measure of courtesy in Congress, but it links civility directly to governance. Events such as the episode with Senator Warren in 2017 or Speaker Pelosi in 2019 may seem dramatic, and they make for riveting moments on C-SPAN. But they were dramatic and riveting because they were so unusual—exceptions that prove the norm.

There is an old joke, the gist of which is: when someone refers to another member as "my esteemed colleague" it means that they actually like that member, but to refer to that person as "my good friend and very esteemed colleague" means the speaker does not like the other member at all.[14] The sincerity of such expressions aside, the norm of courtesy is reflected in a pervasive use of respectful and deferential words and behavior. Jokes about courtesy may actually be a sign that the courtesy norm is still considered "proper behavior and appropriate attitudes" (Yarwood 2014, 45–46). Courtesy on the floor may or may not represent genuine affection or friendliness among members, but it is an active norm of the modern Congress.

SUMMARY: THE FUTURE OF COOPERATION IN THE U.S. CONGRESS

Any observer of contemporary American politics has to be somewhat incredulous about the idea that norms of cooperation are prevalent in the modern U.S. Congress. Yet, the preponderance of interview and survey evidence suggests that norms of apprenticeship, reciprocity, and courtesy are widely understood as appropriate among current and former members and staff, while behavioral indicators of apprenticeship and courtesy, such as waiting period for maiden speeches or adherence to rules of decorum, respectively point to these norms being widely followed. While partisan polarization dominates much of the behavior of and thinking about today's Congress, norms of cooperation continue to play a significant role in member relations with one another and in their conduct as lawmakers. Adherence to these norms is part of what enables the institution to function, and members may agree that they are better off cooperating than not. But norms of cooperation exist also because members of Congress believe it is appropriate to cooperate.

We do not presently live in the era of the *Field of Blood* (Freeman 2018), where members physically threatened and assaulted one another during the antebellum era. This was a period when, in 1856, antislavery Senator Charles Sumner of Massachusetts was nearly beaten to death on the Senate floor by Representative Preston Brooks of South Carolina over the debate on whether to admit Kansas as a slave state (United States Senate Historian 2019b). A nonpartisan House staffer reflected on the era, "There were instances of literally bullying on the floor—surrounding members during votes, brandishing weapons, threatening them. Today, however, courtesy for the most part exists" (Interview 2016). Joanne Freeman finds that "between 1830 and 1860, there were more than *seventy* violent incidents between congressmen in the House and Senate chambers or on nearby streets and dueling grounds" (Freeman 2018, 5, *italics* in original). Maybe it is a low standard, but congressional discord is nowhere near the levels of past violence, intimidation, and acrimony. Norms of cooperation are an important reminder that the Congress of the early twenty-first century is not stricken with as much disharmony as in the past, or as much conflict as is possible. But norms of conflict are also emergent in the twenty-first century. The development and consequences of those norms, examined in the next chapter, will play an important role in whether Congress in the future years of the twenty-first century is one of continued cooperation or further discord.

NOTES

1. Data were compiled by Luke Basham while serving as my undergraduate research assistant during the summer of 2019. For complete data and a compelling analysis of Senate maiden speeches in the period of the 80th through 115th Congresses, see: Luke Basham. 2020. "Maiden Speeches and Apprenticeship: Continuity and Change in the U.S. Senate," Senior Honors Thesis, in requirement for completion of the Bachelor of Arts degree. Washington and Lee University, Lexington, Virginia.

2. There was little evidence of the apprenticeship norm at the state level as well, despite its status as "conventional wisdom" (Hebert and McLemore 1973, 520; Wahlke et al. 1962).

3. "Courtesy" and "comity" will not be used interchangeably here. Comity subsumes two norms, courtesy and reciprocity, but each implies distinct attitudes on cooperation and those informal practices that best facilitate working together toward common objectives. Comity, broadly defined, does exist on Capitol Hill as set of ideas and practices that facilitate members working together. But the definitions of the courtesy and reciprocity provided here express the useful distinctions between the two and it is important to distinguish between them.

4. Ross Baker wrote of the Senate in the 1980s of the manner of courtesy that Senators prefer to interact: "What senators call friendship, and what is vitally important to the smooth operation of the Senate, is a kind of stable business relationship based on trust and reciprocity that grows up between people who may have never exchanged a confidence, or traded volleys on a tennis court, or drunk bourbon together" (Baker 1989, 180). Baker's analysis of the House and Senate of the 1980s came well into the period of the decline of the clubby, social Congress. Still, even with changing rules and changing nature of service in both chambers, courtesy was still upheld. He added, "[T]here are always a few senators in every era pointed to by their fellow members as troublesome and obstructionist, but widespread and enduring uncivility is not characteristic of the Senate" (Baker 1989). Exceptions exist, but the belief in good collegial relationships endures (Baker 1989, 183).

5. There is no statistical difference between male and female respondents in the survey across the battery of questions. However, other scholars have found that the presence of women could make Congress more courteous: "According to a new study by Pamela Ban, a political science professor at the University of California, San Diego, the influx of women could make a definitive difference in committee dynamics, a crucial step in the legislative process" (Simon 2019).

6. Portions of this discussion previously appeared in slightly different form in Alexander 2019.

7. For more detail on the words taken down rule and process, see: Baitinger 2019; *House Practice*, chapter 16, sections 26 and 32; corresponding sections in *Jefferson's Manual* at *House Manual* section 368.

8. The term "courtesy" is not typically used in formal parliamentary language in the House, although it is generally taken as synonymous with "civility" or the more formal term "decorum." See for example: "Members must not only follow all the rules and requirements for the conduct of business in the House, but must also observe the principles of decorum and courtesy in debate, as set forth in rule XVII and by related provisions in Jefferson's Manual" (*House Practice* 2015, chapter 16 section. 21, p. 407).

9. *Notes on data gathering.* I arrived at a classification of violations of the norm of courtesy derived from the words taken down process and developed the search terms for the *Congressional Record* using the HeinOnline data service based on the House Rules, key terms noted by Congressional Research Service (Mulvihill 1999), categories identified by the Annenberg Foundation (2011), and guidance from analysts at the Congressional Research Service and the U.S. Senate Library while I was an American Political Science Association Congressional Fellow (2015–2016). With the exception of admonishments by the chair, only formal motions by a member to have words taken down or charging another member with unparliamentary behavior are included. The selection criteria align with the categories identified in the Annenberg Public Policy Center analysis of the words taken down process to measure "civility" (Annenberg 2011). The words taken down process is used by the Annenberg Public Policy Center in studying what they term "civility": "Because the taking down process is the formal mechanism the House uses to censure inappropriate discourse spoken on the floor . . . it is that measure we use to answer the following . . . Has the level of civility in the House changed in the past three-quarters of a century?" (Annenberg 2011, 2). Key differences in data gathered for the present study allow me to build in unique ways upon that one. Like Annenberg, this study counts both accusations of breaches of decorum and instances where sanctions were subsequently issued of violations of the rule. The present study additionally includes instances of accusers withdrawing the demand before the ruling. Members regularly raise the point of order then withdraw it in the interests of time, or to expedite chamber action, to serve a warning or deterrent against perceived unparliamentary behavior, or to seek some conciliation or recognition that words used were unparliamentary. In addition, this study provides a breakdown of the Annenberg category of requests receiving a ruling into (a) those receiving a ruling that were upheld and (b) those that were overruled. Untimely demands, a subcategory in the Annenberg analysis, are included in the broader category of demands overruled, but a descriptive break-out of this category is included in the full data set. Finally, this study includes cases where no demand was made, but the chair independently admonished the chamber or individual members to adhere rules of decorum; while not common, chair admonishments indicate breaches of decorum and are used as an expedited method to keep the chamber in order.

10. To determine if ideology is a significant contributor to violations of the courtesy norm, an estimation is calculated of ideological distance of members accused of breaching decorum under Rule XVII from the mean ideological score of the chamber

as a whole, using the DW-NOMINATE scale for ideology (Poole and Rosenthal 2007). If ideology were predictive of violations of the courtesy norm, we would see that House members who are ideological outliers are more likely to be accused of Rule XVII violations. A multiple logistic regression is used for a binomial dependent variable (ideological distance of the norm violator from the mean chamber ideology) with binomial and continuous predictor variables (UCLA 2019) in the period of the 80th to the 112th Congresses. Control variables are included for party, tenure, and time based on the Congress when violations occur. The model contains 253 observations and five degrees of freedom and a Pseudo R-square of 0.0861. The predictor variable for ideological distance is not statistically significant (coefficient = -2.725, p = 0.217), nor are other control variables. In short, based on this estimation we cannot attribute norm violations to factors such as ideology, party, or tenure.

11. The current form of the call to order dates to June 14, 1962 (CRS 2018, FN 30). Rule XIX itself emerged after the physical altercation between South Carolina Senators John L. McLaurin and Benjamin R. Tillman erupted on the Senate floor in 1902 (U.S. Senate Historian, Ibid.)

12. While formal calls to order under the Rule are not regularly used, Senators rely upon the rule in other ways to enforce standards of decorum: "Senators have, for example, stated that they considered raising a Rule XIX call to order, indicated their belief that certain words transgressed the rule, cautioned their colleagues to be mindful of Rule XIX when speaking, made parliamentary inquiries of the chair about the application of the call to order mechanism, or directly asked the chair to read from the rule" (CRS 2018, 12). Even here, occasions when Senators mention or allude to the Rule in order to "express their displeasure with a speaker's remarks," are few (Ibid.). Analysis by the CRS analysis finds only twenty-nine examples where the Rule was mentioned but no formal call to order invoked over a period from 1990 to 2018 (CRS, 12–13; Fn. 33).

13. An interesting statistic from the McConnell-Warren episode is the vote on a motion to allow Senator Warren to proceed in order, which was rejected forty-three to fifty along a party-line vote (United States Senate 2017, Roll Call Vote 58). While courtesy may be a norm, evidence also points to the emergence of partisan conflict as a norm as well. The extent to which conflict is emerging alongside norms of cooperation such as courtesy will be taken up in chapter 5.

14. Matthews also points to a variation on this oft-told quip (Alben W. Barkely, *That Reminds Me* (Garden City 1954, 255), in Matthews 1959, 1071), and it remains common to hear some version of it in among congressional observers today.

Chapter 5

Age of Resistance

Emerging Norms of Conflict

Speaker of the House Sam Rayburn's maxim "to get along, go along" (Lingeman 1975) was a sentiment predominant in the Congress of the mid- and late-twentieth century and one still present in the culture of cooperation that exists on the Hill today. The collegial atmosphere of the past is captured in a 1990 column by *Washington Post* writer Peter Carlson: "In a lot of ways, the House is like a small town. Everybody knows everybody else and there are a lot of little cliques. Members hang out with other members from their state, or from their committees, or the members they eat dinner with every Tuesday night. Some members share apartments in Washington, some travel back home together, some campaign for each other, some vacation at each other's houses. The House is a chummy place, a nice place to work, a way of life you'd like to pass on to your children" (Carlson 1990). While norms of cooperation remain important in the modern Congress, few today would describe either chamber like a small town. "Neither get along, nor go along" is an emerging spirit of the twenty-first century Congress. As this chapter examines, all is not well with norms of cooperation in the U.S. Congress and courtesy on Capitol Hill is not what it once was. Norms of conflict are, indeed, a growing part of the Congress of today.

The demise of cooperation is frequently observed by Hill veterans who perceive a change in the institution from their early days. A Democratic chief-of-staff who has served over fifteen years in the House notes, "[There] is certainly a diminishment of civility . . . In the past, members who disagreed politically would acknowledge each in friendly terms. Today those who might disagree on things will just look past each other now" (Interview 2019). Members and staff regularly speak of so-called "better days." Stories are recounted, almost as lore, about a friendship between the liberal Democratic Speaker Tip O'Neill and conservative Republican President Ronald Reagan

(Matthews 2013) or how Republican Leader Bob Michel of Peoria would carpool with Chicago Democrat Dan Rostenkowski back and forth to Illinois in Michael's station wagon, hashing out legislative compromise along the road from Washington, trading turns at the wheel for sleep breaks on a mattress in back (Rogers 2017). Some of these sentiments reflect nostalgia for a past that was far from the rose-colored portrait these stories suggest. Michel's conciliation helped pave the way for Newt Gingrich's rancorous rise (Brownstein 2008). Reagan and O'Neil were far from friends and their private sentiments belie much of the idea that goodwill was driving their relationship (Shirley and Mauer 2017). A long-serving non-partisan Senate staffer told me, "O'Neill didn't like Reagan at all and wouldn't deal with him until he saw how formidable Reagan was. Then he realized he'd have to change his approach" (Interview 2016).

Yet it is true, as evidence in chapters 3 and 4 suggests, that cooperation and the courtesy norm are still predominant on the Hill, whatever the periodic flair-ups and perennial complaints that it is on the wane. But the contrast between the Congress of today and that of the past is not just the product of nostalgic, rose-colored views of days gone by. The demise of compromise perceived by many contemporary observers is tied, no doubt, to broader political conflict in Congress and American politics writ large. But at least in some measure, the increase in conflict on Capitol Hill is tied to the emergence of norms of conflict. Modern observers regularly point to shifts in normative attitudes among congressional actors that are matched in their behaviors. A normative context in which cooperation is prevalent and is being encroached upon by one where conflict is increasingly viewed as appropriate. Reflecting back on Republican partisans of the 1970s and 1980s, a long-term Senate Republican staffer captures this distinction: "Senators Bob Dole [of Kansas] and Howard Baker [of Tennessee] were partisan guys. But at the end of the day, if they saw progress was going to be made on something they would compromise. I don't see that as prevalent today" (Interview 2019). A similar sense of underlying courtesy of the past is captured by William Hoagland, who served from 1982 to 2003 as Republican Staff on the Senate Budget Committee. In an oral history interview with Senate Historian Don Ritchie, Hoagland recounted:

> I left the Senate late one night. We were on the floor finishing up a budget resolution or something. I was by myself and nobody else was around except when I came down the elevator, going down the escalator to get the tram down here, and there were these two senators in front of me, two elderly senators, and they were helping one another. One was having difficulty walking and the other was having difficulty also. They had their arms around each other. It was Jesse Helms and Claiborne Pell. Nobody else was around. They weren't playing for

a photo or the press. I stayed back and I thought to myself, you know, here are two senators probably as far apart as they possibly could be . . . They still have that humanitarian aspect . . . They could go back on the floor and have a rousing debate, but still have that respect for one another as human beings. (United States Senate Historical Office 2007, 23)

Hoagland's anecdote, which dates from the late 1980s or early 1990s, has all the hallmarks of nostalgia for a Congress of the past. That the ultraconservative Republican Helms of South Carolina would walk arm-in-arm with the liberal Pell of Rhode Island speaks to the sense of courtesy and respect that current observers think is increasingly absent in the institution today. It is not that political conflict did not exist—of course, it did. But the normative sense of what is appropriate in relation to political conflict has changed. Indeed, Hoagland closes his story by capturing the sense of what the new normative context means: "[T]here was something different in those days. Not as partisan. Not as political, maybe, as it has become" (Ibid.). Norms of conflict are more prevalent today than they were in the past. In the Congress of the twenty-first century, it is increasingly understood as appropriate to reject cooperation in favor of conflict.

In terms of the normative context of the modern Congress, we live in the age of resistance. This resistance is fueled in part by well-documented ideological and strategic conflict between and even within parties. But this resistance is also driven by a sense of resistance for the sake of resistance. Beyond ideology and beyond strategy, norms of conflict have emerged as a predominant aspect of the modern Congress. For a contemporary lawmaker, norms of conflict are part of the sense of appropriateness, the identities, and the preferences of serving in the modern Congress. Specifically, this context of conflict is embodied in a norm of nonconformity, which is the rejection of cooperation and compromise, and a norm of partisanship itself, which views partisan conflict as appropriate irrespective of ideological or strategic objectives.

A cautionary observation from a previous period of political conflict and incivility in American history illustrates what may be at risk if norms of conflict overtake the institution. An editorial in the Washington *Evening Star*, written at the height of national rancor over Vietnam, observed: "Some people smirk at the exaggerated courtesies practiced in the United States Senate. They think it absurd that two debating senators who are known to have no use for each other exchange flowery flatteries while they go for the jugular, politically speaking. But Americans think too little today of how civilization rests upon unwritten rules of manners. These constitute a compact holding society together against the storms of passion, making life tolerable and democracy possible" (*Evening Star* 1971). While this warning, like others of a similar vein lamenting the loss of courtesy, proved to be an exaggeration, it speaks to the fundamental role that norms play in determining lawmakers preferences: if conflict becomes a preference in its own right, the capacity of the institution to function is weakened or, possibly, in jeopardy.

NONCONFORMITY

Nonconformity exists as a sense that noncooperation is preferred to compromise, that disruption is appropriate, and that violating informal norms or formal rules is an acceptable means of achieving one's ideological or strategic agenda. Nonconformity is exhibited among junior members who use attention grabbing or disruptive tactics to advance their positions relative to other members of both their own and the opposite party, and among minority party members who seek to advance policy agenda in the face of an unwilling majority. An important quality of the nonconformity norm is that Congress functions based on the consent of its members. In both the House and Senate, there are means by which members can willfully drag proceedings to a halt, but this is an ability that members do not frequently exercise. In the Senate, for instance, objections to unanimous consent are one means by which any member could hold up even the most routine proceedings; but it is something which we generally do not witness. In the House, the mechanisms for maintaining legislative business are stronger but, as illustrated in the case of procedural disobedience examined below, a restive minority can hinder the chamber from operating. We take it for granted that elected officials wish for the institution in which they serve to be able to perform its legislative function; but the emergence of the nonconformity norm points to a tendency that rejects this preference.

The nonconformity norm manifests in numerous behaviors on Capitol Hill, ranging from obstructionist tactics in floor or committee hearings, to actions disruptive to or circumventing of leadership outside the formal chamber proceedings, to violation of formal rules and active disruption of legislative proceedings. Nonconformity is illustrated in cases where members willfully obstruct legislative business. For instance, Republican Speaker John Boehner, who faced ongoing challenges of keeping conservatives in the Freedom Caucus on board with other Republicans, called an October 2013 government shutdown, which was pushed by conservative members of his own party who opposed Obamacare, "a very predictable disaster" (Dumain 2014). Boehner did not personally support the move initiated by Freedom Caucus members, but nevertheless witnessed members of his party lead a widely derided cessation of government operations. A long serving Democratic Senate staffer familiar with the negotiations on the shutdown observed: "The main thing Freedom Caucus people wanted to do is stop stuff from getting done. In the past, members wanted to pass legislation. But members of the Tea Party or the Freedom Caucus go home and tell their constituents what bills they stopped, not what they passed" (Interview 2016). Boehner was compelled to go along with the shutdown because, as he put it, "a leader without followers is simply a man taking a walk" (Ibid.). While there were political motives behind the Freedom Caucus, the embodiment of the norm of nonconformity is also on display in the shutdown episode: the will to obstruct takes priority over the requirements of governance.

Other actions which illustrate the norm of nonconformity include the participation in a climate change protest by Democratic Congresswoman-elect Alexandria Ocasio-Cortez of New York, at then Minority Leader Nancy Pelosi's Capitol Hill office in November 2018 (Gaudiano 2018). Another example is Texas Republican Senator Ted Cruz's infamous twenty-one-hour Senate speech against Obamacare in 2013 that included a reading of Dr. Seuss's *Green Eggs and Ham* (Lesniewski 2013). Such actions do not simply reflect ideological or strategic interests, they represent normative attitudes on what is appropriate—in such cases a willingness to engage in obstreperous behavior for ideological or strategic purposes. Nonconformity involves a marked difference from holding ideological or strategic objectives that differ from one's congressional colleagues and entails an additional willingness to breach long-observed norms of cooperation in achieving one's objectives—not every conservative reads Dr. Seuss on the Senate floor. Nonconformity becomes a norm itself when such practices are observed repeatedly across chambers and parties and such behavior is widely understood as appropriate among, even if not widely well regarded. In fact, to be disruptive and unadmired seems as if it is part of the spirit of nonconformity.

Another aspect of nonconformity is what one Democratic Senate staffer described as "leapfrogging." This is when newer members of the House or Senate combine nonconforming behavior with social media in order to gain notoriety and build independent fundraising revenues, circumventing norms that otherwise oblige members to "go along and get along". The Senate staffer described it like this: "A tweet on social media can open up the cash register . . . . Stir up the right attention on Twitter and you unlock huge sums of money. That can be more successful than spending two hours a day in the House gym trying to get to know everyone on the treadmill" (Interview 2019). A former Republican congressman made this observation, "The problem now is that bad behavior gets rewarded. You get up in the State of the Union and yell 'You lie!' and you get all over FoxNews and you raise a million dollars online the next week and you are hailed by the super PACs and the conservative blogs. The bad behavior is rewarded" (Interview 2016). Leapfrogging also entails a willful bypassing of the apprenticeship norm, in which members disregard following cues of more senior colleagues in order to draw attention and accrue public support. If such acts of nonconformity produce returns, such as are enabled by partisan news organizations, social media, and the ability to raise campaign funds, they are even more likely to continue.

Nonconformity as Procedural Disobedience

In September 2018, during Senate Judiciary Committee hearings to confirm Justice Brett Kavanaugh to the Supreme Court, Senator Cory Booker of New Jersey released purportedly uncleared committee documents (Carney 2018). Booker's tactics are what I have termed "procedural disobedience," a form of the nonconformity norm used by the minority party to disrupt House or Senate proceedings (Alexander 2018). Procedural disobedience entails when legislators willfully violate chamber rules and disrupt chamber business for a political purpose. Though acts of procedural disobedience can provide substantial benefits to participants and are rarely punished, they have not happened often. Other such episodes include the 2016 House Democrat gun control sit-in and the October 2019 interruption of impeachment hearings by House Republicans. To date, procedural disobedience has resulted in few meaningful penalties. Given the emergence of nonconformity as a norm in the Congress, rising partisan discord, and the lack of sanction for such acts, it should be unsurprising to see the tactic being deployed more often in the modern Congress. Recent episodes more fully illustrate procedural disobedience as examples of the nonconformity norm in practice.

On June 12, 2016, the United States was confronted with another gun massacre, this time at a nightclub in Orlando, Florida, resulting in the deaths of forty-nine people (Zambelich and Hurt 2016).[1] Meanwhile, in Congress, efforts to advance gun control legislation were stymied by majority party Republican leadership with the backing of gun rights advocates. On Wednesday, June 22, this standstill erupted in confrontation when Democratic members of Congress staged a nearly twenty-six-hour sit-in on the floor of the House of Representatives, demanding action on gun control bills before Congress entered the July 4 recess, breaching rules and grinding formal proceedings to a halt.

The sit-in occurred as a coordinated response by House Democrats over frustration with Republican leadership for not taking up gun control legislation. Shortly after the House convened that Wednesday morning, Georgia Congressman John Lewis, the civil rights icon chosen as the figurehead for the sit-in, offered a floor speech pleading for gun control legislation. Nearly the entire 188-person Democratic caucus participated in the sit-in, including visits from supportive Democratic Senators. Amid chants of "No bill, no break!" they proclaimed they would not budge until the majority leadership allowed consideration of gun control bills (Bade, Caygle, and Weyle 2016).

Republicans, caught off guard, quickly gaveled out and shut off House television cameras. The protest suspended almost all scheduled legislative business until 1 p.m. the next day and left Republican leadership with few options outside the extreme choice of using the Sergeant at Arms to forcibly restore order (which they did not do). Democrats further violated House rules through the use of mobile phones to broadcast live video of the demonstration on social media. This streaming video was widely picked up by news outlets, shared on social media platforms, and aired in its entirety by C-SPAN (Connors 2016).

Republicans widely derided the sit-in (Hawkings 2016b; McPherson 2017). One long-serving former Republican staffer stated: "There are rules, standards of conduct. Jesus Christ, they're out there on cell phones, eating pizza, slouching all over the place. It's like freakin' Woodstock. It's bullshit" (Interview 2016). Yet no formal sanction was issued against the Democratic protestors. The main consequence was in the next Congress when House rules were changed to impose a financial penalty on members using recording devices within the chamber (Bordelon 2017). Rather than illustrating the perils of willful disregard for the rules, the 2016 gun sit-in suggests the potential for the tactics of civil disobedience as a source of minority power in the House of Representatives.

While historically rare, procedural disobedience is not unique to the Democratic sit-in of the last Congress. Other cases include a Republican takeover of the House chamber during a recess in 2008 to oppose an off-shore drilling ban, a 1995 occupation of the House chamber by minority Democrats during a weekend in response to a government shutdown, and a 1968 dispute led by Republicans over televised presidential debates with then-candidate Richard Nixon. What is more, such instances of disruptive, rule-bending behavior have not been met with immediate formal sanctions. On October 23, 2019, Republican House members stormed the secure facility where the Democrat-led impeachment investigation of President Trump was being held to much media fanfare, and the hearing was suspended for five hours (Olorunnipa, Dawsey, and DeBonis 2019). The tactic does not appear to have contributed to legislative victories, but other benefits are achieved. In the interruption of the impeachment hearing, beyond a memo of reprobation from the House Ethics Committee, Republicans involved in the effort received no formal punishment (Tully-McManus 2019). The effectiveness of procedural disobedience is clear: by willfully violating formal rules, a disruptive minority can convey its message to the public, rally its base, and at least temporarily obstruct the agenda of the majority including activity on unrelated legislative business. Procedural disobedience, as these examples illustrate, is an effective legislative tactic of the minority party of the House.

In the Senate, the minority has greater ability within the rules to shape proceedings—most notably the filibuster. Yet even there, we may see a frustrated minority engage the tactic. The confrontation between Democratic Senator Cory Booker of New Jersey and Senate Republican leaders has many hallmarks of procedural disobedience. During the September 2018 Judiciary Committee hearings for Donald Trump's nomination to the Supreme Court, Brett Kavanaugh, who is widely opposed by Democrats, Booker released committee documents that may not have been cleared for the public. In an exchange with Republican Senator John Cornyn of Texas during the hearings Booker stated, "I'm going to release the email about racial profiling and I understand the penalty comes with potential ousting from the Senate. And if Senator Cornyn believes that I violated Senate rules, I openly invite and accept the consequences of my team releasing that email right now" (Bennett 2018).

Although the terms of this case are murky due to competing claims over whether the documents were actually secret when Booker released them (Everett 2018), Booker's public statement and apparent intentions closely align with what we expect from procedural disobedience: frustrated members of the minority party willfully violate chamber rules to achieve legislative or political goals. Regardless of whether Republican leadership would follow through with sanctions, the benefits to Booker are apparent: his stature is raised among the Democratic base who opposes the Kavanaugh nomination; a punishment raises Booker's profile for standing up to Republicans; a lack of punishment calls Republicans on a bluff. Like the gun sit-in and other examples from the House, procedural disobedience may be an effective tactic for members of a restive minority party in the Senate.

Nonconformity, as illustrated in these cases of procedural disobedience, involves both logic of consequences as well as the logic of appropriateness. The politics of cases such as the gun debate and a Supreme Court nomination are unique in many ways, but factors that led to rule-thwarting in each case are endemic to many pressing issues in the modern Congress: polarized public and legislator preferences, mobilization among partisan bases, and highly salient issues (Pew Research Center 2014). Arguably, the consequential logic of congressional decision-making supports such demonstrations when a weak minority party sees procedural, policy, and electoral benefits—with a relatively minimal threat of sanction, at least based on the record so far. In other words, in terms of achieving some narrowly defined objectives, procedural disobedience works.[2] Given such consequential benefits of procedural disobedience, we should expect to see it used more often by a frustrated, weak minority on issues where polarization is highest.

Procedural disobedience is evidence of the rise of nonconformity as a norm in the constitutive sense in the modern Congress. Among the members choosing to engage such nonconformist tactics, the logic of appropriateness is evident in the sense among those lawmakers that disruption and rejection of norms of cooperation is a stronger preference than adherence to long-established norms of cooperation. This is a marked distinction from merely tactical or consequential reasoning: the normative aspect of procedural disobedience is that member preferences reflect the appropriateness of nonconformity. The will to disrupt legislative proceedings does not follow inevitably from rational calculations of partisan conflict and the seeking of legislative outcomes. The will to disrupt is based in an *idea* that it is appropriate to do so and a preference for disruption. The logic of nonconformity is that of a shared sense of appropriateness, not consequences. The action may be strategic, but the preference to engage it is normative.

However, the infrequency of procedural disobedience is also evidence for the enduring power of norms of cooperation. Members often adhere to the rules out of respect for norms, even though norm violations can produce partisan benefits and, as the cases here illustrate, are rarely strongly punished. Beyond the strategic, cost-benefit component of norm adherence, one part of why members of the House minority are reluctant to engage more frequently in procedural disobedience is simply because members respect the norms of the institution irrespective of whether or not adhering to such norms benefits them. Norm adherence is rooted in a sense of what is appropriate or agreed upon as prescribed. The limited cases where acts of nonconformity are undertaken despite strategic advantages of doing so suggests that the logic of appropriateness tilts more strongly, at least for now, to cooperation over conflict.

Nonconformity in a Gridlocked Congress

We should expect to see the nonconformity norm take greater hold in the future. Procedural disobedience, for instance, is evidence of the space between cooperation and conflict that we currently habit. On the one hand, procedural disobedience is effective and seems an inevitable outcome of partisan conflict; on the other hand, that we don't see more of it is evidence for the endurance of norms of cooperation. We take for granted that members find cooperation appropriate. But this could change—the material factors corresponding with nonconformity, such as ideological and partisan conflict, are apparent throughout the Congress and American political life in general. In the past, during the antebellum period violent conflict was part of the norm in Congress (Freeman 2018). This was at a time of ideological conflict that can seem close to that of our own. Norms of cooperation are part of what is keeping the worst tendencies of the modern Congress in check. If these norms start to fade, and norms of conflict become more widely shared, the seeds of conflict may blossom, as evidenced by tactics like the nonviolent sit-in or, worse, those of the violent of the past. As Republican Senate staffer put it, "In the absence of order there is chaos. Anybody can do it, and it can get super ugly. But they don't. Whatever dysfunction there is here, the norm remains to work together, at least somewhat" (Interview 2016).

The logic of consequences also does not totally favor adhering to norms of cooperation. In cases of procedural disobedience, where members willfully violate rules to make a broader political point, fear of penalty for rule violations is not an adequate explanation when the penalties are relatively nonexistent and the political rewards for such behavior so high. Rather, members continue to believe in a sense of cooperation, irrespective of the strategic gains of behaving otherwise.

Like the case of procedural disobedience in the House, while there is an emergence of the norm of nonconformity in the Senate, there is also a prevailing norm of cooperation. For example, much of Senate business, is based on unanimous consent. Any Senator can require a quorum call and tie up business at any time on the claim of the absence of a quorum. But it does not happen. As a nonpartisan Senate staffer put it, "There is more in the Senate Rules for people who want to screw up the Senate than there is for people who want control. But the truth is, we come into session every day and agree to put our weapons down for a little while, at least agree to get somewhere, to start a process of talking" (Interview 2016).

Is nonconformity limited to ideological outliers? Certainly, conservatives like Senator Cruz and liberals like Representative Ocasio-Cortez provide some of the most publicly visible examples of nonconformity. But ideology is not determinant of the behavior. The key constructivist point in these acts is that ideological and other political objectives are not enough to account for such behavior. When almost the entire Democratic caucus engages in a sit-in, this is not behavior exclusive to ideological extremists. The sense of appropriateness regarding disruptive behavior—a norm of nonconformity— also exists.

Long-time Congress observer Chad Pergram, of FoxNews, noted that "It's considered poor form on Capitol Hill for members of one committee to try to impede the business of another committee. Members are typically respectful of this practice" (Pergram 2019b). The Republican disruption of the House impeachment hearing was exactly that. Pergram explains, "The idea is that if you gore someone's ox today, they may gore yours tomorrow" (Ibid.). However, based on the logic of procedural disobedience, more ox goring is exactly what we should expect in the modern Congress. The incentive structure does not fully discourage such disruptive behavior and penalties have been minimal. Moreover, amidst strong partisan tension and a sensationalized media environment where such tactics are bound to gain attention, including among one's political base, the argument in favor of procedural disobedience is quite compelling. The fact that it has not taken off as a more regular tactic may be attributable to the endurance of the norms of cooperation, more so than a consequentialist logic that the penalties outweigh the pay off. If anything, in the cases examined here, it may be the case that disruption is rewarded. We have the norms of cooperation to thank for the fact that Congress isn't more confrontational and disruptive than it already is.

PARTISANSHIP

The modern Congress is widely understood to be the most ideologically partisan and polarized in perhaps at least a century (Azari 2018). The Republican and Democratic parties have steadily become more cohesive and more distant along respective ideologically conservative and liberal lines beginning at least since the 1970s (Desilver 2014). The reasons for such partisan polarization are numerous. Partisan polarization in Congress has its origins in numerous sources. Scholars and political professionals alike point to causes such as gerrymandered congressional districts, a fractured news media environment, the prevalence of independent campaign funding, party-oriented electoral strategies, polarization among political elites and the general public, and other frequently debated sources (Thurber and Yoshinaka 2015; Hawkings 2018). Whatever the sources of partisan polarization in Congress, the result is what congressional observes describe as lawmakers "putting partisan advantage ahead of problem solving" (Mann and Ornstein 2016, 18). In terms of legislative outcomes, as the parties move to the extremes, whether for ideological or strategic purposes, legislative gridlock increases (Binder 2014, 14).

From a consequentialist perspective, partisanship has ideological and strategic origins—members behave in a partisan manner toward other policy and electoral goals, as political science scholars have identified. But what about partisanship as a norm? One view on this proposition came in a discussion with a mid-career senior Senate staffer who has worked for both Democrats and Republicans. In talking with the staffer about the sources and consequences of partisan polarization, the question arose, "Is partisanship a norm?" The response was unequivocal: "Abso-fuckin'-lutely!" Although this author will argue it in less colorful terms, beyond its ideological and strategic nature, partisanship is a norm in the modern Congress. The partisanship norm, in the constitutive sense of the term, entails members of Congress understanding opposition to the other party as a sense of appropriateness and identity, as a basis of preferences, irrespective of other ideological or strategic consequences or objectives. Partisanship as a norm is the sense that party unity is a preference in its own right and that the other party is to be treated as an adversary regardless of the costs or benefits of doing so. Partisan conflict displaces cooperation based on the logic of appropriateness. A retired Democratic member of the House captured the spirit of the partisanship norm this way: "Partisanship isn't just trying to get what you want. It is treating the other party like the enemy. We've always disagreed up here, but what's new is that the other party isn't to be bargained with; they're to be beaten, maybe destroyed" (Interview 2016).

Evidence for partisanship as a congressional norm—a sense of appropriateness, irrespective of consequential motives—comes from several sources, including survey evidence, words of current and former members and staff, and instances where partisan behavior is grounded not in ideological or strategic motives, but in the senses of appropriateness and identities among lawmakers of what it is to be a member of Congress in the current era. This is not to say that partisanship is not consequentialist or that commonly studied ideological and strategic drivers of partisanship do not have invaluable explanatory power. They do. Sources of partisanship and partisan polarization that scholars and congressional observers commonly point to, and such as this book draws from, are a necessary aspect of understanding the modern Congress. But there is also a constitutive aspect of partisanship. Members of Congress are partisan not simply because of the ideological or strategic benefits of being so. They are partisan because it is rooted in a shared social understanding of what is appropriate, a preference on its own, and a quality of the identity of modern lawmakers. Partisanship, in other words, is a norm.

Survey data gathered in 2019 from current and former members of Congress and congressional staff provide evidence of partisanship as a norm. The survey, explained in greater depth in chapter 3, asked respondents with experience in Congress to rate on a scale of appropriateness certain behaviors or attitudes and to consider these attitudes as an abstract proposition, removed from specific ideological and strategic considerations. The partisanship norm is measured in the survey via three proxy questions that indicate the sense of appropriateness regarding the following: voting with the opposition party; reaching bipartisan compromise in order to pass legislation; and, requiring the support of a majority of the majority party for legislation to advance (i.e., the Hastert Rule). In the responses we see consistent evidence of a sense of appropriateness for partisan attitudes and behaviors.

The survey question on "voting with the opposition party," allows us to measure the extent to which members find it appropriate to cooperate with those of the other party. The results of this measurement of attitudes toward a proposition without political context are suggestive of the extent to which members are intrinsically partisan irrespective of consequentialist considerations. Among survey respondents, only 55 percent of all respondents indicate voting with the opposition party is appropriate, leaving a substantial minority unsupportive of the appropriateness such behavior. Notably, within this finding, there is significant partisan difference among Republicans and Democrats in the House, with Republicans statistically less favorable to voting with their Democratic counterparts at a 49.3 percent to 61.6 percent ratio ($p = 0.034^*$; see chapter 3). This latter finding suggests that the partisanship norm, rather than being equally held among parties, is slightly stronger among Republicans.

The extent we observe the partisanship norm is tempered when we consider the question on reaching bipartisan compromise in order to pass legislation. Among both chambers, an average of 89 percent of all respondents find reaching bipartisan compromise as appropriate. Voting with the opposition may be widely viewed as inappropriate, but a strong majority is supportive of the appropriateness of seeking compromise that both sides can agree upon. Within these results, there is a significant difference between chambers, with 97.5 percent of Senate respondents versus 86.0 percent of House respondents responding in supportive of the appropriateness of bipartisan compromise. In the House, the appropriateness of bipartisan compromise is weaker than in the Senate—in other words, the partisanship norm may be stronger in the House. Statistically significant differences between Democrats and Republicans do not exist on this measure.

Another survey question which allows us to sense the strength of partisanship norm in the House is on "requiring the support of a majority of the majority party for legislation to advance," commonly known as the "Hastert rule." The so-called "rule" named after former Speaker Dennis Hastert is actually an unwritten Republican principle whereby the Speaker will not bring a bill to the floor with a support of the majority of the majority (Binder 2013). The survey question on the Hastert rule received the lowest rate of response on the appropriateness scale—only 28.33 percent of all respondents indicate it is appropriate. While the support for this aspect of partisanship is not widely held, the results do point to an important finding regarding differences between the parties on the partisanship norm. Republicans see the Hastert rule as appropriate at 37.5 percent as compared to Democrats at 20.29 percent ($p = 0.002$). Like voting with the opposition, significantly more Republicans support this aspect of partisanship than Democrats.

Additional evidence of the partisanship norm comes in the words of current and former members and staff themselves. As the off-color wording of the Senate staffer above suggests, there is an understanding among those who work and serve on the Hill that partisanship is embodied in a sense of what is appropriate, a preference, even an obligation, irrespective of other interests. In a social theory of Congress, the important distinction is evidence of congressional professionals expressing partisanship as a sense of appropriate-ness, a component of lawmakers' identities, and a preference irrespective of other ideological or strategic consequences. We see this in survey attitudes and how current and former members and staff speak of partisanship. A long-serving congressional reporter whose career started on the Hill captured the essence of the norm this way: "Partisanship has become more of a norm. It's like that Groucho Marx movie 'Horse Feathers,' where they sing the song, 'Whatever you're for, I'm against.'" (Interview 2016). Partisanship is widely viewed to be acceptable and expected in member attitudes and behavior.

There is a sense today that members arrive on Capitol Hill with partisan-ship as part of their identity. There is an expectation in Washington that they will side with their party, as a default position almost without consideration. A House administrative staffer observed, "Partisan is increasingly the world-view of members who get elected. They reflect the America that elects them. Even if that's not really the way to get things done [because] there has to be compromise, there has to be dialogue. Members now come to Congress with the idea that they won't compromise with the other party" (Interview 2016). But there is an aspect of partisanship that goes even further. It is not enough in this context to stick with one's fellow partisans. Rather, it is appropriate, if not expected, to denigrate the opposition. A Democratic House legislative director pointed to a tendency among modern partisans not only to share their party's views, but to demagogue their opponents: "There's a fair number of members who not just vote with their party but go out of their way to dis-parage and abuse members of the other party. The other party is viewed as not worthy, not someone you'd want to find middle ground with" (Interview 2019). Put another way, "More members come in with a partisan attitude of 'he's evil, we're good' than ever before," said a Republican Senate staff who served members of both parties in the House and Senate (Interview 2019).

The emergence of the partisanship norm has emerged over time and works in opposition to the long-standing commitment to cooperation, embodied by other norms of the institution. A senior nonpartisan House staffer observed: "There used to be a belief that government was sort of a joint venture and a partnership. If you had the majority party, you were majority partners in gov-ernance, but the minority party was also a member of the partnership. It was a privilege granted to the minority by the majority to say 'no' which allowed a responsible minority to participate in the collective enterprise of governance" (Interview 2016). This shift became more pronounced in the 2000s, accord-ing to a nonpartisan Senate administrative staffer who works with committees of both parties: "Whereas over the years it was likely to have majority or minority members of the appropriations or budget committees working with me about making the process go forward, that stopped being the norm. What became the norm was the two parties coming in separately and with hostile intentions toward each other. My mindset was still the old mindset—serve the institution and compromise. But that era has passed. Newer members operate from a partisan mindset" (Interview 2016). A House staffer expressed the change this way: "The current norm of people is that their time in Congress is going to be conflictual, to oppose the other party, as opposed to one where compromise will be valued." But it is not just the newer members, they added: "It's everyone. New people, but also people elected into their seventh, eight, tenth term. It's now all of their expectations" (Interview 2016). The partisanship norm stands in marked contrast to norms of cooperation.

Hill actors understand that there is an instrumental aspect of the partisanship norm—the expectation comes with a threat of sanction for violating it. Namely, folks who do not go along with their fellow partisans will find their life in the party more difficult. "You're expected to follow your leadership in the decisions that it makes most of the time. If you're a person who just won't do that, you're not going to be on the inside of everything with your caucus," noted a former Republican Senator (Interview 2019). A senior Democratic Senate staffer echoed the sentiment: "It's harder to be a moderate today . . . if you try to operate as a moderate, you're never really considered a true believer in your own party" (Interview 2019). Operating against the party entails costs, driving up the costs of operating against the partisanship norm, irrespective of other ideological or strategic considerations.

Congressional operatives point to the same things that political scientists point to in explaining partisan polarization; numerous conversations reveal an awareness of common factors thought to explain partisanship. A Democratic Senate staffer summarized views expressed by multiple observers: "There used to be a norm of members of different parties just being friendly and associating with each other. Nowadays, with the way political discourse has developed in the media as well as among the bases, and partly from the pressure to get home every weekend, you don't see that as much. So members don't get to know each other on a personal level as much as they used to . . . and the norm of being friendly is slowly disappearing or has disappeared completely, to the detriment of members' ability to work with each other" (Interview 2019). A senior Senate staffer stated, "I grew up in DC in the seventies and went to school with the children of Senators and Congressman. The parents knew each other. It's a lot harder to punch someone in the face (rhetorically) if you are friends with them. And partisanship is kind of often like a punch in the face. It has become personal. A boundary. And a currency that people are awarded for" (Interview 2016). These sentiments could have been written by the congressional scholar Nelson Polsby, who spoke of factors such as the airplane and members no longer living in Washington, and even the mobility afforded by air conditioning, as reasons Washington is more ridden with conflict than in times past (Polsby 2004). Other causes of partisanship such as the media, the electorate, gerrymandering, and money in politics are also regularly pointed to among congressional professionals as underlying causes of partisan polarization. Scholars who write about polarization in Congress are not just creating elegant academic theories, they are speaking about the perspectives lived by congressional operatives.

If one figure comes repeatedly to the fore of discussions on what has led to the culture of conflict in the modern Congress it is Newt Gingrich. In interview after interview, current and former members and staff regularly point to the shift in tone that Gingrich's rise in the 1980s through the 1990s brought to Capitol Hill. The rise of Gingrich to the Speaker of the House in the Republican electoral victory in 1994 represents not only a sweeping ideological and electoral victory, it fundamentally shifted the sense of appropriateness regarding the manner in which partisan politics is conducted. As a former Republican member of the House who admitted to being on the losing end of several battles with Gingrich put it, "Gingrich established partisanship as a modus operandi, and fundamentally changed the way you should always conduct yourself. And that Gingrich M.O. was opposition at every turn. No matter what. Oppose, oppose, oppose" (Interview 2016). The ideological and strategic character of Gingrich's success alone is not what marks the normative shift. Rather, it is the sense of appropriateness regarding treating the other party as opposition and rejecting cooperation as standard behavior that he introduced to Capitol Hill.

This effect transferred to the Senate, where Republicans that served with Gingrich in the House emerged as "partisan warriors" when they succeeded in running for the Senate (Theriault 2013). These Gingrich Senators exhibited a "pack mentality" based on ideological preferences and exhibited in voting, cosponsorship, and other behavior (Ibid.), which fundamentally altered the character of the Senate. The complementary argument a social theory of Congress makes to this understanding of the effects of this subgroup of Senators is that it is not only ideological preferences or constituency pressure, but a normative sense of what it is to be a lawmaker: specifically, a Republican lawmaker who stands together with fellow Republicans or at the very least in opposition to Democrats. A former Democratic Senator put it, "Gingrich destroyed the political culture that was necessary for the Senate to function—the idea that the majority and minority party had to work together in order to legislate, to govern" (Interview 2016). This marks a fundamental shift in preferences away from cooperation to one of conflict. To be a "partisan warrior," in addition to being driven by electoral and legislative strategies, is to be driven by a norm, in which it is a preference on its own to oppose the other party at all turns.

Based on this account, we can comfortably understand partisanship as a norm in Congress. The idea of opposition to the other party as a part of one's identity as a lawmaker, and a preference, irrespective other interests, is evident in the preceding statements and conforms with attributes of the logic of appropriateness. But the question congressional scholars will be most interested in is whether the partisanship norm accounts for anything about partisan behavior that other behavioralist models of partisanship do not. To exist as a norm it is not necessary to be consequential, but, as in other cases where congressional behavior is affected (such as courtesy or sexual propriety, for example), a norm is more relevant, interesting, and more empirically evident when it does affect outcomes.

Herein lies the difficult rub on partisanship as a norm. When placed among other explanations of partisanship that political science scholars have examined, identifying independent effects of a partisanship norm on Congress and its members remains an open challenge. Competing models of partisanship in Congress look at growing ideological cohesion (Mayhew 1974; Aldrich and Rohde 1999; Cox and McCubbins 2005, 2007) and electoral motivations or strategies of party members (Lee 2009; Koger and Lebo 2017) or even biological attributes of our minds (Klein 2020) to account for the growth of partisan cohesion and partisan conflict in the modern Congress. In order to successfully incorporate or weigh partisanship as a norm in light of such theories, further consideration must be given to identifying and isolating variables that measure the partisanship as a constitutive norm. The challenges of defining a discrete quantifiable variable are widely appreciated by social scientists. For the partisanship norm, if we require a quantitative inferential model as proof, this variable still needs to be found.

Distinguishing ideational from economic behavior is a challenge in this analysis of the partisanship norm—and a problem common to much constructivist research. But the absence of the rigors of statistical inference is not sufficient to deny the normative aspects of partisanship in the presence of other compelling evidence. The idea to be partisan, irrespective of other considerations, has taken hold on Capitol Hill. Normative predispositions such as nonconformity or partisanship are not the inevitable outcomes of ideological or strategic imperatives. They are fundamentally rooted in a sense of appropriateness, in particular ideas of what it means to be a lawmaker and the kinds of behavior and attitudes associated with being a lawmaker. Survey evidence and the words of Hill operatives speak to the way partisanship operates as a constitutive norm: opposing the other party has become a preference in and of itself; members are partisan not only for instrumental purposes, but because it is part of their identities to be so. Future constructivist research to further understand the nature of the partisanship norm as having effects independent of other aspects of partisanship in the polarized Congress would make a valuable contribution to a social theory of Congress. But the evidence presented here offers a compelling basis for the claim that partisanship is not exclusively ideological or strategic. Partisanship is also a norm.

SUMMARY: CONFLICT AND THE
FUTURE OF THE U.S. CONGRESS

Some have argued (e.g., Mann and Ornstein 2016), that Republican Party members, particularly its conservative wing, are more prone to extreme behavior and, therefore, would be more likely to exhibit qualities of the norms of conflict. Certainly, as the examples here illustrate, a particular bent of conservativism exudes the essence of the nonconformity norm—survey results and the legislative style of Newt Gingrich indicate Republicans as embracing of norms of conflict. But Republicans are not alone in exhibiting qualities of nonconformity. The case of procedural disobedience, for instance, shows Democrats taking a strong lead in acting upon norms of nonconformity to engage conflict.

While conflict has its strategic basis, as other scholars have ably demonstrated, in the normative sense argued for here, conflict is ideational. The origins of norms of conflict can perhaps be traced back to Thomas Jefferson. Modern conservativism, particularly that of the strain found among the Tea Party or Freedom Caucus in Congress, embraces the kind of anti-government, anti-authority tendencies of Jeffersonian republicanism. Jefferson biographer Joseph Ellis notes, "the rhetorical prowess of Jefferson's antigovernment ethos should not be underestimated as an influence on the special character of political discourse. Unlike any other nation-state in the modern world, the very idea of government power is stigmatized in the United States. . . . This potent strand of Jeffersonian thought remains alive and well in the conservative wing of the Republican party" (Ellis 1995, 296).

The spirit of resistance is not lacking among liberals, either, as shown by examples such as the stalwart Vermont Independent Senator Bernie Sanders or Bronx Democratic Representative Alexandria Ocasio Cortez. Samuel Huntington interpreted American history and political thought to suggest "the distinct distinctive aspect of the American Creed is its antigovernment character. Opposition to power, and suspicion of government as the most dangerous embodiment of power, are the central themes of American political thought" (Huntington 1981, 33). These are the very qualities of the norms of conflict, now operating among members of the institution of Congress itself. Where previously the normative context of Congress was dominated by cooperation, it has been infected with the infamous Jeffersonian maxim, "a little rebellion now and then is a good thing" (Jefferson 1787).

Perhaps much of this turn to norms of conflict among lawmakers seems unremarkable in the era of partisan polarization and gridlock in Congress and among society in general. But the emergence of norms of conflict in Congress should not be taken as a trivial shift in the culture of the institution. The fact that members find it appropriate to view conflict and noncooperation as acceptable social practice—irrespective of other ideological or strategic objectives—is a dramatic turn in the way members understand their roles in Congress and the very function and purpose of the institution. If partisan polarization contributes to gridlock and dysfunction, the growing presence of norms of conflict will serve only to exacerbate the already downward trend to neither get along nor go along on Capitol Hill.

NOTES

1. A previous version of this account of the gun control sit-in appeared in Alexander 2018.

2. Strategically speaking, there are limited instances when a sufficient number of members would agree upon radically disruptive tactics. Such agreement would seem more likely to occur only where the minority party finds a combination of preference unity, mobilized constituencies, and an important issue. Additionally, if the tactic were used more frequently, the likelihood of formal sanction by the majority would potentially increase—no more allowing the Democrats to "blow off steam," as one observer described the Republican response to the gun sit-in to me. Moreover, it is plausible that public opinion could backfire against members who repeatedly do not allow the institution to function according to its own rules.

Chapter 6

Out of the *Mad Men* Era into the New

Norms of a Changing Culture

One manner in which norms are evident in the U.S. Congress is where values in American society become manifested in the behaviors and attitudes of members and staff. There is a consequentialist aspect to these congressional norms in that members perceived as out of touch from broader societal norms may be penalized by their electorate or sanctioned by their peers. There is, however, also a constitutive aspect, in that members' preferences and identities are rooted in ideas of what is appropriate in the society of which they are a part. These congressional norms do not always directly affect legislative outcomes, but they affect what is acceptable among members and staff as well as the overall culture of an otherwise tradition-oriented workplace.

Evidence of cultural norms affecting norms in Congress can be seen when norms in Congress change in response to shifting cultural attitudes. Two such areas where this shift in cultural norms is evident on Capitol Hill are in norms of *sobriety* and *sexual propriety*. These normative changes are similar to the way attitudes have changed toward race in Congress. Norms of conduct regarding race on Capitol Hill have evolved, for example, from the days of the middle-twentieth century when Democratic Harlem Congressman Adam Clayton Powell, Jr., fought against openly racist and discriminatory behavior on the floor, which included the brazen refusal of Mississippi Democrat John E. Rankin to even sit next to Powell on the Floor (U.S. House of Representatives Office of the Historian 2019). In the twenty-first century, congressional norms now prohibit expressly racist behavior and racial equality is encouraged and presumably valued—even if there remains much room for improvement in attitudes and practices regarding race and racial equality (Mak 2014; Jones 2017; Klar 2019).

In the Congress of the twenty-first century, there have been significant normative shifts regarding alcohol consumption and behavior pertaining to

sexual attitudes and conduct among members and staff. In the Congress of
the past—the era of Mayhew's original study through to a disturbingly recent
time, sexual misconduct and alcohol abuse were commonly practiced and
normatively accepted. At times, a boy's club culture pervaded, and sexism
and alcohol were prevalent. Sometimes they combined, such as at the infamous Quorum Club run by Democratic Senate aide Bobby Baker. Prior to its
exposure in 1963, it was "a private after-hours joint upstairs in the Carroll
Arms Hotel on Capitol Hill, where lobbyists and legislators could repair for a
drink (or three) with attractive women out of the sight of prying journalist's
eyes" (Purdum 2013). The drunken and sexist office culture of the Showtime
television drama *Mad Men* might have been fictionalized, but it is a fiction
not too far removed from fact. The Congress of the past may have had a *Mad
Men* quality, but this is increasingly (and mercifully) less and less the case.

Norms of a changing culture are not directly about policy issues in areas
such as gender (or race), where the country is lagging or policy solutions are
not agreed upon—and nor is it about equality of representation among the
workforce on Capitol Hill, which is also lagging (Bowman 2016; Jones op.
cit.). Rather, these norms are about the attitudes and the conduct of members
and staff thought to be appropriate toward and among one another in the
workplace. There are two approaches to examining these norms. On sobriety,
evidence comes largely the observations and statements of congressional
actors themselves. The norm of sexual propriety can be examined not only
through the observations of members and staff but in the way congressional
rules changed in response to shifting mores regarding gender relations.

SOBRIETY

Stories of Sam Rayburn gathering members in his "Board of Education"
Capitol office, during his lengthy tenure as Speaker of the House during the
mid-twentieth century are legendary. Members would gather to drink and play
poker in room H-128 of the Capitol where the drawers of the Speaker's desk
were filled with bourbon and Scotch (Hallac 2011; House of Representatives
2018). In the Congress of the early 1970s, *New York Times* journalist Richard
Lyons reported, "most Congressmen drink, a small percentage are drunkards
and a few are reformed alcoholics," (Lyons 1973). While alcoholism was not
found to be any more widespread in Congress than the rest of the country,
"Discussions with Congressmen, their staff aides, employees at the Capitol
and legislative hangers-on certainly indicate that drinking is part of the normal way of life in and around the halls of Congress" (Ibid.). A senior staffer
who worked in the Senate since the 1990s recounted how Massachusetts
Democrat Ted Kennedy "could be overheard in the well of the Senate telling

people 'the lantern is lit,' which was the cue to come up to his office and have a drink" (Interview 2016).[1]

Not that the bibulous past should be romanticized as halcyon days. One senior Senate administrative staffer pointed to just some of the less savory aspects of a more alcoholic culture on the Hill:

> They called Republican leader Senator Everett Dirksen's office "The Twilight Lounge." You'd have these evening five o'clock sessions where, particularly, the senior members would come together and have drinks and cigars. They would hash out issues. And there were great benefits to that because a lot of legislative deals were struck in those evening drinking sessions. But there was a downside to it. It was an old white man's club. For women who served at the time, they were excluded from it. So it was very difficult for women like Margaret Chase Smith and Nancy Kassebaum to have an impact on legislation because they were marginalized. (Interview 2016)

The old norm about drinking was a kind of accepted unacceptable behavior, whereby drunken activity or overindulgence of spirits was overlooked or occurred with little repercussion among peers and colleagues (Hocking 2006).

But this has changed. Sobriety is more a part of the workplace than it was in times past. Norms regarding drinking at work or at the Capitol and attitudes toward drunkenness in the workplace have changed. "People aren't sitting around with a glass of bourbon having a chit chat until midnight anymore, figuring it out, making deals and shaking hands," according to a House professional staffer (Interview 2016). The acceptability of the workplace consumption of alcohol, whether in small or large gatherings, has declined on Capitol Hill. "If you talk to people about the forties, fifties, and sixties . . . the workday ended at five o'clock and a member would have you in his office and the portable bar would get rolled out. Again, that's kind of where some of the deal-making was done" (Ibid.). Stephen Hess, a Brookings scholar whose tenure in Washington includes service in the Eisenhower and Nixon administrations, noted in 2006, there is "a great deal less drinking on Capitol Hill than when I got here in the 1950s" (Hocking 2006).

None of this is to suggest that drinking is not a part of Capitol Hill culture (Gale 2015). It is. Congress provides a tempting environment for alcohol consumption with its stress, distance from families, and abundance of socializing after hours (Hocking 2006). Over time, numerous members and staff have struggled with substance abuse (Hohmann 2018), although there is no evidence to suggest the rate of alcoholism on the Hill is any greater than the rest of American society (Ingraham 2015).

Current younger staff who frequent Capitol Hill bars may not find their social milieu to be particularly sober, and Washington is hardly the most temperate of towns (Wilson 2018). In the summertime, as college students and young interns join the staffs of congressional offices, nearby bars beckon. This is true today as it was in the late 1990s, when *Roll Call* wrote, "For these temporary politicos, hitting the bars is an essential part of the Washington experience. As a result, hordes of 18- to 21-year olds wearing suits and try-ing their hardest to look older than they are flood into local watering holes to unwind and network" (Pershing 1999). Indeed, drinking remains part of con-gressional socializing and recreation. Look no further than the ways lobbyists have adapted to gift restrictions (Hocking 2006), staff rituals such as the State of the Union Drinking Game (Walshe and Graham 2017; Melzer and Deutsch 2020), or conduct some field research yourself, such as this intrepid scholar has done, to see the packed happy hours at Capitol Hill bars.

But the days in which moderate consumption or even reckless drunken-ness at the workplace were acceptable (or at least overlooked) are a thing of the past. Along with these shifts, the norm of sobriety has emerged in the modern Congress. This normative shift in congressional workplace alcohol consumptions reflects broader societal trends of lower alcohol consump-tion (Chaudhuri and Maloney 2019). Perhaps surprisingly, despite alcohol consumption historically playing a large part of the culture on Capitol Hill, there is little systematic empirical data on drinking habits and attitudes among members and staff.

The sources of more sobriety on the Hill is the subject of speculation. Lower drinking might relate to growing health-consciousness. In contrast to the past, Senate Historian Don Ritchie said in 2006, "You are much more likely to see someone out literally jogging around the building" than drinking (Hocking 2006). In Washington, greater workplace temperance could also reflect the greater scrutiny placed on public officials in an era of television cameras, pervasive smart phones, and social media. A long-term congres-sional observer attributed the changes in drinking to C-SPAN: "A lot of that ended with television, frankly, because you'd have members that would come to the Senate chamber completely drunk and could not make a speech. But when television started that became so obvious that they were pushed to not let that happen" (Interview 2016). As a senior Senate Democratic aide sum-marized it, "Anything you do can and will be used against you. In the age of camera phones a few drinks at a bar may not be such a good idea" (Interview 2019). Notably, congressional rules cannot be pointed to as a primary source for less drinking on the job. Both House and Senate rules are surprisingly silent on the topic of workplace alcohol consumption and individual offices do not have uniform policies on drinking or enforcement of restrictions at work, if they have one at all (Gangitano 2018).[2] When asked about the rules—or their absence—a congressional aide told me, "I don't know that I've seen any rules. The police are never stopping anyone hauling in cases of whatever . . . I think it's just one of the things they'd rather not have a formal policy on so they can do what they like" (Interview 2020).

In all, while Washington has not gone sober, workplace alcohol consumption on Capitol Hill has changed from what it was in the past. The norm of sobriety embodies this new sense of appropriateness and changed behaviors in the modern Congress.

SEXUAL PROPRIETY

Though the past is troubled, and the present far from equitable, gender norms have shifted across American society toward greater diversity and equality among men and women and people with varying sexual identities. Congress, though improving, is hardly on the vanguard of the sexual revolution—asymmetry in gender representation of Members and staff is pervasive. It is a breakthrough that California Democrat Nancy Pelosi was elected to be Speaker of the House in 2007 during the 110th Congress, and successfully held onto that position in subsequent Democratic majorities. And it is true that a record number of women hold seats in the 116th Congress, with 23.4 percent of House Members (106 of 441, including four of six nonvoting delegates), and 25 out of 100 Senators (Desilver 2018). These numbers mark the biggest jump since the 1990s, yet elected women are still only a quarter of the Congress. Progress is far from uniform or complete. A 2019 analysis of committee staff determines, "Some have gender parity among their aides; some aren't even close" (Burgat and Dukeman 2019, 3). In congressional committees overall, the number of men leads those of women 52.07 percent to 47.93 percent in the House and 55.89 to 44.11 in the Senate. The gender pay gaps exist across all staff committee roles, with one exception: "the only position where women out-earned their male counterparts was administration," (Ibid. 17). Even with a woman Speaker and with Vice President Kamala Harris, the first woman President of the Senate, the institution, like the society it represents, still has a way to go.

Meanwhile, gender controversies erupt on the Hill over even trivial matters like women's sleeveless tops (Shabad 2017) or how it was unacceptable for women to wear pants on the floor of the House up to the 1970s and in the Senate until 1993 (Rollcall Staff 2005). Women House members did not get their own bathroom outside the chamber until 2011 (McKeon 2011) and a 2018 decision to let the first sitting Senator to give birth to bring her baby to the floor set off a "tantrum" as one reporter quipped (Kliff 2018). Such is the progress of gender equity on Capitol Hill.

Related to gender equality, in the past, sexual impropriety was widely accepted among members and staff. People on the Hill looked the other way at sexual indiscretion among members, ignored the philandering of husbands, and did not speak of known homosexual activity in an era when it was considered taboo (Merry 1989). But things have changed. In the 1980s public attention began to turn toward personal behavior among members that was considered sexually inappropriate. Colorado Senator Gary Hart's 1988 presidential campaign faltered on reports of extramarital indiscretion; in 1989 Representative John Tower was rejected by the Senate for Defense Secretary because of womanizing *and* drunkenness (Shapiro 2017). In 1995, the Congressional Accountability Act (CAA) was passed, offering workplace protections on discrimination and prohibitions on harassment more consistent with national law from which Congress previously had exempted itself (Back and Freeman 2018, 2), forcing the institution to uphold a standard mandated in much of the rest of U.S. society.

Norms of sexual propriety evolved within the broader context of expanding gender equity in the chamber. As women become a greater proportion of each chamber, Congress has modified its rules toward greater gender parity and unique considerations brought to Congress by the fact of more women serving. Innovations include seemingly trivial steps on adapting rules on women's' attire to more wide-reaching accommodations such providing lactation rooms in the Capitol complex and accommodation for childcare needs such as daycare and flexible schedules (Vavra 2018). The culture of "boys' club" practices, such as the prohibition of women from the Capitol pool so that, if the reader will forgive the imagery, male Senators and Representatives could swim naked, is largely the stuff of the past (CQ Weekly Report 2018). The Office of Compliance, which oversees implementation of the Congressional Accountability Act and ethics regulations, outlined for *Roll Call* some guidelines for holiday parties in 2014, reminding members and staff of their obligations to adhere rules on sexual propriety. The guidelines to congressional offices included "Employers should keep an eye out for these problem areas: Employees exchanging sexually suggestive or romantic gifts, pressuring staff to kiss under mistletoe, pressuring employees to play games that have a physical contact component like 'Twister,' and excessive teasing or comments about attire or physical attributes" (Gale 2014). One does wonder where concerns about congressional Twister arose, but the overall tenor of the guidelines points to shifting attitudes about what is appropriate—that is, changing norms about sexual propriety on Capitol Hill.

Sexual propriety may be an extension of a broader trend of gender equality and accommodation, but it was strongly ushered in with the #metoo movement which had direct and immediate consequences on Capitol Hill. The #metoo movement, which began in 2006 as a way to draw attention to sexual violence against women but took off on Twitter in 2017 (Shugerman 2017), has accelerated awareness of and adherence to this new norm, even expanding the scope of its meaning and application. Workplace flirtation, romantic liaison, affairs, and pervasive harassment, once a standard on the Hill as elsewhere, are eschewed more now than ever. A long-serving Democratic House staffer said, "In the past you might notice a member getting too friendly with a female staffer during happy hour at Tortilla Coast [a Capitol Hill bar] and pretend you didn't see it. But today I'd be really surprised if you'd see that kind of thing at all" (Interview 2018). A Republican Senate committee staffer noted the new sensibility this way: "Members who are attracted to their staff? A big no-no" (Survey 2019). "Boys-will-be-boys" attitudes, long tolerated in Congress, are now being challenged and called out as unacceptable (McGann 2018). A woman who works as a Republican House committee staffer noted in 2019 that women are "more likely to speak out against abuse, discrimination, or assault than when I started three years ago" (Survey 2019), indicating the rapidity with which norms pertaining to sexual propriety are changing. A female former Senate staffer, who worked on the Hill for twenty years before turning to lobbying, captured the essence of this new normative context: "One norm that has improved dramatically is that there are more women in Congress and they are insisting on being taken seriously and not putting up with some of the behavior and norms their male colleagues insisted on not that long ago" (Survey 2019). Minnesota Senator Al Franken's hasty exit in 2018 following allegations of inappropriate behavior toward women is evidence of the new normative context of sexual propriety (Schor and Kim 2017). The departure of a popular sitting Senator, who once had been considered a contender for the presidency, signaled that something substantial had changed. Certainly, many would rightfully argue that not enough progress has been made on this front, but sexual propriety is an important and developing norm on Capitol Hill.

Norms Formalized as Rules—the Case of Sexual Propriety

Rule changes—the formalization of norms—provide evidence for the development of the sexual propriety norm on Capitol Hill. As the U.S. Constitution states, "Each House may determine the rules of its proceedings" (Art. I, Sec. 5). Such rules may include concurrent resolutions or laws enacted that impose enforceable guidelines on procedural, organizational, and behavioral matters. The 1995 Congressional Accountability Act and the 2018 modification of it are instances where new rules were jointly imposed on each chamber.

Senate and House rules act as the formal embodiment and codification of norms. The Senate largely operates by standing rules that apply from Congress to Congress as well as new precedents as they are adopted. Changes to the Standing Rules of the Senate occur as a simple resolution, adopted by majority vote, but a supermajority of two-thirds of Senators voting, with a quorum of a simple majority, is necessary to close debate on a cloture motion. Therefore, as a simple resolution or as part of another bill, Senate rules may be changed with only a majority vote, but Senate rules on limiting debate can easily require any rule change to pass a super-majority threshold (Beth 2013). Senate procedure may also change based on precedents "that interpret existing rules or other standards differently from before. This might be achieved either by a ruling that directly establishes an altered practice or by one that permits a simple majority to bring the Senate to a vote on a change in rules" (Ibid., ii).

In the House, at the start of every Congress, a resolution containing new rules is passed as part of the first orders of business. CRS notes, "Although a new House largely adopts the chamber rules that existed in the previous Congress, it also adopts changes to those rules" (CRS 2017, 2). There are many reasons rules change, usually incrementally, that affect numerous aspects of the House: "the committee system and its procedures, the floor of the House, budgetary legislation, the administration of the House, and ethical norms of conduct" (Ibid.).

These processes, intentionally complicated, are to limit capricious changes or adopting of rules. When norms, signaling new attitudes toward sexual propriety are incorporated, therefore, it represents a widespread and marked support of not just a new sense of what is appropriate, but a commitment to formally enforcing it. The norm, in this way, becomes the rule. For instance, Annenberg points to the adoption of rules of decorum in the House as a manner in which House members choose to adhere to the norm of courtesy:

> By adopting the rules at the beginning of a new Congress, the membership voluntarily limits the range of rhetoric acceptable on the floor. When Members wonder why they cannot call another Member a liar or a hypocrite even if the evidence justifies the label, the answer is not simply that the rules of the House forbid it; rather, it is that the membership has voluntarily agreed by vote that these are the rules under which the House will operate during that Congress. (Annenberg 2011, 2)

By this logic, members agree to courtesy as a shared sense of what is appropriate. Agreement on rules each Congress implies consent to a set of norms when there is no constitutional obligation to adopt any particular rules. The logic of consequences implies that members may find enforcing particular rules yields more favorable outcomes than if they did not institute such rules. Yet, in rule adoption, we also see the logic of appropriateness when members agree to modify rules based on changing sense of what is appropriate or not.

The case of sexual propriety illustrates the logic of appropriateness and how new norms become formalized in the rules of the Congress. In earlier Congresses, for example, chamber rules were modified to reflect changing gender norms. For instance, House rules were modified in the 111th Congress to provide gender-neutral language in titles and pronouns. Terms such as "Chairman" were replaced with "Chair," and masculine pronouns "he" and "his" in reference to the Speaker or the Sergeant-at-Arms were struck such that a phrase like "his opinion" was replaced with "the opinion of the Speaker," or "his employees" was replaced with "employees of the office of the Sergeant-at-Arms," and so on (House of Representatives 2009).

The rapidity of a normative shift on sexual propriety in Congress is evident in rule changes that occurred in the wake of the #metoo movement. In the 115th Congress, as #metoo was taking off on social media, the House and Senate improved the process for protecting against and responding to sexual harassment and discrimination on Capitol Hill with passage of the Congressional Accountability Act of 1995 (CAA) Reform Act (Marquette 2019). New rules in the act "require offices to post notices of workplace rights, and to implement anti-discrimination and anti-harassment policies and training programs," extending protections to unpaid staff and making members personally liable for acts of discrimination and harassment (Office of Congressional Workplace Rights 2018, 4). The swiftness of such changes in rules points to the way the cultural shift affected the sense of appropriateness regarding sexual propriety and gender relations on Capitol Hill. In the Senate, the measure passed with bipartisan accolades. Republican Majority Leader McConnell called the bill "a landmark agreement," "bipartisan and bicameral," that "strengthens protections for victims" (United States Senate 2018, S7531). Minnesota Democrat Amy Klobuchar praised the bill for "getting rid of a lot of the Byzantine way these cases were being handled—this is going to be better for victims. I am proud the Senate has come together on a bipartisan basis to get this bill done" (*Ibid.* S7548). Even in a hyperpolarized environment there is room for at least some progress on gender equity, as evidenced by new rules that reflect changing norms.

Other rule changes in the 116th Congress reflect evolving norms on sexual propriety. New House rules of the 116th Congress require: mandatory anti-harassment and anti-discrimination office policies, Members to pay for discrimination settlements out of their own pockets, and annual ethics training (House of Representatives, 3 January 2019, H. Res. 6). New bans were also put into place on discrimination on the basis of sexual orientation and on relationships between members and committee staff.[3] Whether these shifts are policy consequential warrants further consideration. But gender norms on Capitol Hill have definitely changed and new rules reflect that.

The reader can decide how much irony they want to attribute to the fact that among the first people held accountable to the new House rules on sexual propriety in the 116th Congress was a woman. Representative Katie Hill, Democrat of California, was forced to resign after the House Ethics Committee opened an investigation into alleged affairs with members of her staff, and salacious information made its rounds on the Internet in relation to an acrimonious ongoing divorce (Caygle, Bresnahan, and Cheney 2019). Democratic House Speaker Nancy Pelosi, who encouraged Hill's resignation, indicated the general sense of the norm, stating, "We must ensure a climate of integrity and dignity in the Congress, and in all workplaces," (Ibid.). This may be viewed as a triumph of new norms over past ways (Murphy 2019). *LA Times* columnist Robin Abcarian, however, thinks Hill "should have earned a slap on the wrist . . . For decades, male lawmakers got away with those sort of shenanigans" (Abcarian 2019). Abcarian points out that as Hill was forced to resign, fellow Californian Republican Duncan Hunter was under investigation for ethics violations about affairs with congressional staff (Kopp 2019). Even if Hill fell to a double standard, it is a standard rooted in a new normative context.

The Sexual Propriety Norm and Gender Progress on the Hill

Sexual propriety has emerged as a norm alongside other changes in gender parity in Congress. But stereotypes about women in Congress have died a slow death. Even the idea that women can perform the job the same as men is not yet fully embraced, well into the twenty-first century. For instance, while Americans are increasingly less likely to view men as better emotionally suited for politics than women, there is still a distinction viewed that is based on gender. "Only about 13 percent of both men and women now think that women are less suited for politics than men—a change of about 37 percentage points since 1975, when the average peaked at almost 50 percent," according to a 2019 study by Georgetown University Center on Education and the Workforce (Carnevale, Smith and Campbell 2019, 3). The report observes "This result is heartening yet disappointing" (Ibid.). Evidence also suggests that men and women may view women candidates differently from men (Thomson-DeVeaux 2019) and weigh their performance along different issues and standards (Dolan 2003). In 2003 a woman Republican Senator, Olympia Snowe of Maine, observed signs of progress: "I think clearly, women have demonstrated the capacity to serve, and have overcome those barriers and perceptions and questions as to whether or not we have the capability to serve." She declared, "I think that's really behind us" (Stevens 2003). But a decade and a half later, still 13 percent of Americans perceive a difference between men's and women's suitability to politics. Vestiges of the barriers Senator Snowe perceived are still evident.

Another perception exists that women may work together differently than men. For example, Representative Susan W. Brooks, a Republican from Indianapolis and member of the bipartisan Women's Caucus, said: "Certainly we know the country is very divided and very polarized . . . But in my experience, the women that I have worked with on substantive issues work incredibly hard to try and find common solutions and results working together" (CQ Weekly Report 2018). New York Democratic Senator Kirsten Gillibrand has claimed that women lawmakers are more productive and more bipartisan (Ramos 2018). Such impressions aside, systematic evidence is mixed on whether legislative behavior varies by gender. There is evidence that women behave differently in committees—interrupting less than men—which may have an effect on committee deliberation (Ban, Grimmer, and Kaslovsky 2018) and that they may gain more bipartisan cosponsors and women may pass more bills than their male counterparts (Klein 2017; Lazarus and Steigerwalt 2018). Other research points to how women lawmakers exhibit the same characteristics as male lawmakers in achieving legislative results and are subject to the same partisan pressures (Lawless, Theriault, and Guthrie 2019). Party is increasingly the determining factor of how one legislatives, with men and women being about equally polarized (Ibid.).

In sum, as gender norms push toward greater sexual propriety and equitability, women are still not afforded a fully coequal place on Capitol Hill. In addition, the policy consequences of women being treated equally and with greater representation remains an important question. Progress on women's representation is marked but relatively slow in Congress. Just over a century ago, in 1916, Jeannette Rankin, Republican of Montana, was the first woman elected to the House, while Hattie Caraway was the first woman elected to the Senate in 1932. A century after Representative Rankin assumed office, women make up about a quarter of all members of the House and Senate. Other progress on gender equity on Capitol Hill has been punctuated with intermittent steps on varying degrees of impact, from restrooms to changing rules on sexual discrimination. Kelly Dittmar, a scholar at the Center for American Women in Politics at Rutgers observed: "We talk about the number of women in office and the importance of increasing women's representation in numerical terms, but as we increase representation, we have to think about how much power they hold" (CQ Weekly Report 2018).

Norms are part of this progress. From the waking months of the #metoo movement in late 2017 to the announcement of new rules of the 116th Congress in January 2019, a normative shift on Capitol Hill is evident in the changing nature of what is appropriate and related changes in rules of the House and Senate that reflect this new sensibility. Sexual propriety is evidence of where norms change and affect the conduct of the members and staff, in this case toward the more equitable treatment of the growing portion of women who comprise the legislature. Inasmuch as gender roles are endemic to society, if norms form the basis and identities that determine preferences, the mere presence of women in the chamber may shift the identities and senses of what is appropriate among an historically male institution (Swers 2013, 237–238). Whether such changes directly affect women's power or whether they have legislative or policy consequences is a larger and more complicated question. However, it is the case that changing norms affect women's abilities to succeed in the chamber and to be treated on more equal footing with their male counterparts.

SUMMARY: CHANGING CULTURE AND THE FUTURE OF THE U.S. CONGRESS

As cultural norms change so too does change the sense of what is appropriate in Congress. The case of sobriety reflects shifts in attitudes toward alcohol consumption—drinking in the workplace has gradually faded from being understood as appropriate in broader society, just as it has on the Hill. Sexual propriety is a norm that strongly reflects the manner in which ideas of what is appropriate affect preferences. As attitudes toward sexual propriety rapidly shifted in the 2016–2018 period as a result of the #metoo movement, bipartisan agreement consolidated around changes to Congressional rules—the formalization of norms—to enforce adherence to a new normative context regarding gender treatment and equality. All norms share in common a degree of ambiguity, but the institutionalization of norms of sexual propriety into formal rules points to the breadth of their acceptance and the importance this norm plays in the modern Congress. Congressional norms are only a small part of the broader movement toward gender equity in the United States, but if we look to Capitol Hill, signs of progress are evident, indeed.

NOTES

1. Further back, during Prohibition, Capitol Hill even had its own bootlegger, George Cassiday, who had a storeroom in the basement of the Cannon House Office Building for convenient distribution to partaking members (Roller and *National Journal* 2014).

2. Alcohol is not directly forbidden on the House or Senate floors, but floor rules do not permit food and beverages, with the exception of water and milk in the Senate (Shapiro and Chang 2020). These rules are adhered to as well as enforced. For instance, in April 2018, Politico reporter Heather Caygle tweeted that door guards

prevented Freshman Congressman Conor Lamb from bringing a (nonalcoholic) coffee cup onto the House floor (Caygle 2018).

3. The presence of two women Muslim lawmakers, a first in the 116th Congress, led to rule changes affecting gender and religion, when the House modified a 181-year ban on headwear in the House Chamber to allow members to wear religious headdress. The new rule thereby permitted newly elected Democrat Ilhan Omar of Minnesota to be the first member of Congress to wear a hijab on the floor (Smith 2019). The new rule was carefully worded to reflect the permission of religious headwear, not a general opening of the dress code. The amendment to Rule XVII states, "During the session of the House, a Member, Delegate, or Resident Commissioner may not wear non-religious headdress or a hat" (Hudiberg 2019, 7). With the introduction of new social groups, the shared sense of what is appropriate can develop as well, and new norms can emerge, which are then reflected in changes in the rules.

Chapter 7

Between Cooperation and Conflict

Norms can bring us together, but norms also can tear us apart. As the preceding chapters have contended, norms play an important role in the behavior of Congress and its members. Norms are not just constraints on behavior that a rational actor will weigh in making economic choices on how to maximize their interests. Norms form part of the bases of those interests in the first place. A social theory of Congress, by bringing norms back into the study of Congress, turns our focus to the role that ideas play in members' identities, their shared senses of what is appropriate, and in the origins of their preferences as lawmakers.

A social theory of Congress posits that norms are both consequential and constitutive. As shared understandings of what is appropriate, norms may constrain a rational lawmaker's behavior based on a calculus of the strategic advantages or disadvantages of adhering to a norm. This is the stuff of rational choice and game theoretic approaches which is well documented in political science and congressional studies. But norms are also constitutive in the sense that they comprise the identities and interests of lawmakers, irrespective of other material or strategic considerations. As such, norms shape lawmakers' senses of what is appropriate; they determine what are interests in the first place. In other words, norms help us consider the role that ideas play in determining what lawmakers want.

Norms widely shared among members of the Congress in the opening decades of the twenty-first century hold in common the idea that cooperation is appropriate and part of what it means to be a member of Congress. Cooperation is evidenced in norms such as courtesy, reciprocity, and apprenticeship, through which members believe it is appropriate to allow other members to fulfill their roles as lawmakers and to enable the Congress to function in such a manner that political conflict can be resolved through the legislative process. By understanding norms of cooperation as appropriate, members indicate their acceptance of the rightful place of the institution of Congress in facilitating political dialogue and of the value in engaging the views of other members in the deliberative process of legislating.

Current and former members and staff may often express a cynicism about the functionality of the modern Congress, views often echoed by political scientists and the general public who hold an overall negative opinion on Congress. In 1999, *Congressional Quarterly* wrote that "[s]cholars and law-makers say politics has rarely been so nasty or cynical" (Bettleheim 1999, 233). Writing of the bitterness of the impeachment probe of President Bill Clinton, they noted "the new brand of politics taking over in Washington. Careful debates on policy matters are increasingly being replaced by nasty confrontations in which politicians lob personal attacks at each other and depict their battles as a choice between truth and lies" (Ibid.) At that time, twenty-four-hour cable news was a primary driver of "salacious gossip" and the coarse rhetoric coming to dominate public political discourse, and Matt Drudge's Internet-based "Drudge Report" could be blamed for put-ting "unconfirmed rumors into play" (Ibid. 241). These observations may seem quaint in the hindsight of an era now dominated by social media, where figures such as Republican Representative Matt Gaetz of Florida and New York Democrat Alexandria Ocasio Cortez have built careers around both social media and cable TV (Butler 2020), but they marked sea changes in the way politics occurred at the time. Shortly later, in 2006, Mann and Ornstein wrote their book on partisan polarization in Congress, *The Broken Branch*, changed the title to *It's Even Worse Than It Looks* in 2012 for a second edition, and then reissued it as *It's Even Worse Than It Was* for another print run in 2016, ten years after the first publication. As the growing alarm in their titles suggests, the sense that congress is on a steady course downward to greater conflict and gridlock is evident in the way close observers have been considering the institution for at least two decades.

But there is something else underlying the perennial lamentations among those on the Hill that Congress is not doing its job well or that it is mired in bitter conflict. Despite cynicism and even despair, there lies a fundamental belief among lawmakers in the legitimacy of the institution, which is exhib-ited in the presence of norms of cooperation. We should not take norms of cooperation for granted. In a social theory of Congress, cooperation is a preference irrespective of other strategic or ideological objectives that mem-bers may hold. Cooperation is not determined exclusively by the structure of institutions, ideological objectives, electoral imperatives, or other behavioral imperatives. To be cooperative, to believe in norms of cooperation, is part of the identity of members of Congress. Cooperation is a preference in and of itself and is manifested in several enduring norms prevalent in the Congress of the past as well as the present. As presented in the preceding chapters, there is ample evidence for widespread, shared understandings on the sense of appropriateness of norms of cooperation. The endurance of norms that have been present at least since Donald Matthews first observed them in the 1950s—especially apprenticeship, reciprocity, and courtesy—should be heartening for anyone who finds Congress unpleasantly contentious or acrimonious.

Against this context of cooperation, norms of conflict are a prevalent aspect of the Congress of the twenty-first century. Nonconformity—a rejection cooperation—has become a fixture among members of both parties and both chambers. Partisanship, typically thought of in strategic or ideological terms, has also become a norm—an understanding that it is part of the identity of lawmakers to oppose the other party, almost as a default setting, and as a preference in its own right. There are clear partisan differences on norms of conflict, with Republicans expressing more support than Democrats for norms of partisanship and pertaining to opposing cooperation with the other party. But Democrats are not unequivocally absent their own support of norms of conflict, and the presidency of Donald Trump may be challenging Democrats' historically more cooperative nature.

Yet, even though norms are not evenly held by each party, norms of cooperation are still widely prevalent across both parties and both chambers. Norms, in this respect, help abate the conflict represented in partisan polarization. Because of norms, members still share the understanding that cooperation is appropriate and part of their identities as lawmakers. Congress may be ridden with conflict, but norms of cooperation prevent this conflict from being even worse.

Norms also reflect the broader culture. This may be true of norms of cooperation and conflict, where Americans, or at least the most politically active of them, are more divided now than at any point in recent history. Members of Congress manifest the broader senses of appropriateness within the society they represent. Norms of sexual propriety and sobriety, which stem from the broader culture, have also made themselves tangibly present on Capitol Hill. Sexual propriety, in particular, elevated rapidly in its importance on Capitol Hill in the wake of the #metoo movement in 2017, ultimately leading to formal rule changes regarding gender relations and sexual harassment. A social theory of Congress requires us to consider both the material and ideational drivers of behavior. If norms have an instrumental purpose—costs and benefits associated with adhering to or rejecting them—they also have an ideational component—they are ideas that inform the nature of preferences in the first place. Norms change as ideas evolve, or even as the culture changes.

CONGRESSIONAL NORMS IN THE TRUMP ERA

Whether the presidency of Donald J. Trump is a symptom or a cause of heightened conflict in American politics is a question that will endure beyond his tenure in office (Tyson 2018; Lelkes 2019). While this book was being written, cases of norm-busting behavior of first Trump the candidate and then Trump the president were a recurring discussion among observers of American politics (Panke and Petersohn 2017; Jenkins 2019). It is beyond the scope of this work to fully engage in this rich, often contentious, and important discussion. But one cannot discuss congressional norms in this period of American politics without inevitably discussing Donald Trump.

The question remains open as to whether the apparent disregard for long-held Washington norms by President Trump is affecting Congress. There is much evidence of norm flouting from the Trump administration and worthy speculation about its broader consequences on American democracy (Sah 2019; Bauer 2019). Presumably more conflictual, discourteous behavior from one end of Pennsylvania Avenue could lead to similar behavior on the other end. The Trump administration could not, of course, be solely to blame for a disregard of cooperation or changing norms in Washington. Acrimony in a time of partisan polarization is not new to the Trump era. Procedural hardball—increases in uses of cloture votes in the Senate (Reynolds 2020), for example, or closed rules in the House (Thorning 2020)—and shifting tactics in partisan warfare were present well before Trump dominated the national scene (see Wolfensberger 2018).

Is Trump a part of a progression from the Gingrich revolution to the Tea Party, to the increasingly obdurate liberal wing among Democrats, and an overall trend of more normatively conflictual and less cooperative American political scene? Or is Trump uniquely Trumpian, and his effect on norms is limited to his period in office? Much of the evidence presented in this book cautions against assuming that things are as bad as they seem. Although norms of conflict, which seem echoed in some of Trump's behavior, are a fixture of the modern Congress, overall norms of cooperation are a prevalent, enduring aspect of life on Capitol Hill.

Generally speaking, it is too early to tell what the long-term consequences of the Trump presidency will be on congressional norms, or other aspects of American political life for that matter. The systematic evidence of the preceding chapters suggests that norms of cooperation are stronger and more widely held than is commonly perceived, but that norms of conflict have emerged as a staple of the U.S. Congress. Within the empirical evidence one data point suggests the direction toward greater conflict that could emerge in Congress because of the Trump presidency. Specifically, the words-taken-down measure for the courtesy norm in the House of Representatives points to a slight

uptick in discourtesy on the floor since Trump took office. In a measurement of demands of words taken down, over the period of the 80th to 115th
Congresses, admonishments from the chair account for 36 (13.09 percent) out
of a total 275 cases. Of these thirty-six, eleven are from the 115th Congress,
the first Congress of the Trump presidency. In each of these cases from the
115th Congress, the Chair is admonishing a member for engaging in personalities against the president, and eight of the eleven are Democratic violators
of the rule. This does not indicate that members have become more discourteous toward one another, but it does suggest, during the Trump presidency
at least, they are substantially more willing than normal to be discourteous
toward the president.

It would be a leap to conclude that this signals a transformation in member
adherence to the courtesy norm, but this measure does suggest that congressional courtesy norm has been tested during the Trump era. Perhaps there
is nothing more to read into this evidence other than House Democrats are
responding in kind to the combative style of Donald Trump. This would not
be unprecedented way for a minority power in the legislature to respond to
the opposing party in the White House; for example, during the Iran-Contra
hearings in 1987, a breakdown in of courtesy was largely between Democratic
critics of then-President Ronald Reagan and his Republican congressional
supporters (Pressman 1987). Perhaps like other episodes of breaches of
courtesy in the Congress, they stand out because they are dramatic but also
unusual. Discourtesy among House Democrats toward the President Trump
may be exceptions that prove the rule. This warrants additional consideration
that the passage of time can help deliver.

THE CHALLENGE OF CONSTRUCTIVISM
AND CONGRESSIONAL STUDIES

The constructivist research agenda, as suggested by a social theory of
Congress, necessitates new ways of considering Congress and its members. If we are to understand the role that identities, ideas, and norms, or
shared notions of what is appropriate, play in Congress new questions and
new research strategies are possible and necessary. For lessons on how to
approach this, we can draw from the experience of constructivist scholars
in international relations theory and both the opportunities and challenges
that a constructivist research agenda promises. Some of the issues faced in a
constructivist approach to Congress are epistemological—if we assume ideas
form interests, by what standards of knowledge can we assess the presence
or the effects of such ideas in identities or behaviors on Capitol Hill? Some
of the issues are methodological—assuming particular epistemological bases

for judging knowledge, what research methods can we employ to empirically establish such knowledge? These are not problems unique to a social theory of Congress, but to constructivist research in general.

The efforts put forward in this book reflect several approaches to addressing these epistemological and methodological challenges. The theoretical proposition has been argued that norms are shared understandings of what is appropriate among congressional actors. On this basis, arguments for the existence of norms have been put forward based on the acceptance of the appropriateness of certain attitudes through survey research, one-on-one interviews, and participant observation (see Klotz and Lynch 2007). Other efforts in this book, borrowed from Finnemore (1996), attempt to demonstrate the presence of a sense of appropriateness of certain ideas based on the lack of compelling alternative behavioral or strategic reasoning behind behavior such as courtesy and nonconformity. In other cases, such as on the norm of sexual propriety, normative attitudes are explored for their effect on changes in formal congressional rules. Each of these methodological approaches enable us to reasonably draw the conclusion that norms are internalized by actors as beliefs or ideas about what is appropriate and serve to inform preferences irrespective of other material or strategic factors.

But these approaches are certainly not exhaustive of the manner by which constructivist arguments regarding norms in Congress can be made. There is a long lineage of constructivist research that attends to issues of how to construct meaningful arguments around a theory which, unlike many other social scientific theories, is not specifically one of inference or cause-and-effect. Norms are ideas that shape preferences and are part of identities, but they do not necessarily yield or lend themselves to measurable outcomes in the sense traditionally examined by the scientific method. In the present work, for instance, norms are not spoken of for their direct policy consequences but for the manner in which they shape member ideas and behavior regarding the institution of Congress and the legislative process, or member interactions among one another on the Hill. In the constitutive sense, ideology or electoral strategy, for example, are not determinants of adherence to courtesy norm, and nor is it argued here that the courtesy norm has an effect on ideological or electoral strategic behaviors. Rather, a norm exists as a shared idea of what is appropriate, irrespective of other material or consequential effects or benefits it may provide. In fact, norms observed here are notable less for their direct policy or ideological outcomes than for the manner in which they facilitate or hinder the functioning of Congress itself. The constructivist assumption is that norms are not just another causal variable that a rational actor weighs in determining the costs and benefits of particular outcomes, the empirical presence of which can then be standard inferential models widely employed in political science (e.g., King, Keohane, and Verba 1994). To the contrary, the logic of inference may prove insufficient in identifying the presence of a norm or the manner by which a norm functions in a social community.

Common criticisms of constructivism in international relations need also to be considered in pursuing a research agenda under a social theory of Congress. For instance, the lack of clarity about the causal nature of constitutive norms, that is, the difficulty of separating out ideas, identities, and norms from materially determined economic or strategic behavior, renders the consequences of norms difficult to isolate with the kind of precision Americanists in political science are typically comfortable with (Hopf 1998). The ambiguity pertaining to what constitutes a shared understanding, such as the ideational content of a norm and among whom specifically is it shared, also raises unique questions about when a particular norm is present in Congress or any given community and how specific actors come to understand a shared idea (Wiener 2004). This book has used survey research and interviews to attempt to measure who shares which norms, but it is not exhaustive of all norms and other measures or epistemologies may exist for identifying, defining, and understanding existing norms and who holds them.

Other considerations regarding constructivism are tied to questions of whether the constructivist approach is anti-rational. That is, if identities and interests are socially constructed, is there a discernable rationality to the manner in which actors behave? Bertucci, Hayes, and Johnson speak to this relationship between constructivism and rationalism: "Constructivism looks beyond the individual as an isolated monad with known and fixed preferences, from its perspective, the narrowly reductionist *homo economicus* of positivist IR [international relations theory]. Instead of taking the individual as given, constructivism moves away from rationality-based explanation and toward socially constructed understanding" (Bertucci, Hayes, and James 2018, 247).

On the one hand, a behavioral or causal approach to socially constituted norms is possible. That is, socially constructed interests may be pursed rationally and with strategic intent, as something such as the electoral imperative or adherence to the courtesy norm can be strategically achieved—the logic of appropriateness can be a rational, strategic endeavor (March and Olsen 1989). On the other hand, however, related to Bertucci, Hayes, and James's meaning, the constructivist argument indicates that it is not exclusively the case that actors behave according to materially determined interests such as is assumed in rational choice approaches to the study of Congress. They can act simply on the basis of an idea. When we remove ends-means calculus from behavior, the importance of a norm in a particular social context may be more difficult to discern. Further consideration is necessary on what is the role of ideas or senses of appropriateness that do not seem to have consequentialist behavioral corollaries.

As has been argued in this book, when we witness adherence to the courtesy norm, or nonconformity, or sexual propriety it may be that we can identify a strategic rationale for an actor or group of actors in following such norms. But this is not necessarily the case—a norm may be a preference in its own right, part of a shared sense of what is appropriate among a community, irrespective of consequentialist outcomes that norm provides the actors that hold it. Adhering to particular norms can occur irrespective of the material or strategic outcomes they yield. For instance, when the norms of sexual propriety shifted radically in 2015, it was not exclusively because of a shift in ideological or strategic contexts—rather, the idea of what people understood to be appropriate changed, and therefore norms changed. By opening congressional studies to constructivism scholars can engage this rich and interdisciplinary dialogue on the constructivist approach. As I hope the present work has shown—and as has undoubtedly been demonstrated in the field of international relations theory—this is an intellectually productive and meaningful discourse, which promises to offer many insights regarding Congress and its members and the role of the institution in American political life.

There also exist questions about the relationship between behavior and ideas or norms—what is the content of the idea that is supposedly reflected in certain patterns of behavior? This phenomenological conundrum raises directly relevant questions about whether the supposedly normative behavior we witness in one period is rooted in the same ideational content as that witnessed in a previous era. For example, as presented in chapter 4, the apprenticeship norm seems to be experiencing something of a resurgence if we look at the waiting period for giving maiden speeches, wherein waiting periods are at near parity in the 2010s as they were in the 1950s, the heyday of Donald Matthews's apprenticeship norm. It warrants questioning whether the sense of the apprenticeship norm or the significance of the maiden speech hold the same meanings in the twenty-first century as they did in the middle of the twentieth century. Rather than resolving such questions once and for all, a social theory of Congress calls on researchers to examine the ideational content of behavior, to better understand what the actors and participants in Congress think, to understand something of the broader culture of the congressional environment, in order to better understand the manner in which ideas, ideology, and culture affect the behavior of members and the policy outputs of the institution. In other words, a social theory of Congress calls for an ethnographic approach, even a genealogical approach (Foucault 1972), to the institution. Much theoretically untapped, fruitful, and provoking work could follow from such a way of understanding Congress and its members.

FUTURE DIRECTIONS

Beyond such theoretical issues in constructivist research, and the various epistemological and methodological questions they also entail, there are specific questions regarding norms in the U.S. Congress that warrant additional consideration. At the most basic level, attention could be focused on additional norms that may be present in the modern Congress. While the present study offers empirically grounded claims about preponderant norms operative in today's Congress, it is not claimed that it is exhaustive of the full universe of those norms. The manner by which norms were identified was rooted in previous scholarship, journalistic accounts, interviews, and in participant observation limited to the researcher's personal experience of Congress, particularly of the 2000s. Additional norms could no doubt be identified. See Appendices IV and V, respectively, for the manner in which past research has attempted to identify norms and the universe of legislative norms uncovered by these approaches.

The research presented in this book classifies norms according to the underlying assumptions on the sense of appropriateness they embody—cooperation, conflict, and cultural values—but perhaps there are other viable distinctions or classifications that can be made. Other scholars, although not writing from a constructivist perspective, point to different typologies of norms that group them based on different functions they serve in the society (Ostrom 2000) or particular institutions (Helmke and Livitsky 2004). A constructivist approach requires that norms reflect a shared sense of appropriateness or the identities of, in this case, lawmakers; the groupings identified here are not necessarily (nor intended to be) exhaustive.

The research presented in this book is also intended to make possible future study of changes in congressional norms. The survey in chapter 3 and the overview of interview and survey work of previous scholars provided in the Appendices provide baselines for future scholarship on the nature of congressional norms. Future studies can compare survey and questionnaire responses to the present to seek out new answer to how changing political, partisan, or other factors may shift support for or presence of particular norms. Questions could be later explored whether changing ideological or political contexts in the United States be mirrored in the norms that members adhere to. If the erosion of existing norms or the emergence of new ones occurs, it would provide insights into how norms change and why some norms are more prevalent at given times than at others.

Better understanding of the institutional, policy, or political effects of constitutive norms would be achieved by additional research that develops empirical cases in which norms of cooperation or conflict are operationalized as causal, independent variables that can be correlated with behavioral outcomes measured by dependent variables. If such norms do matter in the functioning of Congress or the behavior of its members, effective causal arguments would help better articulate the overall role that norms play in the institution and its policy outputs. This book offers a strong start, I hope, but much good work remains ahead.

More research is also necessary on the origins of congressional norms. Specifically, what drives the emergence of norms of cooperation or conflict or the emergence of cultural norms within the institution? In current congressional studies, a characteristic approach to such questions would be to seek correlations between the presence of a particular norm and some other given known interest or driver of behavior, such as ideological or electoral constraints. In such cases, the norm-breaking behavior of a Newt Gingrich or an Alexandria Ocasio Cortez could be measured in ideological terms, with normative attitudes a by-product of some other ideological or strategic agenda. A social theory requires a different approach, however. The expectation of a constructivist approach to Congress would be that standard determinants like ideology scores or electoral pressures would be insufficient and perhaps even unnecessary to predict or yield particular normative beliefs. Moreover, not all ideas become norms, so more research on how an idea propagates into a shared understanding among congressional actors opens additional avenues for future research.

In the constitutive sense, treating norms as shared understandings of what is appropriate or as part of members' identities allows that norms emerge as ideas irrespective of other material or institutional constraints or imperatives. This begs further questions as to whether specific conditions or requirements enable or facilitate the dispersion of a shared idea across a particular community—the Congress as a whole or particular subgroups within it. Certainly, the development of social media, for example, has changed the nature of the ideational content among the community of lawmakers and possibly even expanded who we should include among that community as lawmakers are connected in real-time to people on and off the Hill.

Norms also change, evolve, and are discarded altogether. What nonmaterial factors contribute to the erosion of a norm? Rohde, Ornstein, and Peabody (1985) and Judd Choate (2003) considered how changing ideological dispositions and shifting rules regarding the organization of Congress could yield different norms. Certainly, institutional or electoral imperatives could contribute to the manner in which particular ideas are propagated and shared or not. In some cases, perhaps there is an ecology to norm stability, wherein if enough material factors are present a norm is relatively stable within a community, but if they change, a particular norm is no longer viable among the social community. Wolfensberger, for instance, suggests, "Only a dominant majority will find the magnanimity to be fair and decent to the minority" (Wolfensberger 2007). This ecology, in the constitutive sense, is not consequentially driven as in the game theoretic or rational choice models of norm adherence (Weingast 1979; Sinclair 1989), but rather driven by a community of people who share an idea. Normative change can be explored by considering conditions by which a norm is accepted or not (Sandholtz 2008). For example, there is little evidence today of the norm of institutional patriotism, first identified in the Congress of the late 1950s (Matthews 1960). Perhaps in the context of a polarized and partisan Congress where members frequently run against an institution wildly unpopular with the public, there is little place for the shared sense that the Senate (much less the House) is the world's greatest deliberative body. This warrants further consideration.

In other cases, perhaps new ideas take hold among members, rendering new norms possible and old norms untenable. The combative partisanship of Newt Gingrich in the 1990s or the sudden shift in sexual mores in the wake of #metoo in 2017 were ideas that became widely accepted on Capitol Hill and with relative rapidity took on the status of norms, among their other various attributes and effects. It would be missing an opportunity for a richer understanding of Congress to consider such phenomena as merely the outcomes of ideological or electoral strategies. Such evolution suggests that there are general or particular interrelations between the ideational—or particular norms—and the material—or particular material conditions, which warrant further consideration. A social theory of Congress allows us to consider how ideas take hold to shift identities and shared understandings of what is appropriate, with profound effect beyond what behavioralist models alone might detect.

One answer for how norms emerge or evolve is that Congress embodies the norms of society. Partisanship is an example. As many Americans seem inclined to align with one party or the other, so too in the Congress. A long-serving House administrative staffer spoke to it like this: "Partisanship just seems so baked into society nowadays. You see it in the way the media covers Congress, the way members go to the media and the way people go to the media in to smaller and smaller more fragmented news sources—they go to Fox or to CNN depending on their viewpoints. It's a self-reinforcing thing. You see it in members not socializing or talking to each other. Increasingly members are elected by people who have partisan worldviews. Members are partisan because it's a reflection of the narrow slice of America that elects them" (Interview 2016). Similarly, the rapid evolution of sexual propriety as a norm in the #metoo era, which including passing new rules to represent new values in the 115th Congress, is evidence of how cultural norms are reflected in Congress. The #metoo case also suggests that norms can change slowly, then all at once.

One often hears of the "tribalism" of the growing partisanship in the United States (Packer 2018). In addition to the tangle of the various structural sources of partisan polarization in American politics such as gerrymandering, money in politics, partisan media, geographic sorting, and so on (Thurber and Yoshinaka 2015), there is a sense that Americans are increasingly aligned around core beliefs irrespective of demographic, ideological, or partisan predispositions (Hawkins et al. 2018). It is no surprise, therefore, that such attitudes are permeating the Hill. Much as sexual propriety is reflected in norms and became manifested in the rules of Congress, the institution of Congress as a democratically elected body reflects the society of which it is a part. If "tribalism"—a slightly racist term (Leary 2020), incidentally, which ought to be retired—is afflicting Congress, it warrants greater focus on Congress as a cultural organization of which norms are a key part.

NORMS AND THE IDEALISM OF AMERICAN POLITICS

Norms are a gateway to a greater discussion of the roles of ideas in the behavior of members of Congress. To bring norms back into the discussion of Congress is to steer that discussion into the ideas that motivate interests and the ideals that motivate political action. Behavioralist models look at lawmaker behavior as the economic output of rational choices based on ideological preferences, but frequently do not examine what is the composition of that ideology in the first place. Poole and Rosenthal, for instance, in *Ideology & Congress* (2007), ground their model of congressional behavior on liberal and conservative ideology with very little discussion of the ideas (much less the philosophical richness) of liberalism or conservativism as commonly understood in most conversations of politics or political theory. Behavioralist models of Congress that use ideology scores to find causal patterns in behavior, therefore, are based a concept of ideology that is curiously deficient in ideas.

Such models are, of course, not being dismissed—they are richly descriptive and even predictive of much of the behavior in Congress and American politics more broadly. But such economic models do not speak to the ideas and passions that motivate political actors, that determine their preferences, and that inform how they know what they want in the first place. What actors want is not determined by abstract and quantitatively generalized notions of ideology, nor is it necessarily determined by institutional or material conditions of behavior. To study norms in Congress is to begin to bridge this gap. Actors know what they want based on ideas and norms. A social theory of Congress does not replace or supplant behavioralism; it enriches by bringing into the discussion that thing that makes politics not economics, but human.

While the institutional and electoral barriers that drive partisan polarization in the U.S. Congress seem stubbornly unalterable, if ideas serve to shape preferences, then the existence of norms of cooperation and conflict suggest the promise—or the peril—for norms to affect the direction of American politics. If we recognize an ideational component of both conflict and cooperation, then changes in congressional norms offer either hope for overcoming gridlock or the possibility of furthering its entrenchment. By examining the role of norms in legislative behavior, we expand the scope of what we understand congressional behavior to include. We can look beyond patterns of behavior and institutional imperatives, and toward the beliefs that drive such behavior and how these beliefs are constitutive of the interests that underlie the decisions and behaviors of members of Congress individually and of the institution as a whole.

Institutions, power struggles, reelection, and ideological competition are endemic to the decision-making and behavior of lawmakers. But if ideas matter too, such as in forming the basis of preferences and identities, as argued here, then further consideration of the origins and qualities of those ideas is an important and under-examined area of congressional studies. Returning to the observation of Sarah Binder, if "history and norms become embedded into institutions and then come to shape lawmakers' preferences and priorities" (Binder 2015, 7), then a social theory of Congress helps us to better understand the role of ideas in determining the preferences of lawmakers and the performance of the institution. It is time to bring norms back into the study of Congress.

Appendix I

Methodological Note

The research methodology I have used in capturing contemporary norms of the U.S. Congress is derived from previous research approaches and intended to be repeatable, as much as is possible, in order to provide a basis of comparison upon which future scholars can build. My approach combined direct observation, semistructured interviews, and an anonymous survey. Direct observation was made most possible during my time as a 2015–2016 American Political Science Association Congressional Fellow, where I worked in the office of U.S. Senator Jack Reed (D-Rhode Island). The fellowship provided an incomparable opportunity to view Congress as both a congressional staff member and a scholar, as it entails work responsibilities on par with any staffer and unique learning gained through participant observation. This experience capped other career experience in Washington, DC, relating to Congress in which I worked on government relations and political campaigns, all of which served to influence my impressions and knowledge of the role of congressional norms and their changing character.

Beginning with my PhD dissertation research in 2014, I began incorporating questions on norms in interviews with congressional actors in Washington. These early musings were focused in 2016 when I used my time on Capitol Hill to undertake an interview-based research program on congressional norms. The interview protocol, provided in Appendix II, was carefully crafted to include, wherever reasonable, identically or closely worded questions of previous scholars, while adding new content pertinent to my own theoretical suppositions. Interviews themselves were of a "semistructured" nature, wherein I attempted to closely follow the interview protocol, but would inevitably vary based on the ebbs and flows of conversation or topics that arose.

Previous scholarship that has utilized interviews, questionnaires, or survey research leaves as an instructive but imperfect record upon which to build. Among the studies for which survey or interview questions are available, the closest to a repeated longitudinal question is from Wahlke et al. (1962), when they asked, "We've been told that every legislature has its *unofficial* rules of the game—certain things members must do and things they must not do if they want the respect and cooperation of fellow members . . . What are some of these things—these 'rules of the game'—that a member must observe to hold the respect and cooperation of his fellow members?" (Wahlke et al. 1962, Appendix 6, 495). Variations on this question were used by Hebert and McLemore (1973), and Asher points to it as informing his study (Asher 1973, 500 fn. 6). Other researchers asked open-ended questions to elicit responses, probed on norms previously identified in other research, especially those of Matthews, or inquired about particular norms or the functioning of norms based on the theoretical interests of the researcher (e.g., Asher 1973; Loomis and Fishel 1981; Choate 2003). A full listing of previously asked interview and survey questions is provided in Appendix IV.

Interviews took place in 2016 through 2019, mostly in the beginning and ending of that period, either in-person at offices in Washington, DC, or in conversations over the phone, based on cold calls or other direct means of outreach. The anonymity of respondents is guaranteed to protect identities and to facilitate candor. Respondents were chosen for their ongoing engagement on Capitol Hill as either current or former members or staff. New interviewees were often identified through the "snowball method," wherein at the end of each interview I tried to include the final question, "Is there anybody else you think I should talk to?" This elicited numerous new contacts about whom I might not have been aware or not thought of contacting. Interviews were scheduled for "about 40 minutes," but depending on the respondent lasted as long as two hours, to just a few minutes in the case of some very busy staff and members. Interviewees were promised anonymity, and conversations were audio recorded whenever possible. A total of fifty-six interviews were recorded and transcribed and notes were taken in a dozen other cases where recording was not possible.

There is no perfect number for how many interviews to conduct, but I began to feel confident in the sample when the general tenor of the congressional norms discussed began to repeat or show clear patterns. The efforts of previous scholars on the topic have ranged in the size of their sample. Rohde, Ornstein, and Peabody (1985) conducted fifty-two member interviews at the time of the 93rd Congress, while Choate (2003) interviewed twenty-three House members in the 104th. Matthews's (1960) seminal work on the subject included interviews with fewer than three-dozen members chosen in part based upon "rapport." Where interviews, by their nature, fail to produce discreet variables and, in any case, the size of the interview sample is too small for statistical generalizations, the effort at being systematic was supplemented by the development and implementation of an anonymous survey. Within the interviews, however, are unlimited nuggets of wisdom and interesting stories out there, and much more that I hope to do with the rich data gathered in this process. I am most heartened by the generosity of all the people who enthusiastically took part in this process.

Survey research was conducted over the period May–September 2019 and is further explained in chapter 3 (see footnote 2). As with the semistructured interviews, the anonymity of survey respondents is guaranteed. The survey questionnaire was developed, like the interview protocol, with an eye toward replicating questions on legislative norms that were previously not only asked by other scholars but also tailored to account for the theoretical and research agenda of this project. The nature of the questions included in the survey was also shaped by information gathered during the semistructured interview process, informed by particular ideas or concepts that seemed worthy of focus our attention.

It is challenging to draw direct comparisons among the findings of among the various works on norms—a problem the present work addresses by attempting a degree of replicability that enables methodologically systematic, longitudinal efforts on congressional norms by future scholars. Yet, self-reporting of vested respondents may be vulnerable to several criticisms. A phenomenological problem presents itself when comparing the discrete norms observed in one study with those of another. When relying upon the observations and experiences reported subjects in the field, particularly on qualitative or subjective notions such as "courtesy" or measures of appropriateness, one cannot be certain that they align with the same understandings that others may hold of those concepts. Asking respondents about norms may lead respondents into believing norms exist or matter (Eulau 1995), or phenomenologically no two respondents may be speaking to the same meanings, even if they use the same terms. It is also possible that norms may be so much part of the fabric of lawmaker behavior that they may be unaware when behavior is normative. Finally, such questions may not adequately elicit the role norms play in the behavior of individuals or the functioning of the institution as a whole, as such concerns may be of greater interest to the scholar than the practitioner. Respondents cannot be relied upon to provide adequate direct evidence on the existence, function, or consequences of norms. As Huitt wrote in 1957, "The norms that are not explicit, the 'oughts' that are shared by Senators because they are members of the 'club,' are another matter; perhaps only those members who are in the process of acquiring them understand them at the self-conscious level. They offer quite difficult problems to the non-member student" (Huitt 1957, 314). Open-ended questions, multiple observations, careful survey design, and representative survey samples help to mitigate such problems. The issues become more acute when trying to compare results across time and in the varying contexts of different research projects.

Against this theoretical and methodological backdrop, the survey questionnaire, reproduced in full in Appendix III, is proposed to help meet the needs of historical, longitudinal, and contemporary surveys of norms in the modern Congress.

Appendix II

Legislative Norms Semistructured Interview Protocol

This interview asks question about the role that norms play in Congress. Norms, sometimes known as "rules of the game" or "unwritten rules," are beliefs lawmakers and staff have about what is acceptable or appropriate behavior in the U.S. Congress. The purpose of this research is to help political scientists and congressional scholars better understand the functioning of the institution and the role that norms may or may not play in it.

Your responses are *completely anonymous*. Responses to questions cannot be traced back to the respondent. No personally identifiable information will be reported. Additionally, your responses are combined with those of many others and summarized in a report to further protect your anonymity. Please answer the series of questions openly and candidly.

1. We've been told that every legislature has its unofficial rules of the game—certain things they must do and things they must do if they want the respect and cooperation of fellow members. What are some of these things—these "rules of the game"—that a member must observe to hold the respect and cooperation of his [or her] fellow members? [*Please list or describe as many that come to mind.*]

2. Some members don't seem to have the respect and cooperation of their fellow members because they don't follow the "rules of the game." What are some of the things that may cause a member to lose the respect and cooperation of his fellow members?

3. How do the other members make things difficult for these people when they don't follow the "rules of the game"?

4. It has been said that the [House/Senate] is the greatest legislative and deliberative body in the world. Overall, how much do you agree or disagree with this sentiment.

5. In your estimation, are there norms that are MORE important today than they were when you entered the House/Senate (in years past)? If yes, please list or describe them.

6. Are there norms that are LESS important today than they were when you entered the House/Senate (in years past)? If yes, please list or describe them.

7. Final Question, [Optional. Asked only after all others have been covered]: Partisanship, so prevalent in today's Congress, is viewed by political scientists as largely ideological or strategic—members jockey for policy outcomes, reelection, or power in Congress and therefore see it as strategically logical to behave in partisan ways. But is partisanship also a norm, that is an informal rule that members are expected to adhere to? Please elaborate on your answer.

NOTE: Other information was gathered at the time of the interview and is noted in the interview transcription. This information includes data such as the year the individual first began working on Capitol Hill, whether as member or staff, plus demographic characteristics such as gender, state of origin, age, party, role in Congress (member, staff, chamber), and political affiliation.

Appendix III

Anonymous Survey on Congressional Norms, 2019

The following anonymous survey questionnaire was delivered to current and former House and Senate members and staff in both a paper mail-in format with an accompanying self-addressed stamped envelope and an electronic online survey tool, during the period May through November 2019. The text of the survey is reproduced, verbatim, below.

ANONYMOUS SOCIAL SCIENCE SURVEY ON CONGRESSIONAL NORMS

This anonymous social scientific survey is being conducted by Brian Alexander, PhD, assistant professor of politics at Washington and Lee University. The survey explores the culture of Congress by asking current and former members and staff, as well as other professionals whose work focuses on Congress, about the role that norms play in the U.S. Congress. Norms, sometimes known as "unwritten rules" or informal "rules of the game," are beliefs lawmakers and staff have about what is acceptable or appropriate behavior in the U.S. Congress.

Your confidential input will help political scientists and congressional scholars better understand how Congress functions. The survey should take no more than ten minutes. *Your answers are anonymous and confidential. No information derived from this research will personally identify you and your identity will not be disclosed.* Members' names or offices will not be associated with this information, nor that of any of the staff or other respondents. This survey is voluntary and you can stop participating at any time. Thank you in advance for your help. If you have questions or would like to talk about this research, please contact Brian Alexander at alexanderb@wlu.edu.

List of Statements

Please read the following series of statements about the appropriateness of certain behaviors by members in the House/Senate of TODAY and rate each of them on a scale of 1 to 5. In this case, a one (1) would denote something which is *highly inappropriate* while a five (5) would denote a *highly appropriate* type of activity and a three (3) neither appropriate nor inappropriate. In other words, the higher the number the more appropriate the behavior. Respond based on what *you think* is appropriate or not.

a. Serving an apprenticeship period—that is being more of an observer than a participant when you first enter the legislature.

Highly Inappropriate		*Neither Appropriate nor Inappropriate*	*Highly Appropriate*	
1	2	3	4	5

b. Learning the House or Senate procedural rules.

Highly Inappropriate		*Neither Appropriate nor Inappropriate*	*Highly Appropriate*	
1	2	3	4	5

c. *Senate Only*: Supporting cloture even when one opposes a bill.

Highly Inappropriate		*Neither Appropriate nor Inappropriate*	*Highly Appropriate*	
1	2	3	4	5

d. *House Only*: Requiring the support of a majority of the majority party for legislation to advance (i.e., the "Hastert rule").

Highly Inappropriate		*Neither Appropriate nor Inappropriate*	*Highly Appropriate*	
1	2	3	4	5

e. Specializing in a field or policy area as compared to being a generalist.

Highly Inappropriate		*Neither Appropriate nor Inappropriate*	*Highly Appropriate*	
1	2	3	4	5

f. Never personally criticize a fellow Member on the floor of the chamber.

| Highly Inappropriate | | Neither Appropriate nor Inappropriate | Highly Appropriate | |
| 1 | 2 | 3 | 4 | 5 |

g. Maintaining friendly relationships with members of your own party.

| Highly Inappropriate | | Neither Appropriate nor Inappropriate | Highly Appropriate | |
| 1 | 2 | 3 | 4 | 5 |

h. Voting in a certain way on a bill that you cared little about in order to gain the vote of a fellow member on a bill that you did care about.

| Highly Inappropriate | | Neither Appropriate nor Inappropriate | Highly Appropriate | |
| 1 | 2 | 3 | 4 | 5 |

i. Raising money on behalf of fellow party members.

| Highly Inappropriate | | Neither Appropriate nor Inappropriate | Highly Appropriate | |
| 1 | 2 | 3 | 4 | 5 |

j. Meeting with interest groups or lobbyists representing multiple sides of an issue.

| Highly Inappropriate | | Neither Appropriate nor Inappropriate | Highly Appropriate | |
| 1 | 2 | 3 | 4 | 5 |

k. Voting with the opposition party.

| Highly Inappropriate | | Neither Appropriate nor Inappropriate | Highly Appropriate | |
| 1 | 2 | 3 | 4 | 5 |

l. Reaching bipartisan compromise in order to pass legislation.

Highly Inappropriate		*Neither Appropriate nor Inappropriate*	*Highly Appropriate*	
1	2	3	4	5

m. Maintaining friendly relations with members of the opposing party.

Highly Inappropriate		*Neither Appropriate nor Inappropriate*	*Highly Appropriate*	
1	2	3	4	5

Norms of Today

What are some of the norms—the "unwritten rules" or informal "rules of the game"—of today's Congress? Consider types of behavior that are acceptable or those that are not acceptable in the behavior of members and the functioning of the chamber. Please list or describe as many examples that come to mind in the space below.

{Open ended}

Changing Norms

Are there norms that have changed since you started working on the Hill or in your career pertaining to Congress?

{Open ended}

Demographic Information

If you ever worked or served on the Hill, please indicate your current or most recent position:

U.S. Senator
U.S. Representative
Senate Staff—Committee
Senate Staff—Personal Office
House Staff—Committee
House Staff—Personal Office
Congressional Support Organization (e.g., CRS; House or Senate Library)
Never worked as a member or staff

If you do not currently work as a member or staff, what is your current profession?

I am a current member or staff.
Federal Government (e.g., Executive Branch; Federal Agency)
State/Local Government
Private Sector
Nonprofit
Journalism
Academic/Think Tank
Other

What is your political party?

Republican
Democrat
Independent

In what YEAR did you first start working on Capitol Hill as either a member, staff, or in some other professional capacity (e.g., journalism, government relations, think tank)?

{Open ended}

IF you worked on Capitol Hill but NO LONGER work there, in what year did you leave? (Leave blank if you were never a member or staff.)

{Open ended}

What is your gender?

Male
Female
Other/Prefer Not to Answer

What is your age?

18-29
30–44
45–59
60 and over

You are finished! Thank you so much for your time. Your anonymous input is a key part of this research which will contribute to our scholarly understanding of the U.S. Congress.

If you would like to provide additional information via e-mail or phone or if you have any questions please do not hesitate to contact me.

Appendix IV

Question Bank on Legislative Norms from Previous Scholarship

Since the 1950s scholars have been asking questions about legislative norms in surveys and interviews. While some of these questions are lost to posterity or the format of their inquiry was more open-ended than structured or formal (e.g., Matthews 1959, 1960; Fenno 1962, 1966), other scholars utilized semistructured or formalized questionnaires and survey design to elicit and capture responses. In yet other cases, significant works on legislative norms did not employ surveys or interview-based research methods (e.g., Weingast 1979; Rohde 1988). This Appendix, organized chronologically, catalogs various known formal survey questions asked regarding legislative norms. An effort has been made to be exhaustive, or at least to capture the known questions of the major works on legislative norms. Instruments of some researchers were unavailable for inclusion because they were not included in the published works and efforts to obtain the research questions from the original authors were not possible or not successful. Only those works for which questions could be identified are listed.

WAHLKE, EULAU, BUCHANON, AND FERGUSON (1962, APPENDIX 6, P. 495)

The authors provide the interview schedule and instructions to interviewers in Appendix 6 of their *The Legislative System: Explorations in Legislative Behavior*. Their survey covered a purpose much broader than just legislative norms, although their work includes specific questions on group norms, which they used to develop one of the most substantial early empirical studies in chapter 7, "Rules of the Game." The specific questions on norms included in the survey, are the following:

11. We've been told that every legislature has its *unofficial* rules of the game—certain things members must do and things they must not do if they want the respect and cooperation of fellow members.

    a. What are some of these things—these "rules of the game"—that a member must observe to hold the respect and cooperation of his fellow members?

    b. Would you name four of five of your fellow members, regardless of party or position, who are most widely respected for following these "rules of the game"—I mean people that a new member should look up to when he's just learning the ropes?

    c. Some members don't seem to have the respect and cooperation of their fellow members because they don't follow the "rules of the game." What are some of the things that may cause a member to lose the respect and cooperation of his fellow members?

    d. How do the other members make things difficult for these people when they don't follow the "rules of the game"?

(11)(a) Here we are trying to discover some of the *informal* group norms of the legislature. If R says it is just like any other group situation, probe to find out what kind of behavior he has in mind. Also, probe to determine whether there is any special kind of behavior required in the legislative group.

    (b) Here we are seeking to identify those regarded as conformers and perpetuators of group norms. Emphasis should be placed on being respected *for* following the rules of the game, rather than just being generally respected.

    (c) This is designed to supplement 11a by asking for *proscribed* behavior. Pretesting indicated that R may mention names if probed for examples of "deviant" behavior. Record names if voluntarily given.

    (d) Here we want to discover the sanctions used to enforce the group norms of the legislative body. This may be either individual or group action.

ASHER (1973)

Asher's main purpose was to understand the socialization process that new members of Congress underwent to learn legislative norms. Because this "learning is a longitudinal concern, a two-wave panel design was employed, the first set of interviews conducted in late January and February of 1969, and the second set the following May . . . Of the 37 freshmen in the 91st Congress,

30 were interviewed at t_1 (late January and February) and of these 30, 24 were interviewed at t_2." (Asher 1973, 500).

Asher used a "focused interview approach" to collect information about specific norms. "The main norms investigated were specialization, reciprocity, legislative work, courtesy, and aspects of apprenticeship including learning the House rules, restrained participation, and attendance on the floor and in committee" (Asher 1973, 500–501). However, Asher was concerned that "one cannot simply ask the representative whether a norm of reciprocity exists in the House, for such a label may be without meaning to the legislator" (Asher 1973, 501). Therefore, he developed questions that identified the behavior meant by a particular norm to operationalize its meaning, such as to "attach some behavioral tag to reciprocity" (Ibid.) "The general point to be made here is that questions seeking to uncover information about norms are best framed within a fairly specific behavioral situation. If we cannot observe behavior directly (and most often we cannot), then our questions should be as behaviorally oriented as possible" (Ibid.).

Asher's survey instrument utilized the following question for each of the norms he studied. The corresponding norm is *italicized* for illustrative purposes, although not referenced on the original survey (Asher 1973, 501, fn. 8):

- *Specialization*: Do you think congressmen should specialize in a field or should try to be generalists?
- *Legislative work*: Do you think most of the important work of the House is done on the floor or in committees?
- *Courtesy*: How important do you think it is to maintain friendly relationships with your fellow congressmen?
- *Apprenticeship/Restrained Participation*: Do you think that freshman congressmen should serve a period of apprenticeship, that is, be more an observer than an active participant in the legislative process?
- *Apprenticeship/Learning of House Rules*: How important do you think learning the House procedural rules is?
- *Courtesy*: Would you ever personally criticize a fellow representative on the floor of the House?
- *Reciprocity*: Would you vote in a certain way on a bill that you cared little about in order to gain the vote of a fellow congressman on a bill that you did care about?

Asher also asked a question about institutional patriotism, regarding whether they would ever criticize the House, but he did not include it in his analysis because he concluded "institutional patriotism is far more complex than merely refraining from criticism" (Ibid.).

HEBERT AND MCLEMORE (1973)

Hebert and McLemore (1973) collected data through structured interviews of 181 of 185 members of the Iowa General Assembly, 123 of 124 House members and 58 of 61 Senators during the 1967 session. The first question, inviting an open-ended response, was similar to that of Wahlke et al. (1962):

• We've been told by other members of this legislature that there are some informal, unofficial rules governing a member's conduct IN THIS LEGIS-LATURE. Things that a member is expected to do or not to do in order to get along with the other members of this body. You may call them a code of behavior, if you wish. What, from your point of view, are some of the more important of these rules? (Hebert and McLemore 1973, 512–513).

Hebert and McLemore also included in their survey "a series of fixed-choice items designed to provide additional information regarding selected hypothesized norms" (Ibid., 513). These hypothesized norms were based on "aspects of legislative life which are likely to be the subject of norms in a state legislative body" based on literature on legislative behavior and previous research on norms such as Wahlke et al. (Ibid.). Using the responses, the authors identified items as "norms" if they met the criteria of being widely accepted: "statistical commonality must be evident on any given expectation if it is to be regarded as a norm," indicated here as in their table 2 with a double-asterisk** (Ibid., 515; see pp. 515–518 for tables and statistical criteria). The fixed-choice survey question is the following:

• Now I'd like to read you a series of statements about the operation of the (House or Senate) here in Iowa. Would you rate each of them as I read them using [a] one to 10 scale . . . In this case, a one (1) would denote something which is HIGHLY UNDESIREABLE while a 10 would denote a HIGHLY DESIRABLE TYPE OF ACTIVITY. Thus, the higher the number the more desirable you think this type of behavior is (Hebert and McLemore 1973, 513).
    1. Dealing in personalities in debate or other remarks made on the floor of the chamber.**
    2. Talking on subjects coming before the legislature with which you are not completely informed.**
    3. Talking about decisions which have been reached in private to the press or anyone else.**
    4. Concealing the real purpose(s) of a bill or purposely overlooking some portion of it in order to assure its passage.**

5. Introducing as many bills and amendments as possible during any legislative session.**
6. Giving first priority to your re-election in all of your actions as a legislator.**
7. Seeking as much publicity as possible from the press in order to look good for the people back home.**
8. Being a thorn to the majority by refusing unanimous consent among others.**
9. Being known among other legislators as a "loner" and not having much to do with them outside of the chamber.**
10. Being generally known as a spokesman for some special interest group.**
11. Avoid taking any kind of a stand on legislation before the roll-call.
12. Campaigning against an incumbent legislator in his own district.
13. Voting with the opposition party.
14. Being entertained by a lobbyist.
15. Standing by your commitments even though you may have had a change of heart.
16. Supporting the governor and/or the party leaders by not embarrassing their programs or wishes in the legislature.
17. Serving an apprenticeship period when you first enter the legislature.
18. Following the decisions of your party particularly when they were made in a caucus.
19. Respecting a committee's power over any bill until it has VOLUNTARILY relinquished control over that legislation.

LOOMIS AND FISHEL (1981)

Loomis and Fishel (1981) conducted a survey of members using questions of previous studies (e.g., Asher 1973; Fishel 1973) with some modification. Their data were derived from "questionnaires returned from forty-five of the seventy members of the class of 1974. Follow-up interviews were held with twenty-five of those who returned the questionnaire" (Loomis and Fishel 1981, 83). They focused on incoming members, so their sample "were moderately liberal, relatively young, and disproportionally from New York, California, Indiana, and Iowa, states where substantial electoral gains were made in 1974" (Ibid.). They achieved a high response rate in part because "we did not mail these questionnaires, but rather took them to each office, discussed their contents individually with administrative assistants and members, and made repeated call-backs to the offices to collect them" (Ibid., fn. 6).

The Loomis and Fishel questionnaire is not reproduced in their study but a copy of the questionnaire sent out and completed in the summer of 1976 was provided to the author by Burdett Loomis. The question addressing legislative norms is reproduced below (Loomis, e-mail to author, 3 January 2019).

27. Much has been written about the changing character of informal norms (or "folkways") in the House. Some members feel extensive change has occurred: others feel that informal norms in the House, despite reform, have remained pretty much the same. From your point of view, how important to a member's long-term success and effectiveness are the following:

	Very Important	Somewhat Important	Not Important	Can't Estimate
a. Subject-matter expertise	_____	_____	_____	_____
b. Legislative specialization	_____	_____	_____	_____
c. Seniority (other than chairman selection)	_____	_____	_____	_____
d. Legislative apprenticeship	_____	_____	_____	_____
e. Ability to compromise	_____	_____	_____	_____
f. Personal cordiality and lack of abrasiveness	_____	_____	_____	_____

Loomis and Fishel note that they based their questions from Asher (1973), with some variation on the question regarding seniority (see Loomis and Fishel 1981, 85 fn. 9). To this they added "a follow-up question asking members to identify those norms that were 'most' and 'least' important" (Loomis and Fishel 1981, Table 1, fn. A).

ROHDE, ORNSTEIN, AND PEABODY (1985)

Rohde, Ornstein, and Peabody's (1985) data gathering approach was semistructured interviews with "a prepared list of open-ended questions." Interviews were conducted beginning May of 1973, with a goal of interviewing all senators; and at the time of publication they "completed 52 interviews, 44 with senators who were serving in the 93rd Congress and 8 with senators who served previously" (Ibid., 147, Author's Note).

This author corresponded with Rohde and Ornstein in 2019 and was generously provided typed transcripts of interviews conducted in the summer of 1973, although the original list of open-ended questions was not available. David Rohde indicated that most often the interviews were conducted one-on-one between one member of the research team and the interview subject, although in some cases they were conducted with two interviewers. A preponderance of the interviews were tape recorded and written transcripts of the conversations then made. The wording of prepared questions varied slightly and other questions or comments emerged based on the natural tenor and flow of the conversation on a range of topics pertinent to the researchers' interests. Several questions that repeat across interviews, with slight variation, can be identified that pertain to Senate norms:

- "One of the things that's very interesting about the office—a number of people have written about the Senate that over time it has built up expectations of its members, how they should behave, certain norms that are formally an informally communicated, particularly informally—do you think there's anything to that?" (Rohde, Ornstein, and Peabody, unpublished transcript, July 9, 1973).
- "If a new Senator were to come to you, someone who had just been elected and asked for your advice about how to get ahead in the Senate, how [to] gain the respect of his colleagues, what do you think you would tell him?" (Rohde, Ornstein, and Peabody, unpublished transcript, June 15, 1973).
- "There are some Senators who don't follow those kinds of guidelines—who don't work very hard and who are only out to grab headlines. Is there any way or is anything done to sort of indicate the displeasures of their colleagues at that kind of performance, I mean, are they reprimanded in any way?" (Rohde, Ornstein, and Peabody, unpublished transcript, June 15, 1973).
- "Did you find when you arrived here that and since that time that there is pressure on you to specialize to really dig into the areas within your committees? Or not as much as one might expect?" (Rohde, Ornstein, and Peabody, unpublished transcript, June 20, 1973).

CHOATE (2003)

Choate (2003) undertook semistructured interviews with twenty-three Representatives of the 104th House "of varying parties, region, age, seniority, and committee assignments" (Choate 2003, 28). His purpose was to examine House member attitudes toward the norms of seniority, specialization, and reciprocity (Ibid., 32). Choate's eight interview questions are provided in table 2.2 (Ibid., 33):

1. Generally speaking, what do you think about the learning process of a new member of Congress? Is it easy or difficult to learn the formal and informal rules of the institution?

2. Generally speaking, do you agree with the seniority system with regard to committee chairmanship selection?

3. Please discuss your feelings concerning the new rule limiting committee chairs to six years of continuous service. What members do you think this rule will benefit?

4. What about the five Southern Democrats that changed to the Republican Party? Do you think those members should regain their committee seniority?

5. Have you found it helpful to specialize in a specific policy area? If so, is this specialization based on your committee work?

6. Another norm commonly debated by congressional watchers is reciprocity. What are your feelings concerning the trading of votes?

7. In your estimation, are the three norms mentioned (seniority, specialization, and reciprocity) as important today as they were when you entered the House (in years past)?

8. Finally, if the Democratic Party regains the majority, do you anticipate that they will eliminate the six-year limit on committee chair tenure?

Appendix V

Historical Norms: Index of Legislative Norms Identified in Previous Scholarship

The so-called "canon" of legislative norms (Eulau 1995) emerged within a subset of research on norms over the decades in which the topic has been periodically studied. Not all primary work on legislative or congressional norms focused on norm identification or norm discovery. The universe of identified or presumed legislative norms that may be operative in the U.S. Congress (or other legislatures) is, in fact, quite finite. The index below captures the legislative norms identified in the major works on the topic since the 1950s. Not all work on legislative norms focused on the U.S. Congress, and some of the more groundbreaking studies are based on research in state legislatures. However, legislative norms operative at the federal level may be applicable at the state level, and vice versa, and many norms identified in one context are also observed in the other. The index may not capture all references to particular legislative norms in the congressional literature; rather it points to major research studies in which scholars made a concerted attempt to identify or discover norms or normative behavior. Fenno (1966), Mayhew (1974), or Polsby (2004), for example, speak of norms but such work was not written with the purpose of uncovering congressional norms or explaining particular dynamics of normative behavior; other omitted work, such as Sinclair (1988) or the thoughtful exchange between Schneier (1988) and Rohde (1988) focuses primarily on the dynamics of normative behavior without specific effort at norm discovery or identification.

HUITT (1957)

Huitt (1957) relied upon archival research, contending that "it should be possible to make valid, if crude, inferences about norms for behavior from the printed record which is available to everyone . . . Accordingly, [this] study was made . . . wholly from the printed record" (Huitt 1957, 315) to identify a norm of senatorial allegiance to party presidential candidates. However, the extent to which this norm is generalizable is doubtful given the limited cases Huitt examined and the changes over time of the parties' roles in the presidential nomination process.

MATTHEWS (1959; 1960)

Matthews (1959, 1960) set the course for the study of legislative norms by identifying six "folkways" of the United States Senate: apprenticeship, legislative work, specialization, courtesy, reciprocity, and institutional patriotism. His approach was a series of interviews in 1956 and 1958 with past or present members of the Senate, staff, lobbyists, and journalists. Matthews employed a "focused' type" interview: "No formal interview schedule was used, but standardized topics were raised in each interview as time allowed" (Matthews 1959, 1067 fn. 3). He attempted a rough cross-section of respondents, but favored rapport over a highly representative sample, arguing a greater pay-off given the exploratory nature of his study. Matthews norms provide the substance of much fruitful research in numerous subsequent studies, earning their place, in Eulau's term, as "canonical" in the subsequent literature on the topic.

FENNO (1962)

Fenno (1962) examines the role of norms in the functioning of the House Appropriation Committee, pointing to specialization, reciprocity, and subcommittee unity as means of facilitating integration and decision-making within subcommittees toward the functioning of the overall committee as a whole. Fenno identifies these norms and their functioning through close observation and interviews, applying them to his theory of committee systems, their organization and integration. Fenno relied upon semistructured interviews averaging forty-five minutes each, with forty-five of fifty Committee members in the eighty-sixth Congress, using a flexible interview protocol (Fenno 1962, 311 fn. 4). He does not identify the specific questions he asked.

WAHLKE, EULAU, BUCHANON, AND FERGUSON (1962)

Wahlke, Eulau, Buchanon, and Ferguson (1962) conducted a survey of 474 members of state legislatures in four states during the period January through

June 1957: California (N = 113), New Jersey (N = 79), Ohio (N = 162), and Tennessee (N = 120). A total of forty-two individual norms, or "rules of the game" were identified among respondent answers, which Wahlke ranked in order of frequency (1 to 42; see table 7.1, p. 146–147)) and grouped into seven categories according to function (table 7.6, p. 160–161). The seven categories of function (A-F) with their corresponding norms and the frequency of their appearance by rank (1–42), as listed in table 7.6 are listed below. Many of these forty-two norms repeat or are conceptually related to Matthews's folkways. For example, institutional patriotism, courtesy, and apprenticeship are directly identified and echoed elsewhere in their findings (e.g., courtesy reappears as "impersonality," which includes to not make personal attacks on other members (Ibid., table 7.6)). Legislative work, specialization, and reciprocity are not identified specifically among the forty-two rules of the game of Wahlke et al., although perhaps implied in traits such as "application" or "commitment to job," "restraint in bill-introduction," and "respect for other members' legislative rights," respectively, Matthews's observations are echoed (Ibid.). The reader is referred to the original for detailed explanations the authors provide to each norm listed here.

A. Rules primarily to promote group cohesion and solidarity
- Respect for other members' legislative rights
- Impersonality
- Modesty
- Independence of judgment (Being independent of outside control)
- Unselfish service
- Respect for other members' political rights
- Maintenance of confidences
- Institutional patriotism
- Respect for opposition groups

B. Rules which primarily promote predictability of legislative behavior
- Performance of obligations
- Openness of aims
- Decisiveness
- Advance notice of changed stand
- Openness in opposition
- Avoidance of trickery

C. Rules which primarily channel and restrain conflict
- Conciliation
- Agency for party or administration
- Agency for legislative party
- Apprenticeship
- Seniority

- Acceptance of committee system
- Senatorial courtesy

D. Rules which primarily expedite legislative business
  - Self-restraint in debate
  - Restraint in opposition
  - Application
  - Restraint in bill-introduction
  - Commitment to job
  - Limits to negotiation
  - Compliance with group decisions
  - Limits to partisanship
  - Abstinence from dilatory actions

E. Rules which serve primarily to give tactical advantages to individual member
  - Courtesy
  - Sociability
  - Gracefulness in defeat
  - Caution in commitments
  - Negotiation
  - Self-restraint in goals

F. Desirable personal qualities cited as rules
  - Integrity
  - Personal virtue
  - Objectivity
  - Ability and intelligence
  - Nonvenality

ASHER (1973)

Asher (1973) investigated "specific norms, the determination of which was based upon a survey of the existing literature. The main norms investigated were specialization, reciprocity, legislative work, courtesy, and aspects of apprenticeship including learning the House rules, restrained participation, and attendance on the floor and in committee" (Asher 1973, 500–501). Asher also examined institutional patriotism, "but its operationalization was so narrow that the responses obtained were not very interesting" (Asher 1973, 501 fn. 7). Asher's approach was a two-wave panel of interviews with freshman members of the 91st Congress, with thirty in the first wave and twenty-four in the second wave in February and May of 1969, respectively (Asher 1973, 500).

HEBERT AND MCLEMORE (1973)

Hebert and McLemore (1973) compiled the "ten most frequently mentioned 'unofficial rules' in the [Iowa] House and Senate" (Table 1, p. 514), based on their open-ended survey question derived from the Wahlke et al. (1962) question. They indicate with a double-asterisk** where these norms were among the ten most frequently mentioned in Wahlke et al.'s four state study (Wahlke et al., pp. 146–7, cit. in Hebert and McLemore 1973, 514, table 1). In order of frequency grouped by chamber of the Iowa General Assembly:

House of Representatives:
1. Don't monopolize debate (don't talk too much, don't ramble on)**
2. Don't deal in personalities**
3. Respect for other viewpoints (keep an open mind)
4. Courtesy**
5. Freshmen serve an internship
6. Cooperate with other legislators (don't rock the boat, don't call someone else's motion up)**
7. Treat all legislators with respect (treat others as you want to be treated)**
8. Friendliness
9. Be trustworthy, keep commitments, don't break confidences**
10. Miscellaneous personal behavior and characteristics

Senate:
1. Treat all legislators with respect (treat others as you want to be treated)**
2. Don't deal in personalities**
3. Miscellaneous behavior on the floor, in committees, among others.
4. Be honest in answers, don't lie, don't mislead**
5. Don't lose your dignity (don't get mad, don't be ungentlemanly, don't use rough language)
6. Courtesy**
7. Don't monopolize debate (don't talk too much, don't ramble on)**
8. Respect for other viewpoints (keep an open mind)
9. Be trustworthy, keep commitments, don't break confidences**
10. Cooperate with other legislators (don't rock the boat, don't call someone else's motion up)**

WEINGAST (1979)

Weingast (1979) articulates a norm of "universalism," whereby legislator behavior in the Congress exhibits "unanimous inclusion of representatives' projects in omnibus-type legislation produced by one committee" (Weingast 1979, 246 fn. 1), as compared to game theoretic prediction of minimum (not unanimous) winning coalitions in determining outcomes on distributive legislation. That is, a "norm" exists in which rational, self-interested lawmakers include far more other members in winning coalitions than is necessary for what game theory would predict among purely rational, outcome-maximizing actors. Weingast develops a game-theoretic model to explain why such apparently contradictory behavior is still consistent with rational actor models—the "norm" of universalism in this sense, is still reflective of strategic behavior: "Rational self-interested legislators have compelling reasons to prefer decision making by maximal rather than minimal willing coalitions" (Ibid., 250). Note that Weingast is careful to distinguish 'universalism' from 'reciprocity,' which he, like Mayhew and Polsby, sees as "representatives' deferential behavior toward the legislation of other committees" (Ibid., 246 fn. 1).

LOOMIS AND FISHEL (1981)

Loomis and Fishel (1981) used a survey questionnaire of forty-five of the seventy members of the class of 1974, follow-up interviews with twenty-five who returned the questionnaire, and data provided from previous studies by Asher and Loomis (Loomis and Fishel 1981, 83; see also table 1, p. 86) on the norms of seniority and apprenticeship, with additional consideration of norms of expertise, specialization, ability to compromise, and personal cordiality. In a break with previous work by Fenno and Asher, they argue for a distinction between "expertise" and "specialization" based on member responses and "the fact that many new members believed they possessed expertise on subjects outside committee domains and were more willing to use that expertise when the opportunity developed" (Loomis and Fishel 1981, 88 fn. 14).

ROHDE, ORNSTEIN, AND PEABODY (1985)

Rohde, Ornstein, and Peabody (1985) look at Matthews original six folkways: apprenticeship; legislative work; specialization; courtesy; reciprocity; and institutional patriotism. They analyze how the changing character of Senate membership affects adherence to what they classify as the "general benefit" and "limited benefit" nature of these norms, "on the basis of whether . . . their observance provided benefits to all members in general or only to a subset of members" (Rohde, Ornstein, and Peabody 1985, 179). They find that as the distribution of power shifted, general benefits endured, whereas limited benefit norms eroded due to the shifting nature beneficiaries of such norms.

The study covers the period 1957 to 1974, with a postscript for 1984. Their data gathering approach was semistructured interviews with "a prepared list of open-ended questions." Interviews were conducted beginning May 1973, with a goal of interviewing all senators; and at the time of publication they "completed 52 interviews, 44 with senators who were serving in the 93rd Congress and 8 with senators who served previously" (Ibid., 147, Author's Note). Responses to the interview questions were then analyzed for what they indicated about ongoing adherence to Matthews's folkways.

USLANER (1993)

Uslaner (1993) speaks of a decline of "comity," by which he means "courtesy and reciprocity within a system of norms" (Uslaner 1993, 8), "the six norms of Congressional behavior" identified by Matthews (Ibid., 21). His methodological approach varies, relying upon "impressionistic" (Ibid., 32) evidence among other data.

OVERBY AND BELL (2004)

Overby and Bell (2004) note that retiring Senators do not exhibit a greater propensity to engage in filibuster despite the absence of rational or strategic constraints on such behavior due to their retirement. In their words, therefore, "retiring senators do not entirely and en masse disregard the chamber's norms of comity and cooperation in order to pursue narrowly personal legislative goals . . . The unwillingness of most retiring senators (who were, on average, older and more senior than others in the chamber) to take advantage of the full range of obstreperous parliamentary tactics even when the no longer had to fear future sanctions from their colleagues speaks to the powerful, lasting effects of the internalization of group norms" (Overby and Bell 2004, 920).

AZARI AND SMITH (2012)

Azari and Smith (2012) point to the evolution in the U.S. Senate of a supermajoritarian informal rule. Following the creation of the possibility of filibuster by the adoption of Rule 22 in 1917 requiring a two-thirds vote to end debate (changed to a sixty-vote requirement in 1975), filing of cloture votes was rare during the first four decades of existence. The practice slowly increased starting from the eighty-seventh Congress (1961–62) forward to a modern practice where cloture and a sixty-vote supermajority is routinely required for legislation to advance: "senators have replaced one shared under-standing of acceptable practice—one unwritten rule—with another: 'cloture has gone from taboo to commonplace'" (Azari and Smith 2112, 46; Koger 2010, 46 op. cit.).

Bibliography

Abcarian, Robin. 2019. "Democratic Rep. Katie Hill Messed Up, But She Should Not Have Resigned." *Los Angeles Times*, October 27, 2019. https://www.latimes.com/o pinion/story/2019-10-27/column-katie-hill-should-not-have-resigned.

Abramowitz, Alan I. 2018. *The Great Alignment: Race, Party Transformation, and the Rise of Donald Trump*. New Haven, CT: Yale University Press.

Adler, Emanuel. 1997. "Seizing the Middle Ground: Constructivism in World Politics." *European Journal of International Relations* 3(3): 319–363.

Aldrich, John H. and Rohde, David W. 1999. *The Consequences of Party Organization in the House: Theory and Evidence on Conditional Party Government*. East Lansing, MI: PIPC.

Alexander, Brian. 2016. "Toward a Social Theory of Congress." *PS: Political Science and Politics* 49(1): 162–163.

_____. 2018. "Procedural Disobedience: Minority Resistance in the US House of Representatives. *PS: Political Science & Politics* 51(1): 124–128.

_____. 2019. "The House is More Courteous than You Might Imagine." *Legislative Branch Capacity Working Group*, July 22, 2019. https://www.legbranc h.org/the-house-is-more-courteous-than-you-might-imagine/.

Annenberg Public Policy Center. 2011. "Civility in Congress (1935-2011) as reflected in the Taking Down Process." Annenberg Report No. 2011-1, September 28, 2011. Philadelphia: University of Pennsylvania. https://cdn.annenbergpublicpolicycenter. org/Downloads/Civility/Civility_9-27-2011_Final.pdf.

Asher, Herbert B. 1973. "The Learning of Legislative Norms." *American Political Science Review* 67(2): 499–513.

_____. 1974. "Committees and the Norm of Specialization." *The Annals of the American Academy of Political and Social Science* 411(1): 63–74.

Azari, Julia. 2018. "Politics Is More Partisan Now, But It's Not More Divisive." *FiveThirtyEight*, January 19, 2018. https://fivethirtyeight.com/features/politics-is -more-partisan-now-but-its-not-more-divisive/.

Azari, Julia R. and Jennifer K. Smith. 2012. "Unwritten Rules: Informal Institutions in Established Democracies." *Perspectives on Politics* 10(1): 37–55.

Azari, Julia, Lee Drutman, and James Wallner. 2020. "Do ideas or interests drive our politics?" Politics in Question, April 8, 2020. *Podcast*, 52 minutes. https://www.politicsinquestion.com/episodes/do-ideas-matter-in-politics.

Back, Christine J. and Wilson C. Freeman. 2018. "Addressing Sexual Harassment by Modifying the Congressional Accountability Act of 1995: A Look at Key Provisions in H.R. 4924." *Legal Sidebar*, February 7, 2018. Washington, DC: Congressional Research Service. https://fas.org/sgp/crs/misc/LSB10067.pdf.

Bade, Rachael, Heather Caygle, and Ben Weyle. 2016. "Democrats Stage Sit-in on House Floor to Force Gun Vote." *Politico*, June 22, 2016. https://www.politico.com/story/2016/06/democrats-stage-sit-in-on-house-floor-to-force-gun-vote-224656.

Baitinger, Gail E. 2019. "Words Taken Down: Calling Members to Order for Disorderly Language in the House." CRS Report R45866, August 13, 2019. Washington, DC: Congressional Research Service.

Baker, Ross. K. 1989. *House and Senate*. New York: W.W. Norton & Co.

Ban, Pamela, Justin Grimmer, and Jaclyn Kaslovsky. 2018. "Speaking Up, Speaking More? Female Participation in Committee Hearings." *Harvard University*. Poster Presentation. https://projects.iq.harvard.edu/files/govposters/files/ban_grimmer_kaslovsky2018.pdf.

Barnes, Fred. 2015. "Sasse Finally Speaks." Archives of the *Weekly Standard*. *The Washington Examiner*, November 16, 2015. https://www.washingtonexaminer.com/weekly-standard/sasse-finally-speaks.

Basham, Luke. 2020. "Maiden Speeches and Apprenticeship: Continuity and Change in the U.S. Senate." Senior Honors Thesis, in requirement for completion of the Bachelor of Arts degree. Washington and Lee University, Lexington, Virginia.

Bauer, Bob. 2019. "Rules and Norms in the Trump Presidency: The Risks and Rewards of 'Playing It Straight' on the Inside." *Lawfare*, September 19, 2019. https://www.lawfareblog.com/rules-and-norms-trump-presidency-risks-and-rewards-playing-it-straight-inside.

Bennett, John T. 2018. "Booker Orders Release of Kavanaugh-Related Email in 'Act of Disobedience'." *Roll Call*, September 9, 2018. https://www.rollcall.com/news/politics/kavanaugh-email-disobedience-booker.

Bertucci, Mariano E., Jarrod Hayes, and Patrick James, eds. 2018. *Constructivism Reconsidered: Past, Present, and Future*. Ann Arbor: University of Michigan Press.

Beth, Richard S. 2013. "Procedures for Considering Changes in Senate Rules." CRS Report R42929. Washington, DC: Congressional Research Service.

Bettleheim, Adriel. 1999. "The Issues," Partisan Politics. *CQ Researcher* 9(11): 233–256. CQ Press Library.

Bicchieri, Cristina. 1990. "Norms of Cooperation." *Ethics* 100(4): 838–861.

Binder, Sarah A. 2013. "Oh 113th Congress Hastert Rule, We Hardly Knew Ye!" Washington, DC: Brookings Institution. https://www.brookings.edu/blog/up-front/2013/01/17/oh-113th-congress-hastert-rule-we-hardly-knew-ye/.

_____. 2014. "Polarized We Govern?" Center for Effective Public Management. Washington, DC: Brookings Institution. https://www.brookings.edu/research/polarized-we-govern/.

_____. 2015. "Challenges Ahead for Legislative Studies." *Legislative Studies Quarterly* 40(1): 5–11.

Blake, Judith and Kingsley Davis. 1964. "Norms, Values, and Sanctions." In *Handbook of Modern Sociology*, edited by Robert E. L. Faris, 456–484. Chicago, IL: Rand McNally and Company.

Bordelon, Brendan. 2017. "Constitutional Concerns Raised by House Rule Penalizing Live-Streaming." *Morning Consult*, January 3, 2017. https://morningconsult.com/2017/01/03/constitutional-concerns-raised-house-rule-penalizing-live-streaming/.

Bresnahan, John, Heather Caygle, and Sarah Ferris. 2019. "'Meltdown': Trump-Pelosi Feud Intensifies after Dem Walkout." *Politico*, October 16, 2019. https://www.politico.com/news/2019/10/16/trump-nancy-pelosi-meeting-walkout-048909.

Brownstein, Ronald. 2008. *The Second Civil War: How Extreme Partisanship Has Paralyzed Washington and Polarized America*. New York: Penguin Publishing Group. eBook.

Bullock, III, Charles S. 1970. "Apprenticeship and Committee Assignments in the House of Representatives." *Journal of Politics* 32(3): 717–720.

Burgat, Casey. 2017. "Among House staff, Women are Well Represented. Just Not in the Senior Positions." Monkey Cage. *Washington Post*, June 20, 2017. https://www.washingtonpost.com/news/monkey-cage/wp/2017/06/20/among-house-staff-women-are-well-represented-just-not-in-the-senior-positions/.

Burgat, Casey and Ryan Dukeman. 2019. "Who's On the Hill?" Staffing and Human Capital in Congress's Legislative Committees." Washington, DC: R Street. https://www.rstreet.org/2019/03/14/whos-on-the-hill-staffing-and-human-capital-in-congress-legislative-committees/.

Butler, Jack. 2020. "Matt Gaetz's Constitution." *National Review*, September 17, 2020. https://www.nationalreview.com/corner/matt-gaetzs-constitution/.

Canon, David T. 1989. "The Institutionalization of Leadership in the U.S. Congress." *Legislative Studies Quarterly* 14(3): 415–443.

Carlson, Peter. 1990. "The Least Exclusive Club in the World." *Washington Post*, November 4, 1990. https://www.washingtonpost.com/archive/lifestyle/magazine/1990/11/04/the-least-exclusive-club-in-the-world/76ce9736-0d4c-46b3-bccb-a96845c1722a/.

Carnevale, Anthony P., Nicole Smith, and Kathryn Peltier Campbell. 2019. "May the Best Woman Win?: Education and Bias against Women in American Politics." Washington, DC: Georgetown University Center on Education and the Workforce.

Carney, Jordain. 2018. "Booker Releases 'Confidential' Kavanaugh Documents." *The Hill*, September 6, 2018. https://thehill.com/homenews/senate/405345-booker-releases-confidential-kavanaugh-documents.

Caygle, Heather. 2018. @heatherscope. Twitter, April 18, 2018, 1:07 p.m. https://twitter.com/heatherscope/status/986652525649645568.

Caygle, Heather, John Bresnahan, and Kyle Cheney. 2019. "Rep. Katie Hill to Resign Amid Allegations of Inappropriate Relationships with Staffers." *Politico*, October

27, 2019. https://www.politico.com/news/2019/10/27/rep-katie-hill-to-resign-amid -allegations-of-inappropriate-relationships-with-staffers-000301.

Center for American Women and Politics. 2020. "Women in the Congress 2020." Eagleton Institute of Politics. New Brunswick, NJ: Rutgers University. https://ca wp.rutgers.edu/women-us-congress-2020.

Chaudhuri, Saabira and Jennifer Maloney. 2019. "As Americans Drink Less Alcohol, Booze Makers Look Beyond the Barrel." *Wall Street Journal*, January 17, 2019. https://www.wsj.com/articles/americans-are-drinking-less-alcohol-11547733600.

Chergosky, Anthony J. 2018. "Incivility in Congressional Communication." Unpublished Dissertation in Political Science. University of North Carolina, Chapel Hill, NC.

Choate, Judd. 2003. *Torn and Frayed: Congressional Norms and Party Switching in an Era of Reform*. Westport, CT: Praeger.

CNN. 2009. "Rep. Wilson Shouts, 'You lie' to Obama During Speech." *CNN Politics*, September 9, 2009. https://www.cnn.com/2009/POLITICS/09/09/joe.wilson/.

Cochrane, Emily. 2018. "High Stakes for House Freshman: The Office Lottery." *New York Times*, November 30, 2018. https://www.nytimes.com/2018/11/30/us/politics /freshmen-representatives-office-lottery.html.

Coleman, James S. 1990. "Norm-Generating Structures." In *The Limits of Rationality*, edited by Karen Schweers Cook and Margaret Levi, 250–273. Chicago, IL: University of Chicago Press.

Connors, Tom. 2016. "How Congress' Bad Periscopes Brought Out the Best in C-SPAN." *The Verge*, June 22, 2016. https://www.theverge.com/2016/6/22/12008 592/c-span-congress-periscope-facebook-live.

Cox, Gary W. and Mathew D. McCubbins. 2005. *Setting the Agenda: Responsible Party Government in the U.S. House of Representatives*. Cambridge: Cambridge University Press.

_____. 2007. *Legislative Leviathan: Party Government in the House*. Cambridge: Cambridge University Press.

CQ Weekly Report. 2018. "116th Congress: The Women Are Marching in, Looking to Make a Mark." *CQ Magazine*, November 12, 2018. CQ Press Library.

Crawford, Sue E.S. and Elinor Ostrom. 1995. "A Grammar of Institutions." *American Political Science Review* 89(3): 582–600.

Davidson, Roger H., Walter J. Oleszek, and Frances E. Lee. 2012. *Congress and Its Members*, Thirteenth Edition. Los Angeles: SAGE Publications.

Desiderio, Andrew. 2020. "'This is Bulls—': Bitterness Takes Over Senate as Lawmakers Clash on Rescue." *Politico*, March 23, 2020. https://www.politico .com/news/2020/03/23/senate-coronavirus-rescue-package-144233.

Desilver, Drew. 2014. "The polarized Congress of Today has Its Roots in the 1970s." *FactTank*, June 12, 2014. Washington, DC: Pew Research Center. https://www .pewresearch.org/fact-tank/2014/06/12/polarized-politics-in-congress-began-in-the -1970s-and-has-been-getting-worse-ever-since/.

_____. 2018. "A Record Number of Women Will be Serving in the New Congress." *FactTank: News in the Numbers*, December 18, 2018. Washington, DC:

Pew Research Center. https://www.pewresearch.org/fact-tank/2018/12/18/record
-number-women-in-congress/.

Dionne Jr., E.J., Norm Ornstein, and Thomas E. Mann. 2017. "How the GOP
Prompted the Decay of Political Norms." *The Atlantic*, September 19, 2017. https:/
/www.theatlantic.com/politics/archive/2017/09/gop-decay-of-political-norms/540
165/.

Dodd, Lawrence C. and Scot Schraufnagel. 2013. "Taking Incivility Seriously:
Analyzing Breaches of Decorum in the US Congress (1891-2012)." In *Politics to
the Extreme: American Political Institutions in the Twenty-First Century*, edited by
Scott A. Frisch and Sean Q. Kelly, 71–91. New York: Palgrave Macmillan.

Dolan, Kathleen A. 2003. *Voting for Women: How the Public Evaluates Women
Candidates*. Boulder, CO: Westview Press.

Downs, Anthony. 1957. *An Economic Theory of Democracy*. New York: Harper and
Row.

Drutman, Lee. 2017. "We Need Political Parties. But Their Rabid Partisanship Could
Destroy American Democracy." *Vox*, September 5, 2017. https://www.vox.com/
the-big-idea/2017/9/5/16227700/hyperpartisanship-identity-american-democracy
-problems-solutions-doom-loop.

Dumain, Emma. 2014. "Boehner Tells Leno Government Shutdown a 'Predictable
Disaster'." *Roll Call*, January 24, 2014. https://www.rollcall.com/2014/01/24/boeh
ner-tells-leno-government-shutdown-a-predictable-disaster/.

Ellis, Joseph J. 1997. *American Sphinx: The Character of Thomas Jefferson*. New
York: Alfred A. Knopf.

Eulau, Heinz. 1995. "Legislative Norms." In *Encyclopedia of the American
Legislative System*, Vol. 2, edited by Joel Silbey et al., 585–601. New York:
Charles Scribner's Sons.

Evening Star. 1971. "Civility and Survival." Editorial. *The Evening Star* (Washington,
DC), May 25, 1971, pp. A6.

Everett, Burgess. 2018. "Booker to McConnell on Ethics Charges: 'Bring It!'."
Politico, September 7, 2018. https://www.politico.com/story/2018/09/07/bookeret
hics-probedocument-release-810647.

Evers, Miles M. 2017. "On Transgression." *International Studies Quarterly* 61(4):
786–794.

Fenno, Richard F. 1962. "The House Appropriations Committee as a Political
System: The Problem of Integration." *American Political Science Review* 56(2):
310–324.

_____. 1966. *The Power of the Purse: Appropriations Politics in Congress*.
Boston, MA: Little, Brown and Company.

_____. 1978. *Home Style: House Members in Their Districts*. New York:
Longman.

Finnemore, Martha. 1996. *National Interests in International Society*. Ithaca, NY:
Cornell University Press.

Finnemore, Martha and Kathryn Sikkink. 2001. "Taking Stock: The Constructivist
Research Program in International Relations and Comparative Politics." *Annual
Review of Political Science* 4(June): 391–416.

Fiorina, Morris P. 2017. *Unstable Majorities: Polarization, Party Sorting and Political Stalemate.* Stanford, CA: Hoover Institution Press.

Foucault, Michel. 1972. *The Archaeology of Knowledge and the Discourse on Language.* New York: Pantheon Books.

Freeman, Joanne B. 2018. *The Field of Blood: Violence in Congress and the Road to Civil War.* New York: Farrar, Straus and Giroux.

Gale, Rebecca. 2014. "Tips for Holiday Parties Continued: Office Etiquette, Hot Tickets and What Not to Do." *Roll Call*, December 9, 2014. Factiva.

_____. 2015. "Where the Drinkers Are in Congress." *Roll Call,* December 2, 2015. https://www.rollcall.com/2015/12/02/where-the-drinkers-are-in-congress/.

Gallup. 2019. "Honesty/Ethics in Professions." *Gallup News*, Dec. 2-15, 2019. https://news.gallup.com/poll/1654/honesty-ethics-professions.aspx.

Gangitano, Alex. 2018. "Roll Call Survey: The Culture of Drinking on Capitol Hill." *Roll Call*, June 13, 2018. Factiva.

Gaudiano, Nicole. 2018. "On Her First Day of Orientation on Capitol Hill, Alexandria Ocasio-Cortez Protests in Pelosi's office." *USA Today*, November 13, 2018. https://www.usatoday.com/story/news/politics/2018/11/13/alexandria-ocasio-cortez-nancy-pelosi/1987514002/.

Gibbs, Jack P. 1965. "Norms: The Problem of Definition and Classification." *American Journal of Sociology* 70(5): 586–594.

Gilbert, Margaret. 2008. "Social Convention Revisited." *Topoi* 27(1): 5–16.

Green, Donald and Ian Shapiro. 1996. *Pathologies of Rational Choice Theory: A Critique of Applications in Political Science.* New Haven, CT: Yale University Press.

Green, Matthew N. 2015. *Underdog Politics: The Minority Party in the U.S. House of Representatives.* New Haven, CT: Yale University Press.

Hallac, Joanna. 2011. "Speaker Rayburn's 'Board of Education'." *U.S. Capitol Historical Society.* Blog, December 20, 2011. https://uschs.wordpress.com/2011/12/20/speaker-rayburns-board-of-education/.

Hawkings, David. 2016a. "Holding the Gavel With Nothing to Do." *Roll Call*, April 20, 2016. http://www.rollcall.com/news/hawkings/holding-gavel-nothing.

_____. 2016b. "Inside the House's First Social Media Non-Filibuster." *Roll Call*, June 23, 2016. http://www.rollcall.com/news/hawkings/inside-houses-first-social-media-non-filibuster-democrats-gun-control.

_____. 2018. "The 5 M's for Describing Why Congress Is Broken." *Roll Call*, July 26, 2018. https://www.rollcall.com/news/hawkings/5-ms-describing-congress-broken.

Hawkins, Stephen, Daniel Yudkin, Miriam Juan-Torres, and Tim Dixon. 2018. "Hidden Tribes: A Study of America's Polarized Landscape." *More In Common.* New York. https://hiddentribes.us/.

Hebert, F. Ted and Lelan E. McLemore. 1973. "Character and Structure of Legislative Norms: Operationalizing the Norm Concept in the Legislative Setting." *American Journal of Political Science* 17(3): 506–527.

Helmke, Gretchen and Steven Livitsky. 2004. "Informal Institutions and Comparative Politics: A Research Agenda." *Perspectives on Politics* 2(4): 725–740.

Hocking, Bree. 2006. "Alcohol and Congress: A Long and Troubled History." *Roll Call*, October 5, 2006. Factiva.

Hoffmann, Matthew J. 2017. "Norms and Social Constructivism in International Relations." *Oxford Research Encyclopedia of International Studies*, December 22, 2017. New York: Oxford University Press. https://oxfordre.com/internati onalstudies/view/10.1093/acrefore/9780190846626.001.0001/acrefore-978019084 6626-e-60.

Hohmann, James. 2018. "The Daily 202: As Alcoholism Fells another Congressman, a Reminder That No One is Immune to Addiction." *Washington Post*, May 29, 2018. Dow Jones Factiva.

Hopf, Ted. 1998. "The Promise of Constructivism in International Relations Theory." *International Security* 23(1): 171–200.

Hudak, John. 2013. "Lessons from the Shutdown: Pork and Earmarks Help Break Gridlock." *FixGov*, October 30, 2013. Washington, DC: Brookings Institution. https://www.brookings.edu/blog/fixgov/2013/10/30/lessons-from-the-shutdown-pork-and-earmarks-help-break-gridlock/.

Huder, Joshua C. 2017. "The Housification of the Upper Chamber: The 115th Senate is Basically Unrecognizable." *Legislative Branch Capacity Working Group*, December 21, 2017. http://www.legbranch.com/theblog/2017/12/21/the-housifi cation-of-the-upper-chamber-the-115th-senate-is-basically-unrecognizable.

Hudiberg, Jane A. 2019. "House Rules Changes Affecting Floor Proceedings in the 116th Congress (2019-2020)." CRS Report No. R45787, June 27, 2019. Washington, DC: Congressional Research Service.

Huitt, Ralph K. 1957. "The Morse Committee Assignment Controversy: A Study in Senate Norms." *American Political Science Review* 51(2): 313–329.

_____. 1961. "The Outsider in the Senate: An Alternative Role." *American Political Science Review* 55(3): 566–575.

Huntington, Samuel P. 1981. *American Politics: The Promise of Disharmony*. Cambridge, MA: Belknap Press of Harvard University Press.

Ingraham, Christopher. 2015. "The Jobs Most Likely to Make You Crave a Stiff Drink When the Day is Done." *Washington Post*, April 29, 2015. Dow Jones Factiva.

Jamieson, Kathleen Hall. 1997. "Civility in the House of Representatives." *Annenberg Public Policy Center*, March 1, 1997. Philadelphia: University of Pennsylvania. https://www.annenbergpublicpolicycenter.org/civility-in-the-house-of-representat ives/.

Jamieson, Kathleen Hall and Doron Taussig. 2017. "Disruption, Demonization, Deliverance, and Norm Destruction: The Rhetorical Signature of Donald J. Trump." *Political Science Quarterly* 132(4): 619–650.

Jefferson, Thomas. 1787. "Extract from Thomas Jefferson to James Madison." *Jefferson Quotes & Family Letters*, January 30, 1787. Thomas Jefferson's Monticello. http://tjrs.monticello.org/letter/86?_ga=2.86965848.1570926785.15 86714188-2108108488.1586714188.

_____. 1801. "From Thomas Jefferson to the Senate, 28 February 1801." *Founders Online, National Archives*. https://founders.archives.gov/documents/

Jefferson/01-33-02-0087. Original source: *The Papers of Thomas Jefferson*, vol. 33, 17 February–30 April 1801, edited by Barbara B. Oberg, 101–102. Princeton: Princeton University Press, 2006.

_____. 1801. "From Thomas Jefferson to the Senate, 28 February 1801." *Founders Online, National Archives.* https://founders.archives.gov/documents/Jefferson/01-33-02-0087. Original source: *The Papers of Thomas Jefferson*, vol. 33, 17 February–30 April 1801, edited by Barbara B. Oberg, 101–102. Princeton: Princeton University Press, 2006.

Jenkins, Holman W. Jr. 2019. "Norm Violations Are Now the Norm." *Wall Street Journal*, October 4, 2019. https://www.wsj.com/articles/norm-violations-are-now-the-norm-11570224910.

Jones, James R. 2017. "Black Capitol: Race and Power in the Halls of Congress." Ph. D. Dissertation. Columbia University Graduate School of Arts and Sciences, New York.

Jones, Jeffrey M. 2019. "Job Approval of Congress Reaches Two-Year High." *Gallup Poll*, March 19, 2019. https://news.gallup.com/poll/247928/job-approval-congress-reaches-two-year-high.aspx.

Jung, Hoyoon. 2019. "The Evolution of Social Constructivism in Political Science: Past to Present." *Sage Open* 9(1): 1–10. doi: 10.1177/2158244019832703.

Kane, Paul and Ed O'Keefe. 2017. "Republicans vote to rebuke Elizabeth Warren, saying she impugned Session's character." *Washington Post*, February 8, 2017. https://www.washingtonpost.com/news/powerpost/wp/2017/02/07/republicans-vote-to-rebuke-elizabeth-warren-for-impugning-sessionss-character/.

Kaplan, Fred. 2019. "How Richard Lugar Quietly Saved the World." *Slate*, April 29, 2019. https://slate.com/news-and-politics/2019/04/richard-lugar-obituary-nuclear-policy-barack-obama.html.

Kennedy, John F. 1956. *Profiles in Courage*. New York: Harper & Brothers.

Kim, Seung Min. 2017. "Senate votes to shut up Elizabeth Warren." *Politico*, February 7, 2017. https://www.politico.com/story/2017/02/elizabeth-warren-sessions-silence-234779.

King, Gary, Robert O. Keohane, and Sidney Verba. 1994. *Designing Social Inquiry: Scientific Inference in Qualitative Research*. Princeton, NJ: Princeton University Press.

Klar, Rebecca. 2019. "Clyburn Apologizes After Criticism of 'Tokenism' by Top Democratic Leaders." *The Hill*, June 20, 2019. https://thehill.com/homenews/house/449486-clyburn-walks-back-criticism-of-tokenism-by-top-democratic-leaders.

Klein, Ezra. 2020. *Why We're Polarized*. New York: Avid Reader Press.

Klein, Mariel. 2017. "Working Together and Across the Aisle, Female Senators Pass More Legislation Than Male Colleagues." *Quorum*. https://www.quorum.us/data-driven-insights/working-together-and-across-the-aisle-female-senators-pass-more-legislation-than-male-colleagues/311/.

Kliff, Sarah. 2018. "The Tantrum Over Babies in the Senate Floor, Explained." *Vox*, April 19, 2018. https://www.vox.com/policy-and-politics/2018/4/19/17256390/tammy-duckworth-baby-senate-orrin-hatch.

Klotz, Audi and Cecilia Lynch. 2007. *Strategies for Research in Constructivist International Relations*. Armonk, NY: M.E. Sharpe.

Knight, Jack. 1992. *Institutions and Social Conflict*. New York: Cambridge University Press.

Koger, Gregory and Matthew J. Lebo. 2017. *Strategic Party Government: Why Winning Trumps Ideology*. Chicago, IL: University of Chicago Press.

Kondik, Kyle and Geoffrey Skelly. 2016. "Incumbent Reelection Rates Higher than Average in 2016." *Sabato's Crystal Ball*, December 15, 2016. Center for Politics. University of Virginia. http://centerforpolitics.org/crystalball/articles/incumbent-reelection-rates-higher-than-average-in-2016/.

Kopp, Emily. 2019. "Rep. Duncan Hunter's Affairs With Congressional Staff Raise Sexual Harassment Concerns." *Roll Call*, June 28, 2019. https://www.rollcall.com/news/congress/rep-duncan-hunters-affairs-congressional-staff-raise-sexual-harassment-concerns.

Kratochwil, Friedrich V. 1989. *Rules, Norms, and Decisions: On the Conditions of Practical and Legal Reasoning in International Relations and Domestic Affairs*. New York: Cambridge University Press.

Kraushaar, Josh. 2014. "The Most Divided Congress Ever, At Least until Next Year." *National Journal*, February 6, 2014. https://www.nationaljournal.com/s/627865/most-divided-congress-ever-at-least-until-next-year.

Lawless, Jennifer L., Sean M. Theriault, and Samantha Guthrie, "Nice Girls? Sex, Collegiality, and Bipartisan Cooperation in the US Congress." *The Journal of Politics* 80(4): 1268–1282.

Lazarus, Jeffrey and Amy Steigerwalt. 2018. *Gendered Vulnerability: How Women Work Harder to Stay in Office*. Ann Arbor: University of Michigan Press.

Leary, John Patrick. 2020. "The Troubling Obsession with Political 'Tribalism'." *New Republic*, February 21, 2020. https://newrepublic.com/article/156448/troubling-obsession-political-tribalism.

Lee, Frances E. 2009. *Beyond Ideology: Politics, Principles, and Partisanship in the U.S. Senate*. Chicago, IL: University of Chicago Press.

Lelkes, Yphtach. 2019. "Donald Trump's Election Did Not Increase Political Polarization." *Annenberg School for Communications*, University of Pennsylvania, October 11, 2019. https://www.asc.upenn.edu/news-events/news/trump-did-not-increase-polarization.

Lesniewski, Niels. 2013. "Ted Cruz Takes the Floor, But Don't Call It a Filibuster (Updated)." *Roll Call*, September 24, 2013. https://www.rollcall.com/news/ted-cruz-takes-the-floor-but-dont-call-it-a-filibuster.

_____. 2017. "Marco Rubio: We're Not Rome — Yet." *Roll Call*, October 25, 2017. https://www.rollcall.com/news/politics/rubio-warns-deterioration-norms-like-roman-republic.

Libit, Daniel. 2009. "Won't you be my mentor?" *Politico*, March 30, 2009. https://www.politico.com/story/2009/03/wont-you-be-my-mentor-020639.

Lingeman, Richard R. 1975. "Books of the Times: Going Along with Mr. Sam." *New York Times*, July 29, 1975. https://www.nytimes.com/1975/07/29/archives/books-of-the-times-going-along-with-mr-sam.html.

Loomis, Burdett A. and Jeff Fishel. 1981. "New Members in a Changing Congress: Norms, Actions, and Satisfaction." *Congressional Studies* 8(2): 81–94.

Luke, Timothy W. 2013. "Stultifying Politics Today: The 'Natural Science' Model in American Political Science – How is it Natural, Science, and a Model?" *New Political Science* 35(3): 339–358.

Lyons, Richard D. 1973. "Congressmen Drink, as Ehrlichman Said, But Few on the Hill are Considered Drunkards." *New York Times*, August 9, 1973. Proquest Historical Newspapers.

Mak, Tim. 2014. "Why are black staffers fleeing Capitol Hill?" *The Daily Beast*, September 30, 2014. https://www.thedailybeast.com/why-are-black-staffers-fl eeing-capitol-hill.

Manley, John F. 1965. "The House Committee on Ways and Means: Conflict Management in a Congressional Committee." *American Political Science Association* 59(4): 927–939.

Mann, Thomas E. and Norman J. Ornstein. 2016. *It's Even Worse Than It Looks: How the American Constitutional System Collided with the New Politics of Extremism*, revised edition. New York: Basic Books.

March, James G. and Johan P. Olsen. 1989. *Rediscovering Institutions: The Organizational Basis of Politics*. New York: The Free Press.

Marquette, Chris. 2019. "Workplace Protections for Legislative Branch Employees Take Effect." *Roll Call*, June 21, 2019. https://www.rollcall.com/news/congress/w orkplace-protections-legislative-branch.

Masket, Seth. 2016. "The toughest death of 2016: The Democratic Norms that (used to) Guide Our Political System." *Pacific Standard*, December 27, 2016. https://ps mag.com/news/the-toughest-death-of-2016-the-democratic-norms-that-used-to-g uide-our-political-system.

Matthews, Chris. 2013. *Tip and the Gipper: When Politics Worked*. New York: Simon and Schuster.

Matthews, Donald R. 1959. "The Folkways of the United States Senate: Conformity to Group Norms and Legislative Effectiveness." *American Political Science Review* 53(4): 1064–1089.

_____. 1960. *U.S. Senators and Their World*. Chapel Hill: University of North Carolina Press.

Mayhew, David R. 1974. *Congress: The Electoral Connection*. New Haven: Yale University Press.

McCarthy, Tom. 2018. "Donald Trump and the erosion of democratic norms in America." *The Guardian*, June 2, 2018. https://www.theguardian.com/us-news /2018/jun/02/trump-department-of-justice-robert-mueller-crisis.

McGann, Laura. 2018. "The Still-Raging Controversy Over Al Franken's Resignation, Explained." *Vox*, May 21, 2018. https://www.vox.com/2018/5/21/17352230/al-fra nken-accusations-resignation-democrats-leann-tweeden-kirsten-gillibrand.

McKeon, Nancy. 2011. "Women in the House Get a Restroom." *Washington Post*, June 28, 2011. https://www.washingtonpost.com/lifestyle/style/women-in-the-house-get-a-restroom/2011/07/28/gIQAFgdwfI_story.html.

McPherson, Lindsey. 2017. "Dems Take Photos on House Floor to Protest Proposed GOP Fine." *Roll Call*, January 3, 2017. https://www.rollcall.com/2017/01/03/dems -take-photos-on-house-floor-to-protest-proposed-gop-fine/.

Melzer, Marc and Howard Deutsch. 2020. "The State of the Union Address Drinking Game." Website. 2020. http://www.drinkinggame.us/.

Merry, Robert W. 1989. "CQ ROUNDTABLE: Morality and Politics: A Look Backward." *CQ Weekly*, October 14, 1989, p. 2754. CQ Library.

_____. 2005. "Essay: Senate and Sensibility." *CQ Weekly*, May 9, 2005, pp. 1188–1192. CQ Library.

Monroe, Kristen Renwick, ed. 2005. *Perestroika! The Raucous Rebellion in Political Science*. New Haven, CT: Yale University Press.

Murphy, Patricia. 2019. "Opinion: Why Katie Hill had to Go." *Roll Call*, November 4, 2019. https://www.rollcall.com/news/opinion/why-katie-hill-had-to-go.

Office of Congressional Workplace Rights. 2018. "State of the Congressional Workplace." FY 2018 Annual Report. Statement for the Chair of the Board. Washington, DC: Office of Congressional Workplace Rights. https://www.ocwr .gov/regulations-reports/reports/annual-reports.

Olorunnipa, Toluse, Josh Dawsey, and Mike DeBonis. 2019. "Republicans Storm Closed-Door Impeachment Hearing as Escalating Ukraine Scandal Threatens Trump." *Washington Post*, October 23, 2019. https://www.washingtonpost.com/ politics/republicans-storm-closed-door-impeachment-hearing-as-escalating-ukrain e-scandal-threatens-trump/2019/10/23/29877c06-f5a5-11e9-8cf0-4cc99f74d127_s tory.html.

Olson, Mancur Jr. 1965. *The Logic of Collective Action*. Cambridge, MA: Harvard University Press.

Ordeshook, Peter C. 1986. *Game Theory and Political Theory*. Cambridge: Cambridge University Press.

Ornstein, Norman J. 2018. "The Senate Shreds Its Norms." *The Atlantic*, September 7, 2018. https://www.theatlantic.com/ideas/archive/2018/09/senate-kavanaugh/569 596/.

Orren, Karen and Stephen Skowronek. 2004. *The Search for American Political Development*. New York: Cambridge University Press.

Ostrom, Elinor. 2000. "Collective Action and the Evolution of Social Norms." *Journal of Economic Perspectives* 14(3): 137–158.

Overby, L. Marvin and Laure C. Bell. 2004. "Rational Behavior or the Norm of Cooperation? Filibustering Among Retiring Senators." *Journal of Politics* 66(3): 906–924.

Packer, George. 2018. "A New Report Offers Insights into Tribalism in the Age of Trump." *The New Yorker*, October 13, 2018. https://www.newyorker.com /news/daily-comment/a-new-report-offers-insights-into-tribalism-in-the-age-of-trump.

Panke, Diana and Ulrich Petersohn. 2017. "President Donald J. Trump: An agent of norm death?" *International Journal: Canada's Journal of Global Policy Analysis* 72(4). doi: 10.1177%2F0020702017740159.

Pergram, Chad. 2019a. "Reporter's Notebook: Unprecedented Anger on House Floor, But Things are Looking Up." *FoxNews*, July 17, 2019. https://www.foxnews.com /politics/reporters-notebook-unprecedented-anger-on-house-floor-but-things-are -looking-up.

_____. 2019b. "House GOP's Naked Attempt at Publicity and Its Potential Flaws." *FoxNews*, October 25, 2019. https://www.foxnews.com/politics/house-g ops-naked-attempt-at-publicity-and-its-potential-flaws.

Pershing, Ben. 1999. "Caught in the Dragnet: Hill Bars, Restaurants Stung by D.C.'s Undercover Crackdown on Alcohol." *Roll Call*, August 16, 1999. Factiva.

Petracca, Mark P. 1991. "The Rational Choice Approach to Politics: A Challenge to Democratic Theory." *The Review of Politics* 53(2): 289–319.

Pettit, Philip. 1990. "*Virtus Normativa*: Rational Choice Perspectives." *Ethics* 100(4): 725–755.

Pew Research Center. 2014. "Political Polarization in the American Public." *U.S. Politics & Policy*, June 12, 2014. Washington, DC: Pew Research Center. http:// www.people-press.org/2014/06/12/political-polarization-in-the-american-public/.

Polsby, Nelson W. 1968. "The Institutionalization of the U.S. House of Representatives." *American Political Science Review* 62(1): 144–168.

_____. 2004. *How Congress Evolves: Social Bases of Institutional Change*. New York: Oxford University Press.

Poole, Keith. 2007. "Changing Minds? Not in Congress!" *Public Choice* 131(3/4): 435–451.

Poole, Keith T. and Howard Rosenthal. 2007. *Ideology & Congress*, Second, revised edition of *Congress: A Political-Economic History of Roll Call Voting*. New Brunswick, NJ: Transaction Publishers.

Pressman, Steven. 1987. "Bipartisan Comity Becomes a Casualty... ...In Political Battle Over Reagan Policies." *CQ Weekly*, July 25, 1987: 1646–1647. http://lib rary.cqpress.com.mutex.wlu.edu/cqweekly/WR100401401.

Purdum, Todd S. 2013. "Sex in the Senate: Bobby Baker's Salacious Secret History of Capitol Hill." *Politico*, November 19, 2013. https://www.politico.com/magazine /story/2013/11/sex-in-the-senate-bobby-baker-099530.

Raju, Manu. 2015. "Cruz Accuses Mitch McConnell of Telling a 'Flat Out Lie'." *Politico*, July 24, 2015. https://www.politico.com/story/2015/07/ted-cruz-says-mi tch-mcconnell-lies-export-import-bank-120583.

Ramos, Jill Terreri. 2018. "Do women do better in Congress than men?" *Politifact*, November 16, 2018. Washington, DC: The Poynter Institute. https://www.politifa ct.com/factchecks/2018/nov/16/kirsten-gillibrand/gilibrand-champions-women- legislators/.

Reynolds, Molly E. 2020. "What is the Senate filibuster, and what would it take to eliminate it?" *Voter Vitals*. Washington, DC: Brookings Institution. https://www .brookings.edu/policy2020/votervital/what-is-the-senate-filibuster-and-what-wou ld-it-take-to-eliminate-it/.

Riker, William H. 1962. *The Theory of Political Coalitions*. New Haven, CT: Yale University Press.

Rogers, David. 2017. "Ex-GOP leader Bob Michel, Face of Decency and Public Service, Dies." *Politico*, February 17, 2017. https://www.politico.com/story/2017/02/bob-michel-dies-former-gop-house-leader-234936.

Rohde, David W. 1988. "Studying Congressional Norms: Concepts and Evidence." *Congress and the Presidency* 15(2): 139–145.

Rohde, David, Norman J. Ornstein, and Robert L. Peabody. 1985. "Political Change and Legislative Norms in the U.S. Senate, 1957-1974." In *Studies of Congress*, edited by G. R. Parker, 147–188. Washington, DC: CQ Press.

Rollcall Staff. 2005. "The Long and Short of Capitol Style." *Roll Call*, June 9, 2005. https://www.rollcall.com/news/-9592-1.html.

Roller, Emma and *National Journal*. 2014. "Meet the Man Who Got Congress Its Booze During Prohibition." *The Atlantic*, April 11, 2014. https://www.theatlantic.com/politics/archive/2014/04/meet-the-man-who-got-congress-its-booze-during-prohibition/455610/.

Ruggie, John Gerard. 1998. *World Polity: Essays on International Institutionalization*. New York: Routledge.

Rybicki, Elizabeth. 2003. "Unresolved Differences: Bicameral Negotiations in Congress, 1877-2002." Paper prepared for the History of Congress Conference, University of California-San Diego, December 5–6, 2003.

Sah, Sunita. 2019. "House Impeachment Inquiry May Help Restore the Political and Social Norms that Trump Flouts." *The Conversation*, November 13, 2019. https://theconversation.com/house-impeachment-inquiry-may-help-restore-the-political-and-social-norms-that-trump-flouts-126889.

Sandholtz, Wayne. 2008. "Dynamics of International Norm Change: Rules against Wartime Plunder." *European Journal of International Relations* 14(1): 101–131.

Schmitt, Mark. 2019. "The Watergate Class of '74 Has Valuable Lessons for Freshman Democrats." Opinion. *New York Times*, January 3, 2019. https://www.nytimes.com/2019/01/03/opinion/house-democrats-watergate-1974.html.

Schneier, Edward V. 1988. "Norms and Folkways in Congress: How Much Has Actually Changed?" *Congress and the Presidency* 15(2): 117–138.

Schor, Elana and Seung Min Kim. 2017. "Franken Resigns." *Politico*, December 7, 2017. https://www.politico.com/story/2017/12/07/franken-resigns-285957.

Schwartz, Ian. 2017. "David Brooks: Do the Norms That Governed Politics Reestablish Themselves After Trump, Or Are We Here Forever?" *Real Clear Politics*, July 1, 2017. https://www.realclearpolitics.com/video/2017/07/01/david_brooks_do_the_norms_that_governed_politics_reestablish_themselves_after_trump_or_are_we_here_forever.html.

Shabad, Rebecca. 2017. "Are Sleeveless Dresses 'Appropriate Attire'? Congress Doesn't Think So." *CBS News*, July 7, 2017. https://www.cbsnews.com/news/are-sleeveless-dresses-appropriate-attire-congress-doesnt-think-so/.

Shapiro, Ari and Ailsa Chang. 2020. "Why Milk And Water Are The Only Drinks Allowed On The Senate Floor." *All Things Considered*, January 22, 2020. Washington, DC: National Public Radio. https://www.npr.org/2020/01/22/798644798/why-milk-and-water-are-the-only-drinks-allowed-on-the-senate-floor.

Shapiro, Walter. 2017. "Sexual Harassment from John Tower to Donald Trump - and Beyond." *Roll Call*, November 22, 2017. https://www.rollcall.com/news/opinion/sexual-harassment-lawmakers-shapiro.

Shepsle, Kenneth A. 1989. "The Changing Textbook Congress." In *Can the Government Govern?* edited by John E. Chubb and Paul E. Peterson, 238–266. Washington, DC: Brookings Institution.

Sherman, Jake. 2010. "Stupak Called 'Baby Killer' in House." *Politico*, March 22, 2010. https://www.politico.com/story/2010/03/stupak-called-baby-killer-in-house-034782.

Shirley, Craig and Scott Mauer. 2017. "Liberals Should Admit Tip O'Neill was Reagan's Bitter Enemy, Not His Friend." *The Hill*, September 11, 2017. https://thehill.com/blogs/pundits-blog/national-party-news/350045-liberals-should-admit-tip-oneill-was-reagans-bitter.

Shugerman, Emily. 2017. "Me Too: Why are Women Sharing Stories of Sexual Assault and How Did It Start?" *The Independent*, October 17, 2017. https://www.independent.co.uk/news/world/americas/me-too-facebook-hashtag-why-when-meaning-sexual-harassment-rape-stories-explained-a8005936.html.

Simon, Caroline. 2019. "Are Women Making Congress More Polite?" *Roll Call*, June 3, 2019. https://www.rollcall.com/news/congress/women-making-congress-polite.

Sinclair, Barbara. 1989. *The Transformation of the U.S. Senate*. Baltimore, MD: Johns Hopkins University Press.

Smith, David. 2019. "'My Choice': Ilhan Omar Becomes First to Wear Hijab in US Congress." *The Guardian*, January 3, 2019. https://www.theguardian.com/us-news/2019/jan/03/ilhan-omar-hijab-congress-headwear.

Smith, Steven S. 2007. *Party Influence in Congress*. Cambridge: Cambridge University Press.

Smith, Steven S., Jason M. Roberts, and Ryan J. Vander Wielen. 2013. *The American Congress*, Eighth edition. New York: Cambridge University Press.

Smock, Ray. 2011. "Incivility and Dysfunction in Congress is a National Crisis." *History News Network*, October 2011. Columbian College of Arts and Sciences. Washington, DC: George Washington University. https://historynewsnetwork.org/article/142484.

Sohn, Patricia. 2016. "Methods War: How Ideas Matter within Political Science." *E-International Relations*, November 24, 2016. http://www.e-ir.info/2016/11/24/methods-war-how-ideas-matter-within-political-science/.

Stevens, Allison. 2003. "The Strength of These Women Shows in Their Numbers." *CQ Weekly*, October 25, 2003: 2625–2627. http://library.cqpress.com/cqmagazine/weeklyreport108-000000878472.

Stolberg, Sheryl Gay. 2003. "The Nation; The High Costs of Rising Incivility on Capitol Hill." *New York Times*, November 30, 2003. https://www.nytimes.com/2003/11/30/weekinreview/the-nation-the-high-costs-of-rising-incivility-on-capitol-hill.html.

Stone, Daniel and Miranda Green. 2017. "Congressional Name-Calling, Incivility On the Rise." *Daily Beast*, July 13, 2007. https://www.thedailybeast.com/congressional-name-calling-incivility-on-the-rise.

Swers, Michele L. 2013. *Women in the Club: Gender and Policy Making in the Senate*. Chicago, IL: University of Chicago Press.

Theriault, Sean. 2008. *Party Polarization in Congress*. Cambridge: Cambridge University Press.

_____. 2013. *The Gingrich Senators*. New York: Oxford University Press.

Thomas, Ward. 2000. "Norms and Security: The Case of International Assassination." *International Security* 25(1): 105–133.

Thomson-DeVeaux, Amelia. 2019. "Americans Say They Would Vote For A Woman, But…" *FiveThirtyEight*, July 15, 2019. https://fivethirtyeight.com/features/americans-say-they-would-vote-for-a-woman-but/.

Thorning, Michael. 14 Jan. 2020. "Graveyard Senate? Impeachment-Obsessed House? Or Just Dysfunctional?" *Bipartisan Policy Center*. Washington, DC. https://bipartisanpolicy.org/blog/graveyard-senate-impeachment-obsessed-house-or-just-dysfunctional/.

Thurber, James A. and Antoine Yoshinaka, eds. *American Gridlock: The Sources, Character, and Impact of Political Polarization*. New York: Cambridge University Press.

Trump, Donald J. 2019, 8:27 a.m. @realDonaldTrump. Twitter, July 14, 2019, 8:27 a.m. https://twitter.com/realDonaldTrump/status/1150381395078000643.

Tully-McManus, Katherine. 2019. "GOP 'Storm the SCIF' Stunt Could Jeopardize Classified Briefings." *Roll Call*, November 15, 2019. https://www.rollcall.com/2019/11/15/gop-storm-the-scif-stunt-could-jeopardize-classified-briefings/.

Tully-McManus, Katherine and Lindsey McPherson. 2019. "'I Abandon the Chair': House Floor in Chaos Over Pelosi Speech on Trump Tweets." *Roll Call*, July 16, 2019. https://www.rollcall.com/news/congress/abandon-chair-house-floor-chaos-pelosi-speech-trump-tweets.

Tyson, Alec. 2018. "America's Polarized Views of Trump Follow Years of Growing Political Partisanship." *FactTank*, November 14, 2018. Pew Research Center. https://www.pewresearch.org/fact-tank/2018/11/14/americas-polarized-views-of-trump-follow-years-of-growing-political-partisanship/.

U.S. House of Representatives. 2009. "Adopting rules for the One Hundred Eleventh Congress." H. Res. 5. 111th Congress, First Session. *Congress.gov*, January 6, 2009. https://www.congress.gov/bill/111th-congress/house-resolution/5.

_____. 2018. "Becoming the Board of Education." *History, Art & Archives*, June 18, 2018. https://history.house.gov/Blog/2018/June/6-18-boardofeducation/.

_____. 2019. "Adopting the Rules of the House of Representatives for the One Hundred Sixteenth Congress, and for Other Purposes." H. Res. 6. 116th Congress, First Session. *Congress.gov*, January 9, 2019. https://www.congress.gov/bill/116th-congress/house-resolution/6.

_____. 2019. *Congressional Record*, July 16, 2019, pp. H5851–H5852. https://www.congress.gov/116/crec/2019/07/16/CREC-2019-07-16.pdf.

U.S. House of Representatives Office of the Historian. 2019. "POWELL, Adam Clayton, Jr." History, Art & Archives. https://history.house.gov/People/Listing/P/POWELL,-Adam-Clayton,-Jr--(P000477)/.

UCLA Institute for Digital Research and Education. 2020. "Choosing the Correct Statistical Test in SAS, STATA, SPSS and R." UCLA: Statistical Consulting Group. https://stats.idre.ucla.edu/other/mult-pkg/whatstat/.

United States Senate. 2003. "Maiden Speeches of U.S. Senators." S. Doc. 108-16. Washington, DC: U.S. Government Printing Office.

_____. 2015a. Senator Sasse, speaking on "Syrian Humanitarian Crisis," on September 15, 2015, 114th Cong., 1st sess., *Congressional Record* 161, pt. 132: S6630.

_____. 2015b. Senator Sasse, speaking on "Protecting Affordable Coverage for Employees Act," on October 1st, 2015, 114th Cong., 1st sess., *Congressional Record* 161, pt. 143: S7084.

_____. 2017a. *Congressional Record*, Senate, February 7, 2017: S854. https://www.congress.gov/115/crec/2017/02/06/CREC-2017-02-06-pt2-PgS825.pdf.

_____. 2017b. "Roll Call Vote 58, 115th Congress - 1st Session." Legislation and Records, February 7, 2017. https://www.senate.gov/legislative/LIS/roll_call_l ists/roll_call_vote_cfm.cfm?congress=115&session=1&vote=00058.

_____. 2018. *Congressional Record* Vol. 164, No. 197, 13 December 2018, p. S7531.

United States Senate Historical Office. 2007. "G. William Hoagland: Staff Director of the Senate Budget Committee, Advisor to the Senate Majority Leader." *Oral History Interviews*, November 28, 2006, to August 30, 2007. https://www.senate.g ov/artandhistory/history/oral_history/Bill_Hoagland.htm.

_____. 2019. "History of Maiden Speeches." *Art and History*. https://www.sen ate.gov/artandhistory/history/common/generic/Origins_MaidenSpeeches.htm.

_____. N.D. "The Caning of Senator Charles Sumner." *Art and History*. https ://www.senate.gov/artandhistory/history/minute/The_Caning_of_Senator_Charle s_Sumner.htm.

_____. N.D. "The Censure Case of John L. McLaurin and Benjamin R. Tillman of South Carolina (1902)." United States Senate. https://www.senate.gov/artandh istory/history/common/censure_cases/090Tillman_Laurin.htm.

Uslaner, Eric. 1993. *The Decline of Comity in Congress*. Ann Arbor: University of Michigan Press.

Vavra, Shannon. 2018. "Congress' Wave of Women Wants to Modernize Capitol Hill." *Axios*, December 3, 2018. https://www.axios.com/congress-women-modern -workplace-families-80a44413-f813-48f5-96e6-39c44553eed7.html.

Voteview.com. 2016. "The End of the 114th Congress." *Voteview Blog*, December 18, 2016. https://voteviewblog.com/2016/12/18/the-end-of-the-114th-congress/.

Wahlke, John C., Heinz Eulau, William Buchanon, and LeRoy C. Ferguson. 1962. *The Legislative System: Explorations in Legislative Behavior*. New York: John Wiley and Sons, Inc.

Walshe, Shushannah and David A. Graham. 2011 (2017). "State of the Union Drinking Games." *Daily Beast*, January 25, 2011 (updated July 13, 2017). https:// www.thedailybeast.com/state-of-the-union-drinking-games.

Waltz, Kenneth N. 1979. *Theory of International Politics*. New York: Random House.

Wang, Amy B. 2017. "'Nevertheless, She Persisted' Becomes New Battle Cry After McConnell Silences Elizabeth Warren." *Washington Post*, February 8, 2017. https ://washingtonpost.com/news/the-fix/wp/2017/02/08/nevertheless-she-persisted -becomes-new-battle-cry-after-mcconnell-silences-elizabeth-warren/.

Weingast, Barry R. 1979. "A Rational Choice Perspective on Congressional Norms." *American Journal of Political Science* 23(2): 345–363.

Weingast, Barry R. and William J. Marshall. 1988. "The Industrial Organization of Congress; or, Why Legislatures, Like Firms, Are Not Organized as Markets." *Journal of Political Economy* 96(1): 132–163.

Wendt, Alexander. 1992. "Anarchy Is What States Make of It: The Social Construction of Power Politics." *International Organization* 46(2): 391–425.

_____. 1999. *Social Theory of International Politics*. New York: Cambridge University Press.

Whittington, Keith E. 2019. "Hating on Congress: An American Tradition." *Gallup Blog*, July 20, 2019. Gallup. https://news.gallup.com/opinion/gallup/262316/hating-congress-american-tradition.aspx. Accessed 10 September 2019.

Wickham, Thomas J. 2017. *Constitution, Jefferson's Manual, and Rules of the House of Representatives*, House Document No. 114-192. Washington, DC: U.S. Government Publishing Office. https://www.govinfo.gov/content/pkg/HMAN-115/pdf/HMAN-115.pdf.

Wiener, Antje. 2004. "Contested Compliance: Interventions on the Normative Structure of World Politics." *European Journal of International Relations* 19(2): 189–234.

Wilson, Reid. 2018. "Washington's Heaving-Drinking Ways in Spotlight." *The Hill*, April 28, 2018. https://thehill.com/homenews/news/385223-washingtons-heavy-drinking-ways-in-spotlight.

Wolfensberger, Donald R. 2007. "Incivility Is Symptom Of Larger Problem On Capitol Hill." *Roll Call*, Otober 1, 2007, p. 8.

_____. 2012. "The Culture of Congress: Introductory Essay." *Wilson Center-Bipartisan Policy Center*, April 2012. Washington, DC. https://www.wilsoncenter.org/sites/default/files/cultureofcongresintro_0.pdf.

_____. 2018. *Changing Cultures in Congress: From Fair Play to Power Plays*. New York: Columbia University Press.

Yarwood, Dean L. 2004. *When Congress Makes a Joke: Congressional Humor Then and Now*. Lanham, MD: Rowman & Littlefield Publishers.

Yglesias, Matthew. 2017. "The Wholesale Looting of America: Unchecked by Norms or Political Prudence, It's Smash-and-Grab Time for the GOP." *Vox*, December 19, 2017. https://www.vox.com/policy-and-politics/2017/12/19/16786006/looting-of-america.

Yokley, Eli. 2016. "Moments of Silence on Gun Violence Not Enough, Democrats Say." *Morning Consult*, September 14, 2016. https://morningconsult.com/2016/09/14/dems-moments-silence-gun-violence-not-enough/.

Zambelich, Ariel and Alyson Hurt. 2016. "3 Hours In Orlando: Piecing Together An Attack And Its Aftermath." *The Two-Way*, June 26 2016. Washington, DC: National Public Radio. https://www.npr.org/2016/06/16/482322488/orlando-shooting-what-happened-update.

Index

Abcarian, Robin, 108

alcoholism. *See* sobriety

American politics, norms and idealism of, 124–25

Annenberg Foundation, 76n9

Annenberg Public Policy Center, 64, 76n9

apprenticeship, xiii, 9, 11, 27, 83, 134; as active, 55; and cooperation and, 53, 74, 75n2 (and conflict, 113, 115); decline of, 54; leapfrogging and, 83–84; modern Congress and, 39, 40, 42, 46, 49, 50; significance of, 54–59, 120, 141, 148–50, 152

appropriateness, logic of, xiv, 15n1, 17–18, 129, 131; changing culture and, 100, 103, 104, 106–7, 109, 110, 111n3; conflict norms and, 80–83, 86–92, 94, 95, 97; Congressional norms survey and, 133–36; constructivist approach and, 23, 25, 26, 29, 32–34, 36n1; cooperation and, 53–55, 59–61, 64–66, 69–71, 73, 74, 113–15, 117–23, ; courtesy and, 69–71; modern Congress and, 39, 42–46, 48–50, 51n1; nonconformity and, 86–88; significance of, 1, 3, 5–6, 8, 13–14

Asher, Herbert, 3, 12, 42, 43, 55, 58, 59, 140–41, 144, 150, 152

Axelrod, Robert, 20

Azari, Julia, 12, 153

Baitinger, 68, 76n7

Baker, Bobby, 100

Baker, Ross, 75n4

Ban, Pamela, 75n5

Barkely, Alben W., 77n14

Barnes, Fred, 57

Basham, Luke, 51n2, 75n1

behavioralism, 95, 105, 141; constructivist approach and, 18, 19, 21, 22, 25, 26, 31–35; cooperation and, 54, 59, 65, 71, 74 (and conflict, 114, 118, 119, 122, 123, 124); significance of, xiv–xv, 2, 4, 5, 43, 51n1

Bell, Lauren, 10, 12, 13, 153

Bertucci, Mariano E., 119

Bicchieri, Cristina, 8

Binder, Sarah A., 14, 19, 125

Boehner, John, 82, 83

Booker, Cory, 84, 86

The Broken Branch (Mann and Ornstein), 114

Brooks, Preston, 74

Brooks, Susan W., 109

Buchanon, William, 148

Caraway, Hattie, 109

Carlson, Peter, 79

Cassiday, George, 10n1
Caygle, Heather, 110–11n2
Chang, Ailsa, 110n2
Choate, Judd, 4, 10, 12, 40, 51n1, 122, 145
civility, significance of, 64, 76n9
Cleaver II, Emanuel, 67
Clinton, Bill, 114
Clinton, Hilary, 55
cloture votes, practice of, 153–54
Collins, Doug, 67
comity, 10, 22, 62, 63, 69, 75n3, 153
conflict, norm of, xiv, 13, 29, 34, 39; and nonconformity, 82–84 (in gridlocked Congress, 87–89; as procedural disobedience, 84–87); partisanship and, 89–96; significance of, 79–82; U.S. Congress future and, 96–97
Congressional Accountability Act (CAA) (1995), 104, 105; Reform Act (2019), 107
Congressional Quarterly (journal), 114
Congressional Research Service (CRS), 67, 72, 73, 77n12, 106
consequences, logic of, 53, 54, 119–20; changing culture and, 99, 106; conflict norms and, 86, 88–90; constructivist approach and, 24–25, 33–34; modern Congress and, 38–39, 51n1; reasoning and, 18–23, 27, 29, 30, 31, 87; significance of, xiv, 6, 8, 11
constructivism and Congressional studies, challenges of, 117–20; apprenticeship, 120; rationalism and, 119; sexual propriety and, 120
constructivist approach, xiv, xv; congressional norms and, 23–30; consequentialism and, 19–23; epistemologies and methodologies, 30–35; norms of ideas and, 17–18
cooperation, norm of, xiii, xiv, 77n13, 128, 131, 140, 153; apprenticeship and, 54–59; conflict norms and, 80–

83, 87–90, 92–94, 96, 97, 121–22, 125; constructivist approach and, 17, 21–23, 26, 29–31, 33, 34; demise of, 79; future, in U.S. Congress, 74–75; modern Congress and, 39–40, 46, 48–50, 51n1; as preference, 114–15; reciprocity and, 59–62; significance of, 4, 6–7, 10–14, 37, 53–54, 113–16. *See also* courtesy
Cornyn, John, 86
Cotton, Tom, 63
courtesy, norm of, xiii, 18, 106, 129, 141; as active, 63–65; conflict norms and, 79–82; constructivist approach and, 21–24, 27, 29, 31, 33, 34; cooperation and, 53, 75nn3–4, 77n13, 113, 115–20; evidence, and appropriateness, 69–71; historical norms and, 148–50, 152, 153; on House floor, 66–68; measurement, with words taken down, 68–69, 116–17; modern Congress and, 39, 40, 43, 46, 48, 50; on Senate floor, 71–74; significance of, 2, 9, 13, 62, 76n8; survey evidence of, 66; violation of, 76n9, 76–77n10; in words of participants, 65–66
Crawford, Sue E.S., 7
CRS. *See* Congressional Research Service (CRS)
Cruz, Ted, 63, 83, 88
cultural norms, changing: sexual propriety and, 103–10; significance of, 99–100; sobriety and, 100–103; U.S. Congress future and, 110
cultural norms, significance of, 23
cultural sensibility, 31

Dittmar, Kelly, 109
Drudge, Matt, 114
DW-NOMINATE scale, 77n10

Ellis, Joseph, 96
Eulau, Heinz, 1, 3, 9, 15n2, 148
Evening Star (newspaper), 81

Index

logrolling. *See* vote trading
Loomis, Burdett A., 9, 51n2, 143–44, 152
Lugar, Richard, 55
Lyons, Richard, 100

Mad Men (television), 100
maiden speech, 55–58; waiting period for, 56–58
Manley, John F., 10
material reality, 24–25, 38–39; and interests, 26
Matthews, Donald R., xiii, 2–3, 7, 12, 13, 37, 41, 54, 56, 59, 77n14, 115, 120, 128, 148, 149, 153
Mayhew, David R., 147, 152
McCarthy, Joseph (Senator), 64
McConnell, Mitch, 63, 71–72, 107
McHenry, Patrick T., 63
McLaurin, John L., 77n11
McLemore, Lelan E., 3, 8, 11, 41, 42, 75n2, 128, 142, 151
Merry, Robert, 21–22, 31
#metoo movement, 104–5, 107, 109, 110, 115, 123
Michel, Bob, 80

neorealism, significance of, 21
Nixon, Richard, 85
nonconformity, 7, 11, 13, 34, 71; and conflict norms and, 81, 95, 96 (and cooperation, 115, 118, 120); in gridlocked Congress, 87–89; modern Congress and, 37–38, 40, 43, 50; as procedural disobedience, 84–87; significance of, 82–84
norms: adherence to, 4–8, 10, 19–20, 22, 23, 25–26, 29, 32–34, 53, 55, 66, 69, 70, 71, 74, 87; as ambiguous social facts, 7–8; as constitutive, 5–7; definition of, 3–4; entailing costs and benefits, 4; historical, 147–54; importance of, 11–14; as prescriptive, 3–4; question bank index of questions on,

139–46; rejection of, 4, 5, 8, 19, 25; semistructured interview protocol of, 131–32; as serving institutional purposes, 4–5; significance of, 2–3, 36n1, 113, 115; survey (2019), 133–38; in Trump era, 116–17; types of, 8–11. *See also individual entries*

Obama, Barack, xiii, 55, 57, 63
Obamacare, 57, 82, 83
Ocasio-Cortez, Alexandria, 83, 88, 96, 114, 122
Office of Compliance, 104
Olson, Mancur, 4
Omar, Ilhan, 111n3
O'Neill, Tip, 79
Ornstein, Norman J., 10, 51n1, 122, 128, 144–45, 147–48
Ostrom, Elinor, 7
Overby, Marvin, 10, 12, 13, 153

partisanship: conflict norms and, 81, 84, 86, 87, 89–96; constructivist approach and, 29–30, 34; cooperation and, 50, 60–62, 64, 66, 69, 71–73, 77n13; Gingrich and, 94; as identity, 92; modern Congress and, 37–43, 46, 48–50; as norm, 90–96; polarization and, 64, 89, 90, 93–94, 97, 114–16, 124, 125; significance of, xiv, 2, 10, 11, 13–14, 123–24
Peabody, Robert L., 10, 51n1, 122, 128, 144–45, 147–48
Pelosi, Nancy, 66, 67, 73, 83, 103, 108
Pergram, Chad, 88
Pettit, Philip, 3–4
political ethnography, 13
Politics in Question (podcast), xv
Polsby, Nelson W., 10, 93, 147, 152
Poole, Keith T., 124
Powell, Adam Clayton, Jr., 99
predictability and reciprocity, 60–61
preferences, xiv, xv, 54, 71; changing culture and, 99, 110; conflict as, 50, 82; conflict norms and, 81, 86, 87,

About the Author

Brian Alexander is assistant professor of politics at Washington and Lee University. His research focuses on the intersection of institutions and political power with a concentration on the U.S. Congress. In addition to a career in public policy in Washington, DC, Brian has served as an American Political Science Association Congressional Fellow (2015–16) in the U.S. Senate, and as a research fellow at the International Center for Jefferson Studies at Monticello (2020) for his work on Thomas Jefferson's *Parliamentary Manual*. Brian completed his PhD in political science at George Mason University in 2015. At W&L, he teaches courses in American government and foreign policy and serves as the director of the W&L Washington Term, an undergraduate experiential learning program in Washington, DC. Brian lives with his wife and two daughters in Lexington, Virginia.

www.ingramcontent.com/pod-product-compliance
Lightning Source LLC
Chambersburg PA
CBHW022316280326
41932CB00010B/1121